Rhetoric, Politics and Society

Series Editors
Alan Finlayson
University of East Anglia
Norfolk, UK

James Martin
Goldsmiths, University of London
London, UK

Kendall Phillips
Syracuse University
Syracuse, NY, USA

Rhetoric lies at the intersection of a variety of disciplinary approaches and methods, drawing upon the study of language, history, culture and philosophy to understand the persuasive aspects of communication in all its modes: spoken, written, argued, depicted and performed. This series presents the best international research in rhetoric that develops and exemplifies the multifaceted and cross-disciplinary exploration of practices of persuasion and communication. It seeks to publish texts that openly explore and expand rhetorical knowledge and enquiry, be it in the form of historical scholarship, theoretical analysis or contemporary cultural and political critique. The editors welcome proposals for monographs that explore contemporary rhetorical forms, rhetorical theories and thinkers, and rhetorical themes inside and across disciplinary boundaries. For informal enquiries, questions, as well as submitting proposals, please contact the editors: Alan Finlayson: a.finlayson@uea.ac.uk James Martin: j.martin@gold.ac.uk Kendall Phillips: kphillip@syr.edu

More information about this series at
http://www.palgrave.com/gp/series/14497

Judi Atkins

Conflict, Co-operation and the Rhetoric of Coalition Government

palgrave
macmillan

Judi Atkins
Coventry University
Coventry, UK

Rhetoric, Politics and Society
ISBN 978-0-230-35967-3   ISBN 978-1-137-31796-4   (eBook)
https://doi.org/10.1057/978-1-137-31796-4

Library of Congress Control Number: 2017963622

Cover illustration: Purple Pilchards / Alamy Stock Photo

Printed on acid-free paper

This Palgrave Macmillan imprint is published by Springer Nature
The registered company is Macmillan Publishers Ltd.
The registered company address is: The Campus, 4 Crinan Street, London, N1 9XW, United Kingdom

To Rhianydd,
with all my love

ACKNOWLEDGEMENTS

This book took rather longer to complete than I intended, and I am extremely grateful to my editors at Palgrave Macmillan—Ambra Finotello and Imogen Gordon Clark—for their patience. I also wish to acknowledge the generous support provided by a British Academy/Leverhulme Small Research Grant (award number SG121411), and Coventry University for giving me sabbatical leave in the final stage of the project. The book draws on and develops the arguments presented in two earlier articles, and I thank John Wiley and Sons and SAGE Publications Ltd for permission to reuse this material.

A number of ideas were first tried out at various conferences—including the American Political Science Association, the Rhetoric Society of Europe, the UK Political Studies Association and the one-day event that formed part of this project—and I would like to express my gratitude to participants for their insightful comments and questions. Special thanks are due to the following, who pushed me to refine my thinking on the Coalition and provided much-needed encouragement: Jonathan Dean, Alan Finlayson, John Gaffney, Simon Griffiths, Sophia Hatzisavvidou, Stuart McAnulla, Libby McEnhill, Jim Martin, Dai Moon, David Seawright, Kevin Theakston and Nick Turnbull. I am also indebted to my colleagues in the School of Humanities at Coventry for their support and friendship.

Last but by no means least, I remain deeply grateful to my mum, sister, step-father and my second family, Julia and Ian Garrett, for their unstinting love and support. It means the world to me and I am truly lucky to have you all in my life. However, this book would not have been written without my daughter, Rhianydd. From listening patiently while I tried to get my thoughts straight at the beginning of the project, to tidying up the reference lists at its end, and for being a source of strength and encouragement throughout, I dedicate the book to her.

CONTENTS

CHAPTER 1

The Rhetoric of Coalition Bargaining

Bargaining is the motor of coalition politics. Indeed, negotiation takes place across the lifetime of a coalition (Lupia and Strøm 2008: 58), though the literature to date has focused on its role in government formation. During this stage, the prospective partners must, at a minimum, 'agree on which parties will participate in the government and on the division of cabinet offices. Otherwise, no government could assume office' (Müller and Strøm 2008: 159). The question of 'Who gets in?' has received considerable attention from scholars, many of whom employ game theoretical approaches to predict bargaining outcomes based on the proximity of the parties' policy preferences (e.g. Axelrod 1970; de Swaan 1973), or to analyse the relation between these preferences and the government that is eventually formed (e.g. Budge and Keman 1990; Laver and Schofield 1998). Other coalition theorists, meanwhile, have modelled the allocation of ministerial positions ('who gets what?'), linking this to portfolio saliency (e.g. Druckman and Warwick 2005; Bäck et al. 2010) and to the prestige attached to different cabinet posts (e.g. Warwick and Druckman 2001; Druckman and Roberts 2005).

The parties engaged in bargaining to form a coalition face a dilemma between 'seeking office and seeking votes' (Narud 1996: 499; see also Laver 1989). In other words, entering into a governing partnership requires compromise, but the parties must also be able to compete for votes on the basis of a distinct programmatic stance (Narud 1996:

© The Author(s) 2018
J. Atkins, *Conflict, Co-operation and the Rhetoric of Coalition Government*, Rhetoric, Politics and Society,
https://doi.org/10.1057/978-1-137-31796-4_1

1

520–521). This puzzle corresponds to the unity-distinctiveness dilemma, which confronts the partners during the governance and termination phases of the coalition life cycle. Here, the parties need to work together to govern effectively and present a united public front, while 'maintain[ing] their political distinctiveness, and hence electoral viability' (Boston and Bullock 2012: 350). The tension between co-operation and conflict, unity and distinctiveness, thus pervades the ongoing process of coalition bargaining, and it must be managed if agreements with the governing partner are to be formed and maintained. This in turn suggests that inter-party bargaining is more complex than analyses of payoff distribution are able to capture.

Arthur Lupia and Kaare Strøm define bargaining as 'a process by which actors engage in communication for the purpose of finding a mutually beneficial agreement' (2008: 59). Yet it is precisely this communicative dimension which is neglected in the model-based studies that constitute much of the scholarship on coalition bargaining. The book begins to redress this lacuna by proposing an analytical framework in which coalition bargaining is conceptualized as a negotiation dialogue[1] between the (prospective) governing partners. This dialogue takes place in conditions of uncertainty, and the parties must choose whether to co-operate, or enter into conflict, with each other based on their understanding of the situation at hand. As argued below, language is both a source of this tension and a means for managing it, so the framework developed here offers a new perspective on the unity-distinctiveness dilemma. The role of communicative interaction is overlooked in the literature, which focuses on the institutional mechanisms for dealing with this challenge (e.g. Boston and Bullock 2012; Hazell and Yong 2012), thereby enabling the book to contribute to a second area of coalition studies.

The core contention of this volume is that rhetoric is key to managing the competing dynamics of unity and distinctiveness that permeate coalition bargaining. It takes as its starting point Kenneth Burke's theory of rhetoric as identification, which captures the myriad ways in which 'the members of a group promote social cohesion by acting rhetorically upon themselves and one another' (1969: *xiv*). This account supplements and goes beyond the classical notion of rhetoric as persuasion, and so is suitable for analysing the ongoing negotiation dialogue of coalition politics. The chapter begins by laying the theoretical groundwork for this approach. It then distinguishes three forms of identification and division at work within coalition bargaining, namely: ideological, which is concerned with values; instrumental, which is founded on political expediency; and interpersonal, which focuses on the relations between individuals or groups. These modes are considered in turn, and the discussion is illustrated by reference to the coalition negotiations that followed the inconclusive UK general election result in May 2010. The final section of the chapter outlines the guiding assumptions and structure of the book.

DIALOGUE, RHETORIC AND IDENTIFICATION

Through dialogue, agents may identify and define an issue, and eventually develop a shared understanding. This in turn provides a basis for co-ordinated action (Black 2002: 181). There will, of course, be dialogues that do not work, where the participants are unwilling or unable to arrive at a mutually acceptable understanding of the problem at hand (Black 2002: 182). In these situations, the speakers may agree to differ and co-operation does not follow. It is worth noting that dialogue takes place within a context of ambiguity, where meanings are not fixed and situations can be interpreted in a variety of ways (Hajer and Laws 2006). Consequently, actors must identify the issues at stake before they can begin to address them. This process of selectively emphasizing aspects of a situation can be understood through the concept of the frame. Maarten Hajer and David Laws explain that frames are 'expressed by individuals, but also rooted in and sustained by social interaction' (2006: 259). On this view, the ordering of complex realities is relational, a product of language use, and the sharing of a frame both reinforces and perpetuates its interpretation of the issue at hand.

Alternatively, ambiguity may be managed through storylines, 'narratives on social reality through which elements from many different domains are combined and that provide actors with a set of symbolic references that suggest a common understanding' (Hajer 1997: 62). For instance, 'acid rain' is a storyline that incorporates discursive elements from a range of disciplines, such as physics and philosophy (Hajer 1997: 45–6). By so clustering knowledge, the storyline reduces the discursive complexity of 'acid rain' and makes it appear to be a coherent problem. The resultant narrative not only enables the various actors to understand one other but, through repetition, may become the received interpretation of the issue at hand (Hajer 1997: 63). Storylines thus create 'the possibility of coalition between different actors with different sets of knowledge' (Black 2002: 188–189), a function we return to below.

One approach to the study of dialogue is discourse analysis, which focuses on the 'dynamic, often temporally changeable meanings that shape social practices and that are actively transformed across time and space' (Martin 2014: 11). It also attends to the role of discourses—and indeed storylines—in shaping us as subjects (e.g. as 'politician' or 'protester') and creating positions from which we can speak (or not). Given that discourse theory operates with a relational ontology, it appears well suited to an investigation of how the participants in a dialogue form an interpretation of an issue, and of 'what understandings are shared and by whom ... [and] which are contested and between whom' (Black 2002: 196). However, this perspective pays insufficient attention to the questions of why certain frames, discourses and storylines come to be accepted over others, and of how these dominant interpretations are contested, transformed and (perhaps) superseded.[2] To address them, we need to enter the realm of rhetorical analysis.

Rhetoric is concerned with 'the study of how, in politics, we come to conceive a situation in a certain way, and of how we may get others to conceive it similarly (such that they may act in concert with us)' (Finlayson 2006: 544). There are several approaches to rhetorical study[3] but, for our purposes, the most relevant is Burke's theory of language as symbolic action. This theory proceeds from the premise that 'language reflects, selects, and deflects as a way of shaping the symbol systems that allow us to cope with the world' (Stob 2008: 139). In other words, it directs our attention to some aspects of a situation over others, and so affords us a means of dealing with ambiguity. This function is captured in the concept of a 'terministic screen', which orders reality according to the principles of continuity and discontinuity (Burke 1966: 50). As Burke put it, there are 'terms that put things together, and terms that take things apart' (1966: 49). Crucially, terministic screens—like other ordering devices—may be contested; after all, 'there can be different screens, each with its ways of directing the attention and shaping the range of observations implicit in the given terminology' (Burke 1966: 50).

It is through the opposing principles of continuity and discontinuity that 'A can feel himself [sic] identified with B, or he can think of himself as disassociated from B' (Burke 1966: 49). This statement calls attention to the relational aspect of Burke's theory, at the heart of which is the concept of identification. Here, Burke writes:

> A speaker persuades an audience by the use of stylistic identifications; his [sic] act of persuasion may be for the purpose of causing the audience to identify itself with the speaker's interests; and the speaker draws on identification of interests to establish rapport between himself and his audience. (1969: 46)

There is a strategic element involved, as a speaker will select the signs they believe are most likely to appeal to their audience, and so increase the likelihood of identification occurring. If identification between two people is achieved, they are said to be 'consubstantial': their interests are joined and yet each remains distinct, an 'individual locus of motives' (Burke 1969: 21). Such consubstantiality then provides a basis for co-operative action.

Burke's theory is appropriate to the analysis of the negotiation dialogue between the (prospective) partners in a coalition government, which takes place in conditions of ambiguity. In seeking to order reality, political actors will use a terministic screen based on either the principle of continuity or the principle of discontinuity. This choice lies at the root of the unity-distinctiveness dilemma, as figures from one party must decide whether to co-operate with, or distance themselves from, the other. If they opt for unity, they need to achieve identification with their partner and so facilitate co-operation. Conversely, a strategy based on distinctiveness requires the rhetoric of division, which emphasizes the differences between the parties and facilitates the reassertion of a separate identity. For the purposes of this volume, the concepts of identification and division are disaggregated into three forms—ideological, instrumental and interpersonal—all of which feature in the negotiation dialogue that takes place within coalition governments. Ideology matters because the location of the parties on a left-right continuum not only influences coalition formation and the enactment of policy (Laver and Schofield 1998: 113), but provides a starting point for differentiation during the governance and termination phases. Meanwhile, instrumental concerns are important because 'coalition parties have a common interest to co-operate, but have conflicting interests over the distribution of benefits arising from the co-operation' (Saalfeld 2008: 334–335). Finally, the interpersonal dimension acknowledges the relational aspects of this dialogue, specifically the building (and sometimes undermining) of mutual trust and rapport. These three modes of identification and division are examined next.

IDEOLOGICAL IDENTIFICATION AND DIVISION

According to Ian Budge and Michael Laver, the 'parties' ideological closeness or policy agreement is regarded [by many scholars] as indispensable to the coalition's formation and stability' (1986: 607). Despite this, they continue, analysts rarely treat ideology as a variable in its own right, and instead rely on 'admittedly static and imperfect representations' of the parties' core commitments and policy positions (1986: 608). Budge and Laver's criticism is borne out by studies that conceive of ideologies as 'policy motivations' (e.g. Laver and Schofield 1998: 111) or count them among the parties' 'preferences' (e.g. Strøm et al. 2008). From the perspective of rhetorical analysis, this neglect of ideology is a serious oversight. After all, ideologies are not simply systems of ideas that shape political thinking; they also 'provide actors with a series of locally established "commonplace" arguments, which must be adapted to the demands of the situation'. Furthermore, an ideology supplies a set of criteria for evaluating whether an argument is good or bad (Finlayson 2012: 759), whether it constitutes an appropriate means of inviting identification or fostering division. Alongside these functions, ideology gives an indication of how a party might envisage common ground with a coalition partner, as well as of the tensions that may arise between them.[4] An appreciation of the ideological dimension of coalition politics can therefore shed new light on the competing dynamics of unity and distinctiveness that characterize the negotiation dialogue between the parties involved.

The ambiguity of the political environment is mirrored in the inherent contestability of the concepts present within an ideology. As Michael Freeden explains, the interpretations attached to these political concepts are derived from a potentially limitless and essentially contestable assortment of meanings, and thus will exhibit a wide range of variations (1998: 54). The ideological response to this conceptual indeterminacy takes the form of 'decontestation', a process whereby a specific meaning is assigned to each of the concepts that comprise an ideology (Freeden 1998: 83). Political actors then make use of these decontested concepts in their efforts both to order reality and to persuade others to accept their definition of the issue. In Burke's terms, a politician will employ a terministic screen that stresses the continuity between, say, a policy proposal and a value it is intended to realize. If a (prospective) coalition partner accepts this interpretation, their shared understanding provides a basis for ideological identification. The parties' consubstantiality then paves the way for co-ordinated action. Although ideological proximity is a key determinant of coalition formation and durability, it may come at the cost of electoral distinctiveness—particularly for the smaller party. Hence, the latter may utilize a terministic screen that emphasizes the discontinuity between their values and an initiative proposed by the senior partner, and so directs attention to the ideological differences that exist between the parties.

Through rhetorical strategizing, political actors may play on the ambiguity of ideological claims to bring together competing demands (Atkins 2011: 94), and thus attain consubstantiality. For instance, a socialist may invite identification with a liberal by arguing that their preferred policy will promote 'equality' broadly conceived, as opposed to their specific goal of greater equality of outcome. If a liberal then interprets the argument in terms of their own belief in equal worth and accepts it, the socialist has successfully reconciled the two distinct demands under a single umbrella concept and ideological identification is established. Consubstantiality may also be achieved if the representatives of one party appeal to their (prospective) coalition partner's core commitments in making the case for a favoured objective, even if they do not share those values themselves. This form of rhetorical strategizing may afford an effective means of redefining the situation but, in practice, a party is constrained by the argumentative logics of its own ideology. In other words, if it moves the dispute too far onto the partner's territory it endangers its future bargaining power, while risking the wrath of its supporters. The preservation of ideological distinctiveness thus becomes a matter of partisan interest.

As noted above, ideology shapes a party's view of what constitutes an acceptable common ground with the (prospective) coalition partner. This conception is closely linked to the party's vision for the nation's future, and in turn affects the range of available identification strategies. Taking the 2010 UK general election manifestos as an example, the three main parties committed themselves to the goal of building a stronger society. To this end, the Liberal Democrats advocated a fairer distribution of power, 'be it economic, social, political or financial' (2010: 9), while the Conservative Party pledged to promote individual and social responsibility (2010: *viii*) and Labour asserted that 'active, reforming government … helps make people powerful' (2010: 3). Although prima facie different, the Liberal Democrat and Conservative visions are founded on a belief in limited government. This commitment was central to their conceptions of a beneficial arrangement, as it afforded them a means of promoting their respective goals of greater freedom and responsibility. Indeed, the party leaderships achieved ideological identification during the initial negotiations by linking limited government to reductions in public expenditure. Once in office, their consubstantiality facilitated co-operation on a programme of austerity intended to reduce the size of the state (Atkins 2015: 87; Beech 2011). By contrast, and despite their shared belief in individual empowerment, identification between the Liberal Democrats and Labour would have been difficult. Due to the latter's commitment to state intervention, the quest for common ideological ground would demand substantial compromise, the limits of which are largely determined by the willingness of party members to accept the dilution of their core values (see Laver and Schofield 1998: 24). Considerations of party unity are likely to come into play at this point, highlighting the importance of interests in coalition bargaining.

INSTRUMENTAL IDENTIFICATION AND DIVISION

As Hajer points out, language 'influences the perception of interests and preference. Interests … cannot be assumed as given. Interests are inter-subjectively constituted through discourse' (1997: 59). It follows that political parties engage in internal dialogues about the nature of their political environment, and what their interests are in these circumstances. Given that parties comprise different factions and thus are not 'unitary actors' (Laver and Shepsle 1990: 495), strategies of identification and division will be employed until a compromise is reached. Thus, on entering into coalition negotiations, each team will bring with it a predefined conception of their party's interests and will seek to achieve identification on this basis. As the talks take place within conditions of ambiguity, it is possible that, through dialogue, the actors involved will discover shared interests, and that these in turn will provide a starting point for inter-party agreement and co-operation during the governance stage. However, there is a persistent tension between these newly discovered coalition interests and pre-constituted partisan interests, which the actors must manage if they are to sustain the partnership while preserving their party's distinct identity. It is here that the instrumental forms of identification and division come into play, as we will see next.

At the formation stage, the primary goal is to form an administration. After all, it is widely acknowledged that parties prefer government to opposition, and so 'office may be valued not only because of its intrinsic qualities but because it is a necessary prerequisite for exercising policy influence' (Verzichelli 2008: 237). The negotiating parties will therefore seek to invite identification based on a common interest in achieving power, though the form the government will take is far from certain. So, for instance, one party may see a full coalition as the optimal means of achieving its goals, while the other may be undecided. Using a terministic screen, the former will define the situation so that a coalition appears to be the only viable option, perhaps by calling attention to the need for stability in the face of a national crisis or to the perceived weakness of minority governments. If the latter is persuaded that a coalition is the best course of action, in terms of enhancing its public image, say, or maximizing governmental effectiveness, then instrumental identification has been achieved and the parties are consubstantial.

The governing partners may also share an interest in sustaining the coalition for the duration of the parliamentary term. In the UK, for example, senior Conservative figures believed a substantial period in government would add to their party's authority, while some leading Liberal Democrats were eager to avoid an early general election for financial reasons (Wilson 2010: 176, 140). Although the two parties were instrumentally identified on the need for coalition stability, a major concern for each in the governance stage is to 'enhance their party's electoral prospects and avoid decisions that will have adverse electoral implications' (Müller et al. 2008: 11). As Michael Laver and Norman Schofield explain, 'parties may lose votes if they appear to exert no influence over policy ... [perhaps] by going into a government that enacts policies that differ from those that they promised at election time' (1998: 187). This highlights the importance of maintaining party distinctiveness, particularly for the junior partner whose role in the coalition may be less visible to the electorate (Boston and Bullock 2012). Thus, the smaller party will need to emphasize the discontinuity between their predefined interests and certain policy commitments associated with the senior partner, and so foster instrumental division between them.

Additionally, the Conservatives and the Liberal Democrats attained instrumental identification based on a mutually acceptable understanding of the 'national interest' (Atkins 2015). This is evident in their claim that the gravity of Britain's economic difficulties demanded the two parties should 'put aside their differences on economic policy and work together in the national interest to heal the national finances and rebalance the economy' (Gamble 2012: 67). Specifically, the party leaderships defined the 2008 global financial crisis as a 'crisis of debt' which, they argued, was caused by the alleged fiscal irresponsibility of the previous Labour governments and could only be addressed by significant cuts to public spending (Beech 2011: 271–273). This narrative incorporated elements from domains such as economics, politics and social policy, and so simplified the crisis while giving it an apparent coherence. The deficit thus functioned as a storyline that, through repetition, became the received understanding of the situation (Gamble 2012: 67). In an example of identification through antithesis (Burke 1972: 28), it also enabled the coalition partners to overcome their differences and to unite behind the cause of deficit reduction in opposition to a common enemy, namely the Labour Party. We return to the storyline of the deficit in the next chapter.

INTERPERSONAL IDENTIFICATION AND DIVISION

This form of identification is concerned with the relations between individuals or groups. It is pertinent to the study of coalition politics because:

> Uncertainty about the credibility and opportunism of (potential) coalition partners are particular problems in coalition bargaining processes, especially as parliamentary parties are at least in partial competition with each other and because party leaders need to win the support of their backbenchers for inter-party agreements at leadership level. (Saalfeld 2008: 335)

Therefore, the parties must endeavour to build a rapport with the prospective partner. A failure to do so may increase the risk of personal conflict and early cabinet termination, though as Erik Damgaard points out, the latter phenomenon is often overdetermined and 'many of the participants [in the government] have strategic reasons to conceal the real forces at work' (2008: 312). With this caveat in mind, we turn to the interpersonal aspect of the negotiation dialogue that characterizes coalition politics.

The interpersonal mode of identification and division encompasses such continua as trust-mistrust, admiration-disapproval and respect-disrespect.

It is somewhat nebulous in comparison to the ideological and instrumental forms, as it stems from personal chemistry (or a lack thereof) as much as it does from rhetorical strategizing. Nevertheless, these sentiments can be created rhetorically, perhaps through the use of a terministic screen that demonstrates a similar understanding of the issue at hand or through the giving of the signs of consubstantiality. They can also arise as 'a by-product of a situation which has other chief aims' (Brockriede 1968: 2), among which may be the establishment of another form of identification. For the purposes of this discussion, the goals of interpersonal identification and division are termed 'rapport' and 'friction' respectively.

Rapport is an important consideration when selecting a negotiating team, as the leader and the wider membership need to trust the participants to represent their party's values and interests, and so to bargain effectively on their behalf. While all three UK parties chose their negotiators on this basis (Laws 2010: 14–15; Wilson 2010: 52; Adonis 2013: 33) the Liberal Democrats were the best prepared, having assembled their team in late 2009 (Laws 2010: 13). Consequently, the negotiators were able to build a rapport and reach a shared understanding of their party's interests in advance of the general election. A significant omission from the team was Vince Cable, the Treasury Spokesperson, which Labour's Andrew Adonis attributes to a difficult relationship with the Liberal Democrat leader, Nick Clegg (2013: 83). However, Cable's absence ensured that 'none of the prominent figures from the left were included in the negotiating team' (Wilson 2010: 37), which arguably facilitated the party's talks with the Conservatives.

During the formation stage, former adversaries need to ascertain whether they can govern together. The creation of rapport is vital here, and to this end the members of a negotiating team must persuade their counterparts that they take the talks seriously and, moreover, are receptive to the idea of forming a partnership. Such an attempt at interpersonal identification was evident in the 2010 negotiations,[5] which opened with William Hague telling the Liberal Democrats that the Conservatives 'sincerely want this to work' (quoted in Laws 2010: 67). This declaration set the tone for the talks, and indeed David Laws was gratified to discover that the Conservative negotiators were 'able to engage in a sensible, mature and respectful way with our team' (2010: 67; see also Wilson 2010: 105). The participants' demonstrations of an open, constructive attitude thus enabled them to establish rapport, which was mirrored in the warm relationship between Clegg and the Conservative leader, David Cameron

(Paun 2011: 254). While important for coalition formation and unity, this interpersonal identification would contribute to a loss of electoral distinctiveness for the Liberal Democrats, who by late 2010 were widely seen as 'a gang of Tory stooges' (d'Ancona 2013: 64). So, although some interparty friction at the senior level can provide a basis for differentiation, too much can impede the functioning of government and perhaps result in its early termination (Damgaard 2008: 304).

Interpersonal friction was a key factor in the Liberal Democrats' decision not to enter into a coalition with Labour. As Clegg put it, the Prime Minister, Gordon Brown, was 'impossible to deal with' (quoted in Laws 2010: 122; see also Adonis 2013: 5), while Laws claims that Labour's negotiating team 'seemed determined to wreck or undermine the very talks which they were engaged in' (2010: 273–274). However, Adonis challenges Laws's account, speculating that the Liberal Democrats used interpersonal division as an alibi for their decision to go with the Conservatives, rather than form a progressive alliance with Labour (2013: 154; see also Wilson 2010: 77). Nevertheless, the friction between Clegg and Brown is well documented and this, in conjunction with the Liberal Democrats' concern that a 'traffic light coalition' would soon fall apart (Laws 2010: 158), effectively ruled out a governing partnership with Labour. Interpersonal and instrumental divisions thus outweighed the parties' apparent ideological convergence on economic policy and electoral reform (see Adonis 2013: 27).

It is worth noting that the three modes of identification and division are neither hierarchical nor mutually exclusive, as the complexities of real-world politics mean that their importance will vary between different negotiations. This is due to factors such as how the parties defined their interests, the strength of their commitment to 'red line' issues and the degree of rapport between their representatives. Additionally, more than one form of identification or division may be at work within the same rhetorical situation. Indeed, the presence (or absence) of interpersonal identification 'may have a profound influence on whether other dimensions vary, as well as on how they vary' (Brockriede 1968: 2). Similarly, these conditions of ambiguity entail that the imperatives of unity and distinctiveness are present within all three of the modes discussed above, making this framework a useful tool for investigating the rhetorical dynamics of coalition bargaining.

The Structure of the Book

At every stage of the coalition life cycle, 'the outcome of the bargaining process depends on the past as well as the present. The past determines the resources that different players have available to them' (Lupia and Strøm 2008: 59). This book proceeds from the assumption that Lupia and Strøm's claim is equally applicable to rhetorical resources. As Dennis C. Grube put it, 'political actors do not start with a clean sheet of paper each time that they formulate a piece of political rhetoric—their rhetorical choices are encumbered by the ways they have shaped their rhetoric previously' (2016: 535). It is important to note that, for Grube, 'rhetorical path dependency is not deterministic; it does not suggest that words are unchangeable, but it does argue that they are sticky' (2016: 533). That is, an actor will employ a particular rhetorical formulation to define a situation or articulate their party's policy response to it, and proceed to reinforce this choice by honing and repeating the initial rhetoric in speeches, political interviews and parliamentary debates (Grube 2016: 532–3). Such consistency can benefit a politician by contributing to an image of trustworthiness, but equally the success of their earlier rhetoric precludes the easy adoption of a new strategy even if the situation demands it (Grube 2016: 531). Nonetheless, Grube argues, 'there remains room for actors to exercise agency in reshaping their earlier rhetoric to try and reframe a particular issue in a way that at least provides the illusion of consistency'. In short, some formulations are stickier than others (2016: 536).[6]

A second assumption underpinning this book is that the partners in a multi-party government use the legislative process as a means for managing the unity-distinctiveness dilemma. Lanny W. Martin and Georg Vanberg explain that parliamentary debate affords the leaders an opportunity to show their MPs and supporters that 'the party has successfully defended their interests and that it has been able to secure favourable compromise policies as part of coalition negotiations—in other words, that the party has stayed true to its principles'. This is of particular import when a proposed policy is ideologically divisive, as the leaders must justify their backing for the compromise and persuade their members that they fought hard to protect the party's interests. These endeavours are reflected in higher levels of participation in the parliamentary debates on that policy, as the leaders must make a convincing argument in order to maintain their party's support (2008: 505).

In their analysis, Martin and Vanberg use the length of parliamentary speeches 'as a proxy for the extent to which parties employ debates to communicate with their constituents' (2008: 513). This book instead explores the dynamics of debate behaviour by focusing on the *content* of these speeches, specifically the role played by the three modes of identification and division considered above. In the UK's House of Commons, a senior government figure proposes a motion, which is then debated and voted on. By attending to these opening statements and the subsequent deliberations the book offers an analysis of the rhetorical strategies employed by the Executive and Coalition MPs, as well as of the inter- and/or intra-party divisions they were intended to create or to resolve. These discussions are illustrated with representative examples of the arguments made during the debates. The book also considers the language of unity and distinctiveness in key speeches made by senior Conservatives and Liberal Democrats, so shedding light on the Coalition's 'externally facing' rhetoric and the image it was designed to project.

Chapter 2 applies the framework to the negotiation dialogue that preceded the formation of the Coalition. It begins by discussing the commitments presented first in the parties' 2010 manifestos and then in the *Programme for Government*, identifying the overlaps between them and any areas of compromise. The chapter proceeds to examine how senior figures used appeals to ideological and instrumental identification, in conjunction with the storyline of the deficit, to construct an image of unity and join together the Coalition's constituent parties in opposition to Labour. Next, the book turns to the governance phase of the coalition life cycle and, using the approach elaborated above, considers the rhetorical strategies employed by the leadership and backbench MPs in four areas of policy. In so doing, it pays particular attention to how political actors sought to make sense of ambiguity, the extent to which the bargains made during the formation stage shaped subsequent agreements and the presence (or indeed absence) of rhetorical path dependency.

Thus, Chap. 3 is concerned with higher education funding, which was an 'agree to disagree' issue in the negotiations and would prove problematic for the Liberal Democrats. Nonetheless, the junior partner defended the policy, and so demonstrated ideological and instrumental consubstantiality with the Conservatives. Chapter 4 discusses constitutional reform, an agenda that was primarily associated with the Liberal Democrats. Here, partisan interests took precedence over Coalition unity, giving rise to an inter-party conflict over House of Lords reform that turned on contrasting interpretations of the Coalition Agreement. Chapter 5 turns to Europe, a policy area dominated by the Eurosceptic Conservative Party and where, contrary to expectations, there was a broad consensus with the pro-European Liberal Democrats. The dissenting voices instead came from the Conservative backbenches as MPs employed ideological division to distance themselves from the Coalition leadership, whose case for Britain's EU membership relied on appeals for instrumental identification.

Chapter 6, meanwhile, considers foreign policy, which was an area of broad consensus between the parties. Of particular concern are the debates over intervention in Libya and Syria, the outcomes of which turned on the efficacy of appeals for identification through antithesis, which were based on the storyline of the 2003 Iraq war. Chapter 7 focuses on the termination phase of the coalition life cycle and examines the rhetoric of the 2015 general election campaign, during which the parties had to defend their record while reasserting their distinctive identities. This was straightforward for the Conservatives, but the Liberal Democrats' strategic options were severely limited by previous bargaining outcomes and rhetorical choices. Finally, Chap. 8 reflects on the legacy of the Coalition, paying particular attention to higher education policy and the 2016 referendum on Britain's continued membership of the EU. It then turns to the rhetoric of the confidence and supply agreement between Theresa May's Conservative minority government and the Democratic Unionist Party, before identifying lessons for a future coalition and highlighting potentially fruitful areas for further research.

NOTES

1. According to Doug Walton, 'the goal of the negotiation dialogue is to make a deal to reach some kind of agreement that both parties can live with even if it involves compromises' (1992: 89). It thus differs from persuasion dialogue, the primary objective of which is to 'persuade the other party that your point of view is right by means of arguments' (Walton 1992: 90).
2. This oversight is evident in Hajer and Laws's discussion of ordering devices (2006). Meanwhile, Julia Black notes that analyses of regulatory conversations should attend to the rhetorical techniques employed in the development and contestation of these understandings (2002: 196), but does not consider them herself. Similarly, Hajer acknowledges the importance of argumentation (1997: 53–54) but places 'appeals to collective fears or

senses of guilt' under the definition of a storyline (1997: 63), rather than recognizing them as persuasive techniques in their own right—that is as appeals to the emotions of an audience, or pathos. Meanwhile, Ernesto Laclau's theory of discourse is primarily concerned with the naming of 'empty signifiers'—the rhetorical trope of catachresis (Finlayson 2012: 756)—rather than with persuasion per se. In contrast, rhetorical study 'explores the moments at which discursive "regimes" are introduced and reproduced through argument', and so 'permits analysis of concrete interventions that aspire to become effective, perhaps dominant discourses' (Martin 2014: 12).

3. See, for instance, Atkins (2011); Finlayson (2007); Martin (2015); and Turnbull (2017).

4. It is important to note that 'political parties are themselves not unitary actors, so attention should also be paid to the priorities of different wings of the two movements' (Paun 2011: 258; see also Laver and Shepsle 1990).

5. The Conservative negotiators were the MPs William Hague, Oliver Letwin and George Osborne, and Cameron's chief of staff, Ed Llewellyn, while the Liberal Democrat team comprised the MPs Danny Alexander (chair), Chris Huhne, David Laws and Andrew Stunnell (Laws 2010: 52–53).

6. It is possible to adopt an historical approach to the analysis of rhetorical path dependency. One might, for instance, examine the rhetorical formulations employed by successive governments in the area of welfare policy, or study Conservative Party rhetoric on Europe since 1979. However, such investigations are beyond the scope of the present volume, which instead seeks to illuminate the extent to which the Coalition's early bargains and rhetorical formulations shaped those of the governance and termination stages.

REFERENCES

Adonis, A. (2013). *5 Days in May: The Coalition and Beyond*. London: Biteback Publishing Ltd.

Atkins, J. (2011). *Justifying New Labour Policy*. Basingstoke: Palgrave Macmillan.

Atkins, J. (2015). 'Together in the National Interest': The Rhetoric of Unity and the Formation of the Cameron-Clegg Government. *The Political Quarterly*, *86*(1), 85–92.

Axelrod, R. (1970). *Conflict of Interest*. Chicago: Markham.

Bäck, H., Debus, M., & Dumont, P. (2010). Who Gets What in Coalition Governments? Predictors of Portfolio Allocation in Parliamentary Democracies. *European Journal of Political Research, 50*(4), 441–478.

Beech, M. (2011). A Tale of Two Liberalisms. In S. Lee & M. Beech (Eds.), *The Cameron-Clegg Government: Coalition Politics in an Age of Austerity* (pp. 267–279). Basingstoke: Palgrave Macmillan.

Black, J. (2002). Regulatory Conversations. *Journal of Law and Society, 29*(1), 163–196.

Boston, J., & Bullock, D. (2012). Multi-Party Governance: Managing the Unity-Distinctiveness Dilemma in Executive Coalitions. *Party Politics, 18*(3), 349–368.

Brockriede, W. E. (1968). Dimensions of the Concept of Rhetoric. *Quarterly Journal of Speech, 54*(1), 1–12.

Budge, I., & Keman, H. (1990). *Parties and Democracy: Coalition Formation and Government Functioning in Twenty States.* Oxford: Oxford University Press.

Budge, I., & Laver, M. (1986). Policy, Ideology, and Party Distance: Analysis of Election Programmes in 19 Democracies. *Legislative Studies Quarterly, 11*(4), 607–617.

Burke, K. (1966). *Language as Symbolic Action: Essays on Life, Literature, and Method.* Berkeley and Los Angeles: University of California Press.

Burke, K. (1969). *A Rhetoric of Motives.* Berkeley and Los Angeles: University of California Press.

Burke, K. (1972). *Dramatism and Development.* Barre: Clark University Press.

Conservative Party. (2010). *Invitation to Join the Government of Britain: The Conservative Manifesto 2010.* London: The Conservative Party.

Damgaard, E. (2008). Cabinet Termination. In K. Strøm, W. C. Müller, & T. Bergman (Eds.), *Cabinets and Coalition Bargaining: The Democratic Life Cycle in Western Europe* (pp. 301–326). Oxford: Oxford University Press.

d'Ancona, M. (2013). *In It Together: The Inside Story of the Coalition Government.* London: Viking.

de Swaan, A. (1973). *Coalition Theories and Cabinet Formations.* Amsterdam: Elsevier.

Druckman, J. N., & Roberts, A. (2005). Context and Coalition-Bargaining: Comparing Portfolio Allocation in Eastern and Western Europe. *Party Politics, 11*(5), 535–555.

Druckman, J. N., & Warwick, P. V. (2005). The Missing Piece: Measuring Portfolio Salience in Western European Parliamentary Democracies. *European Journal of Political Research, 44*(1), 17–42.

Finlayson, A. (2006). 'What's the Problem?' Political Theory, Rhetoric and Problem-Setting. *Critical Review of International Social and Political Philosophy, 9*(4), 541–557.

Finlayson, A. (2007). From Beliefs to Arguments: Interpretive Methodology and Rhetorical Political Analysis. *British Journal of Politics and International Relations, 9*(4), 545–563.

Finlayson, A. (2012). Rhetoric and the Political Theory of Ideologies. *Political Studies, 60*(4), 751–767.

Freeden, M. (1998). *Ideologies and Political Theory: A Conceptual Approach.* Oxford: Clarendon Press.

Gamble, A. (2012). Economic Policy. In T. Heppell & D. Seawright (Eds.), *Cameron and the Conservatives: The Transition to Coalition Government* (pp. 59–73). Basingstoke: Palgrave Macmillan.

Grube, D. C. (2016). Sticky Words? Towards a Theory of Rhetorical Path Dependency. *Australian Journal of Political Science, 51*(3), 530–545.

Hajer, M. A. (1997). *The Politics of Environmental Discourse: Ecological Modernization and the Policy Process.* Oxford: Oxford University Press.

Hajer, M., & Laws, D. (2006). Ordering Through Discourse. In M. Moran, M. Rein, & R. E. Goodin (Eds.), *The Oxford Handbook of Public Policy* (pp. 251–268). Oxford: Oxford University Press.

Hazell, R., & Yong, B. (2012). *The Politics of Coalition: How the Cameron-Clegg Government Works.* Oxford: Hart Publishing Ltd.

Labour Party. (2010). *The Labour Party Manifesto 2010: A Future Fair for All.* London: The Labour Party.

Laver, M. (1989). Party Competition and Party System Change: The Interaction of Coalition Bargaining and Electoral Competition. *Journal of Theoretical Politics, 1*(3), 301–324.

Laver, M., & Schofield, N. (1998). *Multiparty Government: The Politics of Coalition in Europe.* Ann Arbor: University of Michigan Press.

Laver, M., & Shepsle, K. (1990). Government Coalitions and Intraparty Politics. *British Journal of Political Science, 20*(4), 489–507.

Laws, D. (2010). *22 Days in May: The Birth of the Lib Dem-Conservative Coalition.* London: Biteback Publishing Ltd.

Liberal Democrats. (2010). *Liberal Democrat Manifesto 2010.* London: Liberal Democrats.

Lupia, A., & Strøm, K. (2008). Bargaining, Transaction Costs, and Coalition Governance. In K. Strøm, W. C. Müller, & T. Bergman (Eds.), *Cabinets and Coalition Bargaining: The Democratic Life Cycle in Western Europe* (pp. 51–83). Oxford: Oxford University Press.

Martin, J. (2014). *Politics and Rhetoric: A Critical Introduction.* London: Routledge.

Martin, J. (2015). Situating Speech: A Rhetorical Approach to Political Strategy. *Political Studies, 63*(1), 25–42.

Martin, L. W., & Vanberg, G. (2008). Coalition Government and Political Communication. *Political Research Quarterly, 61*(3), 502–516.

Müller, W. C., Bergman, T., & Strøm, K. (2008). Coalition Theory and Cabinet Governance: An Introduction. In K. Strøm, W. C. Müller, & T. Bergman (Eds.), *Cabinets and Coalition Bargaining: The Democratic Life Cycle in Western Europe* (pp. 1–50). Oxford: Oxford University Press.

Müller, W. C., & Strøm, K. (2008). Coalition Agreements and Cabinet Governance. In K. Strøm, W. C. Müller, & T. Bergman (Eds.), *Cabinets and*

Coalition Bargaining: The Democratic Life Cycle in Western Europe (pp. 159–199). Oxford: Oxford University Press.

Narud, H. M. (1996). Electoral Competition and Coalition Bargaining in Multiparty Systems. *Journal of Theoretical Politics, 8*(4), 499–525.

Paun, A. (2011). United We Stand? Governance Challenges for the United Kingdom Coalition. *The Political Quarterly, 82*(2), 251–260.

Saalfeld, T. (2008). Institutions, Chance, and Choices: The Dynamics of Cabinet Survival. In K. Strøm, W. C. Müller, & T. Bergman (Eds.), *Cabinets and Coalition Bargaining: The Democratic Life Cycle in Western Europe* (pp. 327–368). Oxford: Oxford University Press.

Stob, P. (2008). 'Terministic Screens', Social Constructionism, and the Language of Experience: Kenneth Burke's Utilization of William James. *Philosophy and Rhetoric, 41*(2), 130–152.

Strøm, K., Müller, W. C., & Bergman, T. (Eds.). (2008). *Cabinets and Coalition Bargaining: The Democratic Life Cycle in Western Europe*. Oxford: Oxford University Press.

Turnbull, N. (2017). Political Rhetoric and Its Relationship to Context: A New Theory of the Rhetorical Situation, the Rhetorical and the Political. *Critical Discourse Studies, 14*(2), 115–131.

Verzichelli, L. (2008). Portfolio Allocation. In K. Strøm, W. C. Müller, & T. Bergman (Eds.), *Cabinets and Coalition Bargaining: The Democratic Life Cycle in Western Europe* (pp. 237–267). Oxford: Oxford University Press.

Walton, D. N. (1992). *Plausible Argument in Everyday Conversation*. New York: State University of New York Press.

Warwick, P. V., & Druckman, J. N. (2001). Portfolio Salience and the Proportionality of Payoffs in Coalition Governments. *British Journal of Political Science, 31*(4), 627–649.

Wilson, R. (2010). *5 Days to Power: The Journey to Coalition Britain*. London: Biteback Publishing Ltd.

CHAPTER 2

The Formation of the Coalition

The 2010 general election produced a hung parliament with the Conservatives as the largest party. In these conditions of uncertainty, Cameron made a 'big, open and comprehensive offer' to form a government with the Liberal Democrats (quoted in Laws 2010: 49), and so opened up five days of intense inter-party bargaining. The eventual outcome of these negotiations was by no means guaranteed (see Paun 2011: 251) but, on 11 May 2010, Britain had its first peacetime coalition since the 1930s. Using the framework elaborated previously, this chapter explores the rhetorical dynamics of unity and distinctiveness that were present within the talks, focusing on the policy areas of higher education, constitutional reform, Europe and foreign affairs. Given that a number of those involved in, or close to, the negotiations have published detailed accounts (e.g. Laws 2010; Wilson 2010; Adonis 2013),[1] this analysis includes verbatim quotations where possible. After considering the four areas of policy in turn, the chapter examines how senior politicians employed the rhetoric of identification and division to construct an image of unity, and to join together the Coalition's constituent parties in opposition to Labour.

HIGHER EDUCATION

The 2010 manifestos demonstrate that both parties were ideologically consubstantial on the principle of fair access to higher education for all, regardless of an individual's background or parental income (Conservative

© The Author(s) 2018   21
J. Atkins, *Conflict, Co-operation and the Rhetoric of Coalition Government*, Rhetoric, Politics and Society,
https://doi.org/10.1057/978-1-137-31796-4_2

Party 2010: 17; Liberal Democrats 2010: 39). However, they differed on the question of how this was to be achieved, with the Conservatives promising to 'consider carefully the results of Lord Browne's review into the future of higher education funding [in England]' (2010: 17) and the Liberal Democrats pledging to 'scrap unfair university tuition fees for all students taking their first degree, including those studying part-time' (2010: 39). This latter change would be implemented over six years, ensuring that 'the change is affordable even in these difficult economic times, and without cutting university income' (2010: 39). The Liberal Democrats also proposed to introduce a National Bursary Scheme, with awards made on the basis of whether a student is studying for a degree in a 'strategic subject' such as science or mathematics, and if they are experiencing financial hardship (2010: 39).

Given the divisiveness of the university funding issue, it was first discussed in private by Cameron and Clegg. As the talks reached their end and the negotiators were drafting the Coalition Agreement, the parties agreed on a formulation based on principles as opposed to policies, and deferred the decision until the publication of the Browne report (Laws 2010: 185). This position was taken from the Conservative manifesto, but both parties agreed that Browne's proposals should be assessed against a number of criteria. Among these were the need to promote social mobility, increase the proportion of students from disadvantaged backgrounds, ensure that the universities are properly funded and improve teaching quality (HM Government 2010: 31–32). If the Liberal Democrats were unable to accept the Government's response to the report, then 'arrangements will be made to enable Liberal Democrat MPs to abstain in any vote' (HM Government 2010: 32). This is an example of instrumental co-operation, as it enabled the negotiations to continue while delaying a difficult decision until October 2010. By this time, the Business Secretary, Vince Cable, had started to acknowledge publicly what senior Liberal Democrats had admitted in private, namely that tuition fees would have to rise (see Laws 2010: 185–186).

CONSTITUTIONAL REFORM

Electoral reform was perhaps the most contentious issue in the negotiations. In their manifesto, the Conservative Party supported the first-past-the-post system for general elections because it 'gives voters the chance to kick out a government they are fed up with' (2010: 67). This position is founded on a 'populist' notion of fairness, which demands that 'voters, not party leaders, should choose governments'. Post-election bargaining is therefore seen as unfair because it removes the power to choose a government from the electorate and places it in the hands of party leaders (Blau 2004: 167). The Conservatives also committed themselves to 'fair vote' reforms, pledging to 'equalize the size of constituency electorates' and 'conduct a boundary review to implement these changes within five years' (2010: 67). These measures drew on a conception of fairness as equality, according to which every MP should represent an equal number of voters and each citizen's ballot carries the same weight. Reinforcing the ideological commitment to these proposals was a belief that first-past-the-post best served the Conservatives' interests by giving them 'regular opportunities to hold power' as a majority government and, moreover, that the boundary changes would work to their electoral advantage (Laws 2016: 88; Hazell and Yong 2012: 159–160).

Like the Conservatives, the Liberal Democrats promised to introduce 'fair votes', but they differed in their view of how this was to be achieved. Specifically, their manifesto advocated proportional representation for Westminster elections in the form of the Single Transferable Vote system, which would also reduce the number of parliamentary seats by 150 (Liberal Democrats 2010: 87–88). This proposal is based on the 'equality' conception of fairness, which requires that 'each citizen and party should be treated equally, as in the idea of "one person, one vote, one value"' (Blau 2004: 167). As such, it is consistent with the core liberal belief in the equal worth of all individuals. The Liberal Democrats also had partisan interests involved, as they believed that a change in the electoral system would compensate for the loss of support resulting from their participation in a coalition government (Rennard in Laws 2016: 86; d'Ancona 2013: 75). So, although both parties justified their proposed political reforms in terms of fairness, their divergent understandings of this contested concept entailed very different means of achieving their objectives.

The Liberal Democrats have a longstanding commitment to electoral reform, and indeed it would be one of their four 'bottom-line negotiating issues' in any coalition talks (Laws 2010: 88; Kavanagh and Cowley 2010: 215).[2] Before the 2010 general election, Laws had advised Clegg and the other members of the Liberal Democrat negotiating team that there was only one way of persuading the Conservatives, to whom proportional representation was anathema, to accept a referendum on reform for Westminster elections. This was to

Push for a referendum on the most modest form of electoral reform—the Alternative Vote ... and to link this to Lib Dem support for the Conservatives' own reform plan, which was to reduce the number of parliamentary seats and to remove Labour over-representation. (Paraphrased in Laws 2010: 100; see also Wilson 2010: 161)

In Burke's terms, the Liberal Democrat strategy involved using a terministic screen based on continuity to join the two parties' proposals together. This would then provide a ground for instrumental identification by offering the Conservatives 'something which would be likely to offset any loss of seats that AV might deliver' (Laws 2010: 100). Equally, and given that the Liberal Democrats regarded the Alternative Vote (AV) system as fairer than first-past-the-post, this proposal represented an ideologically acceptable compromise. It also accorded with their perceived partisan interests; indeed, Clegg described AV as a 'baby step in the right direction' towards the reform of Westminster elections (quoted in Bogdanor 2011: 101).

In the light of their divergent views on electoral reform it is unsurprising that the talks between the Conservatives and Liberal Democrats soon became deadlocked, jeopardizing their preferred option of a partnership government (Wilson 2010: 164; Laws 2010: 99–100). Both had instrumental reasons for favouring this outcome, with Cameron believing that a coalition would deflect attention from the Conservatives' failure to win an outright majority, while the Liberal Democrats' commitment to proportional representation meant they had a 'vested interest in showing the public that coalitions could work in practice' (Hazell and Yong 2012: 31). The latter had already ruled out a confidence and supply arrangement, as it would result in them 'taking no credit for the government's achievements, but all the pain for sustaining it in office' (Huhne quoted in Laws 2010: 18; Clegg 2016: 147). In short, the Liberal Democrats perceived this option as damaging to their electoral interests.

Thus, on 9 May, the Liberal Democrats implemented Laws's strategy, and Danny Alexander told the Conservative team that 'we will support your proposals on redrawing the constituency boundaries, to make voting fairer. But in return, we want your support for a referendum on a reformed first-past-the-post system' (quoted in Laws 2010: 101).[3] Here, Alexander employed a terministic screen that directed his listeners' attention to the continuity between AV and the existing electoral system (viz. 'reformed first-past-the-post'). By doing so, he perhaps sought to downplay the impact of the change and make it more agreeable to the Conservatives. Likewise, by bringing together the demands of the two parties under the umbrella of 'fairness' (broadly conceived), the Liberal Democrats invited ideological identification with the Conservatives, on the basis of which the two parties could work together to 'usher in a new and more co-operative politics and a fairer voting system' (Alexander, paraphrased in Laws 2010: 101).

However, Alexander's effort to redefine the issue of voting reform was rejected, with Hague asserting that 'the Conservatives are opposed as a party to both the Alternative Vote and proportional representation. And calling AV "reformed first-past-the-post" won't change our people's minds!' (quoted in Laws 2010: 101). Here, Hague was constrained by the argumentative logics of Conservative ideology, and in particular its commitment to preserve traditional institutions. As such, the Liberal Democrats' attempt to invite identification was unsuccessful, and that Party's negotiating team therefore had to change their tactics. It was perhaps with this ideological constraint in mind that Laws responded:

> Surely most Conservative MPs are opposed to PR and not AV? AV is a far more incremental and modest change. And in a coalition, the old assumptions on how people use their second preferences could change. AV might not be bad for the Conservatives under those circumstances. (Quoted in Laws 2010: 102)

With these words, Laws appealed to both the Conservatives' belief in gradual change and their electoral interests, and so sought to persuade them to identify ideologically and instrumentally with the Liberal Democrats on their proposals for a referendum on AV.

Again, this identification strategy was unsuccessful and the talks reached an impasse. For George Osborne, 'the best Conservative offer on this is going to be equalization of seat size and a free vote in the Commons on an AV referendum', while Laws's position was that: 'We cannot persuade Lib Dem MPs to vote for a Lib Dem-Conservative coalition without [electoral reform]' (both quoted in Laws 2010: 103; see also Wilson 2010: 162–163). Faced with the prospect of the Liberal Democrats reaching an agreement with Labour, on 10 May David Cameron sought the assent of his parliamentary party to offer a referendum on AV (Wilson 2010: 219; Kavanagh and Cowley 2010: 213–214). While a number of senior figures supported the move, in general Conservative MPs adhere to the traditional view of the constitution. As such, they 'do not regard the political system as broken and, if there is to be change, it should be incremental, tackling proven ills, not radical change fundamentally challenging the basics of a nation's constitutional underpinnings' (Norton and Thompson 2015: 130; see also Wilson 2010: 218). In essence, then, the parliamentary Conservative Party was confronted with a choice between pragmatism and principles.

To persuade backbench MPs to support the offer of a referendum, the Conservative grandee Sir Malcolm Rifkind invited instrumental identification based on a conception of the national interest, saying:

> The Conservative Party's judgement has always been that in any crucial decision we have to address the public interest, not the party interest. And the public interest is economic stability, the prospect of a government that can govern at any particular moment. (Quoted in Wilson 2010: 220)

Although many MPs had grave misgivings about crossing their party's 'red line' on voting reform, few voiced their concerns and the Conservative leadership proceeded to offer the Liberal Democrats a deal on AV (Wilson 2010: 220–221; Kavanagh and Cowley 2010: 214). The silence of these backbenchers demonstrates the rhetorical power of appeals to the 'national interest', given that 'open dissent ... could be construed as an expression of narrow self-interest that would damage [them] personally' (Atkins 2015: 88) and, furthermore, risked causing serious harm to the Conservatives' image as a credible party of government.

For the Liberal Democrats, meanwhile, intra-party divisions centred on the choice of coalition partner. The majority of MPs favoured the Conservatives for instrumental reasons; in Clegg's words:

> If we were ever to become a credible party of government, then we would need to show that we could govern in tough times, and finally put an end to the perception of us as a nice but ineffectual party of opposition. (Clegg 2016: 178; see also Laws 2010: 77)

However, others—notably the former party leaders and many members of the House of Lords—advocated a partnership with Labour, based on their longstanding conviction that 'the future of progressive politics lies in the realignment of the centre-left' (Clegg 2016: 165; see also Laws 2010: 197). In the event, at a meeting of MPs and peers held on 11 May, the

Liberal Democrats almost unanimously agreed to enter into a coalition with the Conservatives (Laws 2010: 198; Kavanagh and Cowley 2010: 220). Critical to allaying the Party's doubts was the intervention of a former leader, Paddy Ashdown, who expressed instrumental identification with the negotiators by declaring that a coalition with the Conservatives was 'the only sensible outcome to the predicament in which we found ourselves' (Clegg 2016: 177; see also Laws 2010: 197). Thus, each parliamentary party was, for the most part, instrumentally consubstantial, but their identification was based on different grounds.

In the Coalition's *Programme for Government*, the parties pledged to bring forward measures to create 'fewer and more equal sized constituencies' and to hold a referendum on AV (HM Government 2010: 26). The Liberal Democrats had agreed to the proposed boundary changes because they were already committed to reducing the number of MPs, and they shared the Conservative Party's belief that 'the present unequal size of constituency electorates just wasn't fair' (Laws 2010: 101). As such, they were ideologically identified with the Conservatives on the basis of a shared conception of fairness as equality. However, the Liberal Democrats were unable to persuade the Conservatives to accept AV as a matter of principle, and so failed to achieve ideological identification on this part of their agenda. This is because the equality conception of fairness tends to clash with the populist idea endorsed by the Conservatives, as 'fairness in translating votes to seats may lead to unfairness in translating seats to power' (Blau 2004: 173). Thus, the inherent ambiguity of 'fairness' that had enabled the parties to achieve consubstantiality on the issue of equalized boundaries created ideological division over electoral reform. On this issue, the Conservatives and Liberal Democrats instead were instrumentally consubstantial, as an agreement on an AV referendum would enable the parties not only to take power, but to demonstrate that they could set aside partisan concerns and act in the national interest (Laws 2010: 199; Wilson 2010: 210–212). This in turn would enhance their standing in the eyes of the public, while contributing to the Coalition's early narrative of governmental unity.

EUROPE

In opposition, the Conservatives were a 'soft' Eurosceptic party which supported Britain's EU membership but opposed any further integration (Lynch 2011: 218). Thus, their manifesto asserted that 'Britain's interests are best served by membership of a European Union that is an association of its Member States', and that a Conservative government would 'never allow Britain to slide into a federal Europe' (Conservative Party 2010: 113). To this end, they pledged to hold a referendum on any future treaty that transferred further powers to the EU—a 'referendum lock'—and to introduce a Sovereignty Bill that would affirm the ultimate authority of the UK Parliament (Conservative Party 2010: 113–114). In addition to these measures, they would seek to repatriate social and employment policy, on the ground that 'the steady and unaccountable intrusion of the European Union into almost every aspect of our lives has gone too far' (Conservative Party 2010: 114).

Meanwhile, the Liberal Democrat manifesto stated that 'European co-operation is the best way for Britain to be strong, safe and influential in the future', and promised to ensure that 'we use our influence to achieve prosperity, security and opportunity' (2010: 66, 57). This position reflected the Party's deeply-held belief in internationalism, as well as its ideological commitment to economic liberalism (Goes 2015: 98). However, the Liberal Democrats' pro-Europeanism was tempered by the recognition that the EU was in need of reform, specifically in relation to its 'accountability, efficiency and effectiveness' (2010: 66). The manifesto also contained pledges to offer an in/out referendum in the event of a 'fundamental change in the relationship between the UK and the EU' and, when the economic conditions were right, to hold a plebiscite on whether Britain should join the Euro (2010: 67).

During the formation stage, the sensitivity of the European question meant that it was left to the party leaders to discuss. As Clegg explains, he and Cameron sought to lay the issue to rest in order to prevent it from blighting the Coalition's time in office (2016: 205), and they subsequently agreed that 'the UK would move neither significantly towards nor significantly away from the rest of the European Union' (Laws 2016: 238). This pragmatic approach was equally evident in the Coalition's *Programme for Government*, which expressed the view that 'Britain should play a leading role in an enlarged European Union, but that no further powers should be transferred to Brussels without a referendum' (HM Government 2010: 19). This entailed a 'referendum lock' on the further transfer of sovereignty, which was an 'absolute red line' for the Conservatives (Wilson 2010: 273; Lynch 2011: 221), and indeed the pledge was reproduced verbatim from their manifesto. As the Liberal Democrats had advocated an in/out referendum, the difference between the parties was simply a matter of degree.

A number of compromises were present, as the Conservatives' desire to repatriate powers became a commitment to 'examine the balance of the EU's existing competences' (HM Government 2010: 19) after Clegg 'insisted that there should be no renegotiation of EU membership under the Coalition' (Lynch 2015: 244), and the Sovereignty Bill was reduced to a pledge to 'examine the case' for such legislation. However, both parties agreed to rule out joining the Euro in that Parliament and, as Philip Lynch correctly points out, there was 'common ground on EU reform, notably global competitiveness, completion of the single market [and] budget reform' (2015: 245). This suggests that the Conservatives and the Liberal Democrats had achieved instrumental identification based on a shared view of Britain's national interest, while their ideological divisions over the principle of sovereignty were concealed beneath ambiguous language. Therefore, the Coalition claimed that its approach 'strikes the right balance between constructive engagement with the EU to deal with the issues that affect us all, and protecting our national sovereignty' (HM Government 2010: 19).

FOREIGN POLICY

In their 2010 manifestos, both parties used a terministic screen based on discontinuity to distinguish their foreign policy agenda from that of New Labour. Thus, the Conservatives offered an approach founded on 'liberal Conservative principles' (2010: 109), which was:

> Liberal, because Britain must be open and engaged with the world, supporting human rights and championing the cause of democracy and the rule of law at every opportunity. But Conservative, because our policy must be hard-headed and practical, dealing with the world as it is and not as we wish it were. (2010: 109)

This pragmatism was also present in the Party's scepticism towards 'grand utopian schemes to remake the world' (2010: 109), whereby the rhetoric of ideological division served to distance them from New Labour's ill-fated efforts to promote democracy in the Middle East. The Conservatives instead would seek to promote British values and interests by 'developing and strengthening our alliances and reforming international institutions' (2010: 109–110). In policy terms this involved, for instance, establishing closer relationships with India and China, supporting the reform of the UN Security Council and maintaining a 'strong, close and frank relationship with the United States' (2010: 110).

Meanwhile, the Liberal Democrats acknowledged the damage done to Britain's international standing by the 2003 invasion of Iraq and promised to 'put British values of fairness and the rule of law back at the heart of our foreign policy, (2010: 67). Here, they implied that New Labour had lost sight of these values, both of which were core Liberal Democrat beliefs, and so created ideological division between the parties. Such discontinuity was also evident in their pledge to co-operate with the international community in its efforts to prevent Iran from becoming a nuclear power. Here, the manifesto stated that: 'We would follow a diplomatic route of active engagement, and are ready to back targeted sanctions, but we oppose military action against Iran' (2010: 68). Among other policy proposals were a commitment to a two-state solution to the Israeli-Palestinian conflict, a tougher regime of arms control and 'a full judicial inquiry into allegations of British complicity in torture and state kidnapping', which would help to restore Britain's 'reputation for decency and fairness' (2010: 68) following the extraordinary rendition scandal of the New Labour era.

The 'Foreign Affairs' section of the *Programme for Government* opened by expressing the Coalition's belief that 'Britain must always be an active member of the global community, promoting our national interests while standing up for the values of freedom, fairness and responsibility' (HM Government 2010: 20). These principles provided the ideological foundation of the new government, and they would be realized through Britain playing a constructive role in international organizations such as NATO and the UN, working to promote security and stability, and 'pushing for reform of global institutions to ensure that they reflect the modern world' (HM Government 2010: 20). The Coalition's policy pledges indicated that the parties had also achieved instrumental identification on a shared conception of Britain's national interest, as they included commitments to strengthen relationships with the emerging powers, support global nuclear non-proliferation efforts and never to condone the use of torture (HM Government 2010: 20).

THE COALITION'S NARRATIVE OF UNITY

In their first joint press conference since taking office, Cameron and Clegg offered a 'radical' programme that would mark the beginning of a 'new politics'. This programme, they claimed, was based on the values of freedom, fairness and responsibility and, moreover, would provide Britain with the strong, stable leadership it needed for the long term (Cameron and Clegg 2010). The overriding aim of this press conference was to present a united front, both to the grassroots members of the Coalition's constituent parties and to audiences beyond. In particular, the two leaders sought to foster coalition cohesion while reassuring the financial markets and the public that the new government could take the action necessary to tackle Britain's economic problems. Given the novelty of coalition government in the UK, Cameron and Clegg also had to persuade a sceptical media that their partnership would hold together for the duration of the parliament. This show of unity posed considerable challenges for the parties involved, but it was vital in creating the first impressions that would influence perceptions of the Coalition far beyond the formation stage.

Ideological Identification and Shared Values

Following the formation of the Coalition, writes Simon Lee, Cameron and Clegg 'sought to demonstrate that their partnership was born out of genuine political conviction rather than an expedient marriage of convenience' (2011: 13). To this end, both leaders employed the principle of continuity to frame the compromises made during the negotiations in a positive light, rather than as the dilution of their parties' cherished commitments. As Cameron put it, 'the more we talked, the more we listened, the more we realized that our visions for this country and the values that inspired them are strengthened and enhanced by the act of the two parties coming together' (Clegg et al. 2010). Such displays of ideological identification were central to the construction of an image of unity, which was intended to reassure the party faithful and the electorate that the partners could work well together and, moreover, that the Coalition would stay the course.

The influence of the two parties' ideological traditions was evident in the guiding principles of the Coalition. While a commitment to freedom was common to both, fairness was primarily associated with the Liberal Democrats and responsibility with the Conservatives. At the press conference for the launch of the *Programme for Government* on 20 May 2010, senior Coalition figures invited identification with these values, and each concept is now discussed in turn. For Clegg and the Conservative Home Secretary, Theresa May, freedom was defined in terms of individual choice and empowerment. In Clegg's words, 'we will disperse power and restore freedom, and so build a stronger society where people are once again trusted to take control of their own lives' (Clegg et al. 2010). This was a definition with which Conservatives and Liberal Democrats could readily identify and, in practice, it entailed a better balance between individual freedom and national security, together with the restoration and protection of our civil liberties. As we will see below, the parties' shared belief in freedom from state control also supplied the ideological basis for significant reductions in public expenditure.

Meanwhile, Cable explained that fairness was about 'being a society where we protect the weakest, the most vulnerable and where everybody has the opportunity to fulfil their potential' (Clegg et al. 2010). Indeed, he claimed, 'without agreement on ... the concept of fairness, the coalition would never have happened' (Clegg et al. 2010). This statement was critical because Cable was associated with the social democratic tradition within the Liberal Democrats. As such, his prominent role in the new government offered reassurance that these values would be upheld, and so invited the Party's left wing to identify with the Coalition and support its policy programme. This reassurance was important, as the Liberal Democrat leadership had recently come to accept the Conservatives' plan for tackling Britain's budget deficit. While Cable noted that this was the Coalition's first priority, he was quick to emphasize that:

> The success of the government won't simply be measured by whether we deal with the budget deficit, but how we deal with it ... And the approach is that the burdens have got to be fairly shared—and in the difficult times ahead, we won't balance the books on the backs of the poorest. (Clegg et al. 2010)

Although fairness was a core Liberal Democrat value, Cable's use of the pronoun 'we' implied that both party leaderships were identified with this commitment and, furthermore, that it would guide the Coalition's deficit reduction programme.

On Cameron's view, the most important of the three principles was responsibility, as it was a core Conservative value and the mainstay of the 'Big Society'. This concept was explicated by Cameron and Osborne at the launch of the *Programme for Government*, which reflected both their ideological identification and the Conservatives' status as the senior partner within the Coalition. Cameron defined responsibility in terms of the obligations we owe to each other, the fulfilment of which will supply the foundations of a strong society. At the same time, he continued, those who are unable to play their part would receive the help they needed

(Clegg et al. 2010). This statement is consistent with the Liberal Democrats' belief in fairness, and so invited identification with Cameron as the embodiment of a modernized, compassionate Conservative Party that would promote responsibility while protecting the vulnerable.

Whereas Cameron focused on social responsibility, Osborne, as Chancellor of the Exchequer, was primarily concerned with the economy. Thus, he pledged that 'this coalition will put everything it does through this simple test: if it encourages responsibility we should do it; if it encourages irresponsibility, we shouldn't' (Clegg et al. 2010). In particular, he continued, 'we will bring responsibility to … creating a new economic model, where we save and invest for the future instead of building an economy on debt' (Clegg et al. 2010). This promise was mainly targeted at Conservative supporters but, in the wake of the 2008 global financial crisis, the notion of financial responsibility also resonated with a wider audience. By tapping into this, Osborne invited the public to identify ideologically with the Coalition, while seeking to cultivate an image of economic competence.

Underlying the Coalition's guiding principles was a belief in limited government, which facilitated the discovery of common ideological ground between the two parties and, moreover, afforded them a means of promoting their goals of freedom and responsibility. For Clegg, the dispersal of state power would ensure that people are 'free to make their own choices' (Clegg et al. 2010), while Cameron and Osborne viewed cuts to public spending—notably to the welfare budget—as vital to fostering personal and social responsibility. However, it would soon become apparent that the retrenchment of the social democratic state was at odds with the Coalition's publicly-expressed commitment to fairness. As Libby McEnhill argues, the Liberal Democrats could have responded either by openly reaffirming their belief in this core value, so preserving their distinctiveness, or by maintaining coalition unity at the expense of their reputation as the party of social justice (2015: 101). That they chose the second option led to ideological division within the Liberal Democrats and, in the longer term, caused serious damage to their public image and electoral prospects alike.

Although values are undoubtedly important, Cameron asserted that, 'above all, [the Coalition is] united in the purpose of bringing strong, stable, decisive government to our country' (Clegg et al. 2010). This, he claimed, is 'something that all Conservatives believe in profoundly', and as such his statement invited MPs and party supporters to identify ideologically with the new government. Equally, it can be interpreted as an attempt to carve out a place for the Coalition within the myth of the British political tradition, according to which strong, effective (single-party) government is intrinsically desirable, and so to reassure a wider audience that the partnership would not collapse within months. Either way, Cameron's words suggest that his administration was ideologically consubstantial, that it was united by shared values as well as a common goal, and that therefore it would endure for a full parliamentary term.

Instrumental Identification and the 'National Interest'

Using a terministic screen based on the principle of continuity, senior party figures linked the Coalition's stated aim of providing strong, stable government to the idea of the national interest. In Cameron's words,

> Given the massive challenges this country faces, particularly the deficit, the national interest was not served by a minority government limping along. It was served by strong, stable, decisive government that could really act in the long-term interests of our country. (Clegg et al. 2010)

Likewise, Clegg asserted that:

> At a time of such enormous difficulties, our country needed a strong and stable government. It needed an ambitious government determined to work relentlessly for a better future. That is what we have come together in this coalition to provide. (Cameron and Clegg 2010)

These claims indicate that the two leaders had agreed on a definition of the problems facing Britain, and had also attained instrumental identification based on a mutually acceptable conception of the 'national interest'. Indeed, their vision of the 'national interest' afforded a useful means of transcending ideological conflict and partisan interests, and so provided listeners with an alternative basis for identification.

In addition to bringing stability, Clegg claimed, the Coalition would be a 'radical reforming government' where needed (Cameron and Clegg 2010). As such, it would usher in a 'new politics' where, as Cameron put it, 'the national interest is more important than the party interest, where co-operation wins out over confrontation, where compromise ... is not a sign of weakness, but a sign of strength' (Cameron and Clegg 2010). It is worth noting that both leaders emphasized the novelty of the Coalition's approach, using the principle of discontinuity to portray it as a departure from the in-fighting of previous governments and as a source of hope for the future. This representation was designed to create a sense of optimism, which would increase the receptivity of their audience to the idea of a 'new politics' and, in turn, promote identification with the Coalition itself.

Cameron and Clegg presented the rapport between them as exemplary, as standing for the 'new politics' as a whole. Thus, Cameron emphasized their shared desire to 'put aside party differences and work hard for the common good and for the national interest' (2010), while Clegg observed that 'we have just been through an election campaign and now we have a coalition. Until today, we were rivals; now, we are colleagues. That says a lot about the scale of the new politics that is now beginning to unfold' (Cameron and Clegg 2010). On one level, these displays of interpersonal identification enabled the two leaders to project an image of coalition unity. On another, Cameron and Clegg's changed relationship provided a model for their parliamentary parties to emulate, encouraging them to overcome partisan rivalry and co-operate with their former adversaries to deliver the strong, stable government that Britain needed.

The allocation of ministerial portfolios is a source of potential conflict for any government, but arguably more so for a coalition. In a bid to neutralize discontent among backbench MPs, Cameron explained that:

> There are five Liberal Democrat Secretaries of State in Cabinet working hand in hand with Conservative colleagues to address the big challenges that Britain faces ... I think this is a sign of the strength and depth of this coalition and our sincere determination to work together constructively to make this coalition work in our national interest. (Cameron and Clegg 2010)

This depiction of inter-party co-operation within the Cabinet again served as an example to MPs, inviting them to set aside any ill-feeling and identify with Cameron's conception of the national interest. After all, any open dissent at this early stage could have been construed as an expression of narrow self-interest that would damage MPs personally and, moreover, risked destabilizing the Coalition at a time when unity was paramount.

At the launch of the *Programme for Government*, Clegg addressed the electorate directly, saying:

> New politics is about delivering the change you want ... You will get a referendum on the voting system, so you have a greater say on who represents you in Parliament. Government will be transparent. You will be able to get

your hands on all the information you need. You will be able to sack MPs who abuse the rules and we will pass a Freedom Bill to restore and protect your liberties. (Clegg et al. 2010)

Here, Clegg invited the public to identify instrumentally with the Coalition by enumerating the positive changes the 'new politics' would bring to their lives. After acknowledging the scale of the economic challenges facing Britain, he depicted deficit reduction as the precondition for the Coalition's 'ambitious programme for change and renewal' (Clegg et al. 2010). More specifically, austerity was presented as the means for achieving the government's goals of 'a stronger society, a sound economy, an accountable state, and power and responsibility in the hands of every citizen', and thus as being in the national interest (Clegg et al. 2010). We return to this argument in the next section.

There were, of course, individual and partisan interests involved on both sides, but they were downplayed by the two leaders in their efforts to portray the Coalition as a strong, united partnership. For Cameron, the formation of the coalition enabled him to deflect attention from his failure to win an overall majority and, in the words of Timothy Heppell and David Seawright, to 'minimize the impact of opposition from the parliamentary right [of his party] by diluting it with the support of the Liberal Democrats' (2012: 9). More broadly, Robert Hazell and Ben Yong note that the Conservatives could not have enacted their austerity programme as a minority government, and so needed to be the larger party in a full coalition (2012: 118). From the Liberal Democrats' perspective, meanwhile, Ruth Fox observes that the parlous state of their finances 'meant that the party could not afford a quick second election' (2010: 610). They also needed to show that coalition politics could work, given their commitment to electoral reform and their desire to secure a 'Yes' vote in the forthcoming referendum on AV. To voice these concerns in public would have risked making the leaders' decision to form a coalition appear self-serving, so they instead presented partnership government as the only means of advancing the national interest at a time of great uncertainty, and invited instrumental identification on this basis.

Identification Through Antithesis: The Storyline of the Deficit

The Coalition built a crisis narrative around Britain's structural deficit and employed it to invite identification through antithesis. This storyline consisted of two parts—a common cause and a common enemy—and we consider them in turn. As Paul 't Hart and Karen Tindall correctly point out, political parties will 'seek to mould and exploit ... crises in ways that suit their interests' (2009: 9) and, moreover, are compatible with their values and goals. Thus, in their 2010 manifestos, the Conservatives and the Liberal Democrats defined Britain's ongoing economic problems as a 'crisis of debt' that necessitated measures to reduce public expenditure (Conservative Party 2010: 3; Liberal Democrats 2010: 14). This response would have been seen as likely to compound the nation's difficulties had the situation been portrayed as a 'crisis of growth', but it appeared to be an entirely logical solution to a 'debt crisis'.[4] As a result, the parties' claims that cuts to government spending were in the national interest were more likely to gain traction with a wide audience.

On entering into coalition, the development of this storyline was facilitated by the ideological proximity of Conservative modernizers and the *Orange Book* Liberal Democrats. Of particular importance were the values of individual freedom and a smaller, less centralized state, which both factions believed could be realized through reductions in public expenditure. As Matt Beech explains, the idea was that the 'retrenchment of the state will gradually enable entrepreneurs and private firms to engender growth and for the voluntary sector and businesses to begin to provide more goods and services to the British people where previously the state had dominated' (2011: 273). The congruence of the two parties' thinking ensured that their commitment to austerity acted not only as the cornerstone of the Coalition, but as the overarching goal that would sustain the partnership through the inevitable conflicts and compromises ahead.

According to the *Programme for Government*, 'the deficit reduction programme takes precedence over any of the other measures in this agreement' (HM Government 2010: 35). Through a terministic screen based on continuity, this primacy was linked to the national interest, with Cable supporting the immediate implementation of austerity on the ground that 'the problem of the financial crisis in Europe over the last few weeks has underlined the absolute priority for establishing confidence in the country' (Clegg et al. 2010). Cable's statement marked a startling about-face for the Liberal Democrats, who had campaigned vigorously against immediate spending cuts before the general election. On this basis, Mark Stuart suggests that the Party may have used the emerging Eurozone crisis as a fig leaf to justify their acceptance of the Conservatives' economic policy and the subsequent formation of a full coalition government (2011: 48). It is also worth noting here Andrew Gamble's claim that senior Coalition figures exaggerated the threat this developing crisis posed to Britain 'in order to establish a new definition of political reality and a new set of policies' (2012: 69). Nevertheless, the alignment of core party values with the leaders' conception of the national interest constituted a compelling invitation to MPs and grassroots members to identify with the Coalition, and so to unite behind the cause of deficit reduction.

In bringing the parties together to tackle the economic crisis, the storyline also joined them together against a common enemy, namely the Labour Party. 't Hart and Tindall explain that 'apportioning blame is an integral part of contemporary politics in times of crisis' (2009: 9) and, given that the financial crash occurred on Labour's watch, it was relatively easy for the partners to direct their listeners' attention to the purported connection between them. To this end, writes Ben Kisby, Coalition figures repeatedly claimed that:

> The vast government debt that now needs to be tackled is the result of an over-mighty state and not due to the previous government's need to spend hundreds of billions of pounds precisely to prop up banks and the money markets to enable the free market to keep functioning. (2010: 485)

Thus, the Labour government's fiscal stimulus, which as Gamble notes was previously seen as the 'necessary means to avoid financial collapse', was redefined as the problem that the Coalition needed to overcome in order to restart economic growth (2012: 67).

To further undermine Labour's reputation, Coalition figures attributed the crisis not only to its alleged incompetence and mismanagement, but to moral failure. As Osborne put it:

> So many of the great problems we face as a country today ... come back to a lack of responsibility. Our enormous debts, our massive welfare rolls ... at the root of these problems may be one person, a collection of people, or even a whole culture, saying, 'Let's do what we want, instead of what is right'. (Clegg et al. 2010)

In contrast, he continued, the Coalition would bring responsibility 'back to the heart of our national life' by reducing the size and power of the state, reforming the welfare system and demonstrating that Britain can 'tackle its debts and live within its means' (Clegg et al. 2010). The suggestion here is that because responsibility was one of the Coalition's guiding principles, it alone could be trusted to act in the national interest and take the difficult decisions required to transform the economy and restore sustainable growth. In this way, identification through antithesis served to minimize inter-party divisions by inviting MPs and supporters to unite behind the values and goals of the Coalition, in opposition to the 'fiscally irresponsible' Labour Party that had 'wrecked' Britain's economy.

However, writes Stuart, 'what [the Liberal Democrats] seemed unable to realize at the time was that their central concession to the Conservatives on the economy—agreeing to cut the deficit further and faster than Labour—trumped all their anorak manifesto commitments put together' (2011: 53). It also came at the cost of their commitment to fairness which, as noted above, was subordinated to the Coalition's goal of reducing the size of the state. Although a degree of ideological realignment may be inevitable for the junior partner, a process that was facilitated in this case by the proximity of the Conservative leadership and the *Orange Book* Liberal Democrats, the latter could arguably have defended their core principle more vigorously. After all, claims Stuart, the Conservatives 'needed the maximum degree of parliamentary support possible for [their] tough decisions on public spending ... [and calculated that] the best means of securing that was through a strong and stable coalition' (2011: 48). This suggests that the Liberal Democrats could have demonstrated more influence over the direction of the government than they perhaps believed possible, and that they could have done so without fear of the partnership's collapse. But, in the early days of the new government—and in public at least—the two parties needed to present a united front; there would be plentiful opportunities for them to assert their distinctiveness later on.

CONCLUSION

This chapter has examined the rhetorical dynamics of unity and distinctiveness at work within the negotiating dialogue between the Conservative Party and the Liberal Democrats. Here, the issue of higher education funding was controversial, and the leaders deferred the decision in order to enable the talks to continue. Also contentious was constitutional reform but, through rhetorical strategizing, senior Conservatives and Liberal Democrats were able to achieve ideological identification on the equalization of constituency boundaries. They also discovered a shared interest in promising to hold a referendum on AV and, moreover, succeeded in winning their MPs' support for the deal. On Europe, Cameron and Clegg 'essentially decided that policy ... should be put in the deep freeze' (Laws 2016: 238), though they were instrumentally consubstantial on their definition of the national interest. On this basis, the Coalition pledged to co-operate with the EU to address such challenges as economic competitiveness, climate change and global poverty (HM Government 2010: 19). Finally, the parties were ideologically consubstantial in the area of foreign policy, due to their common beliefs in the rule of law and international co-operation. In instrumental terms, they shared a pragmatic commitment to distance the Coalition from New Labour, and so to repair the damage wrought to Britain's reputation by the 2003 Iraq war.

Once the negotiations were completed, senior Coalition figures employed a range of strategies to invite party members and the wider electorate to identify with the new government. Thus, they mobilized the Coalition's guiding principles of freedom, fairness and responsibility—together with their shared commitment to reduce the size of the state—in a bid to foster ideological identification. The partners also used constructions of a 'new politics' and the 'national interest' to downplay the role of partisan interests in their decision to form a full coalition, as well as to quell intra-party dissent. Finally, the chapter considered the Coalition's use of identification through antithesis, which was based on the storyline of Britain's debt crisis. This storyline served to unite party supporters behind the cause of deficit reduction, in opposition to the 'reckless' and 'incompetent' Labour Party. The following chapters will explore how the strategies of identification and division employed in the formation stage shaped the rhetorical opportunities and constraints available to the coalition partners in the governance phase, starting with higher education policy.

NOTES

1. Laws's account is based on transcripts and detailed notes of the meetings, and the accuracy of his recollections is verified by others involved in the negotiations (2010: 9–10). The chapter draws primarily on this text though, as far as possible, only verbatim quotations from the coalition talks and intra-party debates are included in the analysis. For verification purposes, these are triangulated with other sources.

2. The other 'red line' issues for the Liberal Democrats were the Pupil Premium, tax cuts for low earners and 'action to restore the public finances and create a sustainable economy' (Laws 2010: 88).

3. The argument that AV is a form of first-past-the-post was also made by Chris Huhne and Nick Clegg (Wilson 2010: 162, 207), lending support to Laws's account of the Liberal Democrats' pre-election strategizing.

4. On the framing of the 2008 global financial crisis, see Hay (2013).

REFERENCES

Adonis, A. (2013). *5 Days in May: The Coalition and Beyond*. London: Biteback Publishing Ltd.

Atkins, J. (2015). 'Together in the National Interest': The Rhetoric of Unity and the Formation of the Cameron-Clegg Government. *The Political Quarterly*, *86*(1), 85–92.

Beech, M. (2011). A Tale of Two Liberalisms. In S. Lee & M. Beech (Eds.), *The Cameron-Clegg Government: Coalition Politics in an Age of Austerity* (pp. 267–279). Basingstoke: Palgrave Macmillan.

Blau, A. (2004). Fairness and Electoral Reform. *British Journal of Politics and International Relations*, *6*(2), 165–181.

Bogdanor, V. (2011). *The Coalition and the Constitution*. Oxford: Hart Publishing Ltd.

Cameron, D. (2010, May 11). *General Election Victory Speech*. Retrieved from http://www.britishpoliticalspeech.org/speech-archive.htm?speech=217

Cameron, D., & Clegg, N. (2010, May 12). *Press Conference Given by Prime Minister David Cameron and Deputy Prime Minister Nick Clegg*. Retrieved from https://www.gov.uk/government/speeches/pm-and-deputy-pm-press-conference--2

Clegg, N. (2016). *Politics: Between the Extremes*. London: The Bodley Head.

Clegg, N., May, T., Cable, V., Osborne, G., & Cameron, D. (2010, May 20). *Press Conference on the Coalition: Our Programme for Government*. Retrieved from https://www.gov.uk/government/speeches/the-coalition-our-programme-for-government-press-conference

Conservative Party. (2010). *Invitation to Join the Government of Britain: The Conservative Manifesto 2010*. London: The Conservative Party.

d'Ancona, M. (2013). *In It Together: The Inside Story of the Coalition Government*. London: Viking.

Fox, R. (2010). Five Days in May: A New Political Order Emerges. *Parliamentary Affairs*, *63*(4), 607–622.

Gamble, A. (2012). Economic Policy. In T. Heppell & D. Seawright (Eds.), *Cameron and the Conservatives: The Transition to Coalition Government* (pp. 59–73). Basingstoke: Palgrave Macmillan.

Goes, E. (2015). The Liberal Democrats and the Coalition: Driven to the Edge of Europe. *The Political Quarterly, 86*(1), 93–100.

Hay, C. (2013). Treating the Symptom Not the Condition: Crisis Definition, Deficit Reduction and the Search for a New British Growth Model. *British Journal of Politics and International Relations, 15*(1), 23–37.

HM Government. (2010). *The Coalition: Our Programme for Government*. London: Cabinet Office.

Hazell, R., & Yong, B. (2012). *The Politics of Coalition: How the Cameron-Clegg Government Works*. Oxford: Hart Publishing Ltd.

Heppell, T., & Seawright, D. (2012). Introduction. In T. Heppell & D. Seawright (Eds.), *Cameron and the Conservatives: The Transition to Coalition Government* (pp. 1–15). Basingstoke: Palgrave Macmillan.

Kavanagh, D., & Cowley, P. (2010). *The British General Election of 2010*. Basingstoke: Palgrave Macmillan.

Kisby, B. (2010). The Big Society: Power to the People? *The Political Quarterly, 81*(4), 484–491.

Laws, D. (2010). *22 Days in May: The Birth of the Lib Dem-Conservative Coalition*. London: Biteback Publishing Ltd.

Laws, D. (2016). *Coalition: The Inside Story of the Conservative-Liberal Democrat Coalition Government*. London: Biteback Publishing Ltd.

Lee, S. (2011). 'We Are All in This Together': The Coalition Agenda for British Modernization. In S. Lee & M. Beech (Eds.), *The Cameron-Clegg Government: Coalition Politics in an Age of Austerity* (pp. 3–23). Basingstoke: Palgrave Macmillan.

Liberal Democrats. (2010). *Liberal Democrat Manifesto 2010*. London: Liberal Democrats.

Lynch, P. (2011). The Con-Lib Agenda for Europe. In S. Lee & M. Beech (Eds.), *The Cameron-Clegg Government: Coalition Politics in an Age of Austerity* (pp. 218–233). Basingstoke: Palgrave Macmillan.

Lynch, P. (2015). The Coalition and the European Union. In M. Beech & S. Lee (Eds.), *The Conservative-Liberal Coalition: Examining the Cameron-Clegg Government* (pp. 243–258). Basingstoke: Palgrave Macmillan.

McEnhill, L. (2015). Unity and Distinctiveness in UK Coalition Government: Lessons for Junior Partners. *The Political Quarterly, 86*(1), 101–109.

Norton, P., & Thompson, L. (2015). Parliament and the Constitution: The Coalition in Conflict. In M. Beech & S. Lee (Eds.), *The Conservative-Liberal Coalition: Examining the Cameron-Clegg Government* (pp. 129–144). Basingstoke: Palgrave Macmillan.

Paun, A. (2011). United We Stand? Governance Challenges for the United Kingdom Coalition. *The Political Quarterly, 82*(2), 251–260.

Stuart, M. (2011). The Formation of the Coalition. In S. Lee & M. Beech (Eds.), *The Cameron-Clegg Government: Coalition Politics in an Age of Austerity* (pp. 38–55). Basingstoke: Palgrave Macmillan.

't Hart, P., & Tindall, K. (2009). From 'Market Correction' to 'Global Catastrophe': Framing the Economic Downturn. In P. 't Hart & K. Tindall (Eds.), *Framing the Global Economic Downturn: Crisis Rhetoric and the Politics of Recessions* (pp. 3–19). Canberra: ANU E Press.

Wilson, R. (2010). *5 Days to Power: The Journey to Coalition Britain*. London: Biteback Publishing Ltd.

CHAPTER 3

Higher Education Policy

The funding of higher education in England was a key issue for the Liberal Democrats in the run-up to the 2010 general election. Indeed, all 57 Liberal Democrat MPs—including Nick Clegg and Vince Cable—had signed a National Union of Students (NUS) pledge to 'vote against any increase in fees in the next parliament and to pressure the Government to introduce a fairer alternative' (NUS 2010), and were photographed doing so. They thus identified themselves ideologically with the students' cause, based on a common commitment to fairness. This move was consistent with the Liberal Democrats' self-image as a radical, progressive party that was outside the political mainstream. It also differentiated them from Labour and the Conservatives, both of whom were 'distinctly noncommittal on student fees and kept their options open' (Hazell and Yong 2012: 173; see also d'Ancona 2013: 61). Clegg later became the 'face' of his party's policy when he appeared in a YouTube video for the NUS annual conference on 13 April 2010. Here, he invited instrumental identification based on the claim that it is not in people's interests to leave university with 'this dead weight of debt, around £24,000, round their neck' (quoted in Watt 2010). This strategy proved very effective, as the Liberal Democrats attracted high levels of support from students, which in turn contributed to the outbreak of 'Cleggmania' as the campaign progressed.

© The Author(s) 2018
J. Atkins, *Conflict, Co-operation and the Rhetoric of Coalition Government*, Rhetoric, Politics and Society,
https://doi.org/10.1057/978-1-137-31796-4_3

In the *Programme for Government*, the Coalition partners deferred the decision on university funding until the publication of the Browne Report. This chapter begins by outlining Browne's recommendations and the Coalition's policy response to them. It then considers the rhetoric of identification and division at work within the December 2010 parliamentary debate on the reforms. Next, the chapter examines the identification strategies employed by Vince Cable, the Liberal Democrat Secretary of State for Business, Innovation and Skills (BIS), and David Willetts, the Conservative Minister of State for Universities and Science, in keynote speeches delivered between 2010 and 2012. Finally, it discusses Clegg's public apology for the Liberal Democrats' U-turn on tuition fees, which was broadcast in September 2012 and, as far as possible, was intended to 'draw a line under the issue ... well before the general election' (Laws 2016: 205). In so doing, the chapter demonstrates that while both parties appealed to conceptions of 'fairness' and to a range of economic interests, the Liberal Democrats made frequent use of interpersonal identification in a bid to foster understanding of their changed position on higher education funding.

The Browne Report and the Coalition's Response

The Browne Review published its report, entitled *Securing a Sustainable Future for Higher Education: An Independent Review of Higher Education and Student Finance*, on 12 October 2010.[1] This document 'modelled an 80 per cent cut in the teaching grant to universities', thereby shifting the bulk of the financial cost of higher education away from the state and onto individual students (Griffiths 2011: 82). Browne also argued that there should be no limit on tuition fees, although a levy should be imposed on institutions charging fees of more than £6,000, and that they should not be payable upfront. Instead, fees should be repaid in the form of a loan (Brown with Carasso 2013: 90). The threshold for the repayment of loans (with interest) was increased from £15,000 to £21,000, and any outstanding debt would be written off after 30 years. Notably, Browne rejected the alternative option of a graduate tax, on the ground that it 'would not provide a mechanism to improve student experience, whereas a loan system empowers the student as consumer' (Griffiths 2011: 82; see also Collini 2017: 181).

According to the Browne Committee, their proposals would benefit the higher education sector in three ways. First, they would enable it to expand, as the number of places should increase by 10 per cent, while support for part-time and low-income students should be improved. Second, the proposals would improve quality by creating:

> Genuine competition for students between [Higher Education Institutions, or HEIs], of a kind that cannot take place under the current system. There will be more investment available for the HEIs that are able to convince students that it is worthwhile. This is in our view a surer way to drive up quality than any attempt at central planning. (The Browne Report, quoted in Brown with Carasso 2013: 91)

Third, higher education would be financially sustainable in the long term, as increased contributions would be sought from those who could afford to make them. Furthermore, the blanket government subsidy would be removed from all courses, though public investment in priority subjects would continue (Brown with Carasso 2013: 91).

With regard to student support, the Browne Committee prosed to simplify the maintenance loan system by establishing a single flat-rate entitlement of £3,750. Students who were only applying for a loan would not be means tested, and this maintenance loan would be repayable on the same terms as the tuition fee loan. The Committee also recommended that the maximum grant for students from low-income backgrounds, which would be available in addition to the maintenance loan, should increase to £3,250. Where household income was below £25,000 students would be eligible for the full grant, while a partial grant would be available up to a household income of £50,000. Finally, 'all students should receive at least as much cash in hand as at present' from the combined maintenance loan and grant (Brown with Carasso 2013: 91–92).

In response to Browne's recommendations, the Coalition proposed an absolute cap on fees of £9,000 per annum, though it emphasized that most universities would be expected to charge £6,000. Those institutions charging more than this sum would be required to contribute to a National Scholarship Programme to support students from low-income backgrounds. In addition, there would be a 'stricter regime of sanctions encouraging high-charging universities to increase participation' (Griffiths 2011: 82), and the Government's Office for Fair Access (OFFA) would be responsible for monitoring this new regime. These measures were introduced in an effort to ensure that students from poorer backgrounds would not be deterred from applying to university, an issue that was of 'real importance to the Liberal Democrats' (Hazell and Yong 2012: 175) given their ideological commitments to fairness and opportunity for all. However, the Party's acceptance of Coalition policy was in direct violation of their manifesto pledge to abolish tuition fees and, as we will see below, it would prove problematic for senior Liberal Democrats seeking to persuade their MPs to identify with the Government and support its reforms.

The Parliamentary Debate on Higher Education Funding, 2010

On 9 December 2010, MPs debated the draft Higher Education (Basic Amount) (England) Regulations 2010, which would allow universities to increase tuition fees to a maximum of £9,000 from September 2012.[2] Prior to this, three Parliamentary Private Secretaries—two Liberal Democrats and one Conservative—resigned in order to vote against the Coalition's proposals. The debate took place against the backdrop of two protest marches in central London, which were organized by the NUS and the University of London Union and were expected to involve up to 40,000 demonstrators (Walker and Paige 2010). For much of the day the demonstrations were 'tense but peaceful'. However, once the result of the vote was announced, they descended into violence as protesters clashed with the police. In total there were 26 arrests, and at least 38 demonstrators were injured (Wintour and Watt 2010).

As Secretary of State for BIS, Cable was responsible for steering the proposals through the Commons. Despite the provision in the *Programme for Government* that Liberal Democrat MPs could abstain in the parliamentary vote, Cable insisted he would support the measures on the ground that 'the system he was introducing was better than the one it was replacing' (Cowley and Kavanagh 2016: 105). In making the case for higher tuition fees, Cable employed both instrumental and ideological forms of identification. Taking these strategies in turn, he presented the Coalition's proposals to Parliament as the best available option in light of the scale of Britain's economic difficulties. Given that BIS was facing a spending reduction of around 25 per cent, he claimed that the government could have reduced the number of university places by 200,000, or cut the financial support available to students. Alternatively, it could simply have reduced the funding to universities 'without giving them the means to raise additional income through a graduate contribution'. This approach would inevitably lead to their decline, and for Cable was 'unacceptable' (HC Deb., 9 December 2010, vol. 520 col. 544). After seeking to create rapport with MPs by acknowledging that 'we have had to make very difficult choices', Cable asserted that the Coalition's policy 'provides a strong base for university funding and makes a major contribution to reducing the deficit, while introducing a significantly more progressive system of graduate payments than we inherited' (HC Deb., 9 December 2010, vol. 520 cols. 548–9). Thus, it would be in the interests of the universities, as it would enable them to maintain their level of funding without the need for reductions in student numbers. The new fees regime would also benefit the nation's economy by easing the pressure on the public finances, and Cable invited MPs to identify instrumentally with these conclusions.

Cable also sought to foster ideological identification with the Coalition's reforms, on the ground that they provide 'a more progressive system of graduate contributions based on people's ability to pay' (HC Deb., 9 December 2010, vol. 520 col. 540). The claim that the policy was 'progressive' was central to Cable's argument, and in the following statement he repeated it no fewer than four times:

> The first thing that I asked [Lord Browne] to do was to see how we could make the existing system of graduate payments more *progressive* and more related to future graduates' ability to pay. He undertook to do that, and we have done further work to develop the *progressivity* of the system. As a result, the Institute for Fiscal Studies was able to conclude that the package that we have produced is more *progressive* than the existing system and more *progressive* than the Browne report. (HC Deb., 9 December 2010, vol. 520 col. 541, emphasis added)

Here, 'progressive' is defined in terms of fairness, which is understood as not placing an excessive financial burden on graduates. The concept of fairness is a core Liberal Democrat value, and it is perhaps not too much of a stretch to suggest that Cable's reluctance to employ it was indicative of his concerns about how his Party would react to the Government's proposals. Indeed, for many Liberal Democrats, the Coalition's policy hardly constituted the 'fairer alternative' demanded in the NUS pledge, so these appeals to 'progressivity' afforded Cable an alternate means of inviting ideological identification.

The shift away from 'fairness' was evident in Clegg's (2010) Hugo Young lecture, where he created an antithesis between 'old' and 'new' progressives. As Clegg put it: 'Old progressives measure success by the power and spending of the central state. New progressives measure it by the power and freedom of individual citizens'. Clearly Labour were to be seen as 'old' progressives, while the *Orange Book* Liberal Democrats and the Conservative modernizers were classed as 'new' progressives due to their shared belief in individual freedom and a small state. In turn, Clegg continued, this classification entailed a redefinition of fairness, 'from a static, income-based definition of fairness to an approach focused on mobility and life chances' (2010). This modified concept underpinned the Coalition's higher education reforms, in which the market took precedence over the state in the provision of a public good and consumer choice was paramount. Clegg's distinction also mirrored the division between the *Orange Book* Liberal Democrats and the Party's social liberal wing, the latter of which was ideologically consubstantial with the NUS on the basis of the 'old' progressive conception of fairness.

It is not surprising that only a minority of the Liberal Democrats' parliamentary party supported the proposals. One such MP was Duncan Hames, who cited the Coalition's constructive response to his efforts to persuade them to make the reforms fairer. Although he recognized that more work was needed, he declared he was confident that 'Ministers will continue to engage with the issues. That is why I will join them in the Aye Lobby' (HC Deb., 9 December 2010, vol. 520 col. 608). In contrast, most Conservatives backed the Government, and indeed some MPs praised the policy as 'progressive'. Rehman Chishti, for example, supported the reforms 'on the basis that they are fair, just and progressive' and would ensure that 'anyone who wants to go to university will be able to do so, and will be able to reach their true potential' (HC Deb., 9 December 2010, vol. 520 col. 598). Likewise, Alok Sharma rejected the claim that the proposals would reduce social mobility, citing the abolition of upfront fees, and argued that 'everyone, whatever their background, will be able to take advantage of the opportunities offered by a university education' (HC Deb., 9 December 2010, vol. 520 col. 591). Here, both Conservative MPs endorsed the 'new' progressive conception of fairness as opportunity and social mobility, and so demonstrated their ideological consubstantiality with the Coalition's approach.

Many Conservative backbenchers also identified with the Coalition on instrumental grounds, claiming the reforms would bring a range of benefits. Thus, using a terministic screen based on continuity, Sharma argued that the proposed changes would 'go further towards making universities more accountable to students as customers' (HC Deb., 9 December 2010, vol. 520 col. 591), and David Evennett stated that they would 'encourage a genuine market that will provide academic excellence and reinforce the international success of British universities' (HC Deb., 9 December 2010, vol. 520 col. 560). These views are consistent with the neoliberal belief that 'market competition may improve quality as institutions respond to students … by improving quality of service' (Brown with Carasso 2013: 125), and so Sharma and Evennett presented the Coalition's proposals as being in the interests of students and universities alike. Indeed, Willetts reinforced this position by observing that: '53 university leaders from across England have made it clear that they support the … shift towards a more progressive graduate contribution scheme as the way to provide a more sustainable higher education system' (HC Deb., 9 December 2010, vol. 520 col. 623).

Willetts also invited instrumental identification on the basis of the national interest, contending that: 'Labour left a mess in the public finances, and the Government must tackle it. If we do not tackle it in the way we propose … it will simply mean less funding for universities or more Government borrowing', which would have increased the deficit further (HC Deb., 9 December 2010, vol. 520 cols. 623–4). A number of Conservative MPs sought to undermine Labour in this way, implying the Party that had created the present 'economic mess' was not in a position to criticize the Coalition's 'sustainable solution' to the question of higher education funding.[3] This use of identification through antithesis drew on the storyline of the deficit and served to unite the 'fiscally responsible' coalition partners against the 'profligate' Labour Party, while simultaneously creating an ideological contrast between the 'new' and the 'old' progressives.

However, the reforms were subjected to heavy criticism from several Coalition MPs, who distanced themselves from the reforms while seeking to reassure the students and their constituents that they, at least, remained true to their principles. For instance, the Liberal Democrat Greg Mulholland employed a terministic screen based on the principle of discontinuity to challenge the Government's linkage of higher fees to 'all those positive things, which are in the proposals and are progressive in terms of the graduate contribution'. Indeed, he argued, 'it is simply not true to say, "You cannot have one without the other" and that is the crucial flaw in the Government's argument today' (HC Deb., 9 December 2010, vol. 520 col. 565). Mulholland then dismissed the claim that the proposals would contribute to deficit reduction as a budgetary sleight of hand, and he refused to support the Coalition for this reason (HC Deb., 9 December 2010, vol. 520 col. 566). Similarly, the Conservative back-bencher John Baron expressed the concern that, 'by increasing the tuition cap, participation levels among lower and middle-income students will fall away' (HC Deb., 9 December 2010, vol. 520 col. 544).[4] While these objections can be contested, the main point here is not their validity. Rather, they are important because they demonstrate a lack of instrumental identification with Cable's conclusion that the Coalition's policies were in the interests of students and the universities and, more-over, would benefit the country as a whole.

A number of MPs challenged Cable's assertion that the new system would be more progressive. Thus, Mulholland drew on the 'old' progressive definition of fairness to object that 'I simply cannot accept that fees of up to £9,000 are the fairest and most sustainable way of funding higher education' (HC Deb., 9 December 2010, vol. 520 col. 565), while others called attention to the loss of the Aimhigher scheme. This initiative was intended to widen participation in higher education and, as the Conservative MP Steve Brine put it, 'I think it works and that it has been proved to work, and it worries me that it is disappearing' (HC Deb., 9 December 2010, vol. 520 col. 598). He therefore cast doubt on the Liberal Democrats' claim to be 'new' progressives who supported social mobility. Indeed, these MPs' objections show that they did not identify ideologically with Cable's position on the basis of either the 'old' or the 'new' progressive definition of fairness.

In the event, Cable was unable to persuade the majority of Liberal Democrat MPs to support the Coalition's proposals in the parliamentary vote. This intra-party conflict was manifested in a three-way split, with 28 MPs voting in favour of the policy, 21 opposing the changes and eight either absent or exercising their prerogative to abstain as per the *Programme for Government* (Griffiths 2011: 83). Among those who voted against the policy were the former Liberal Democrat leaders Charles Kennedy and Sir Menzies Campbell (d'Ancona 2013: 64), both of whom were associated with the 'old' progressive wing of the Party. The legislation was passed with a majority of 21 votes but, as Robert Hazell and Ben Yong point out, 'had all the [Liberal Democrats] abstained … the vote would have been lost' (2012: 175). Although the passage of the legislation maintained the stability of the Coalition in the early months of the Parliament, it came at a high price for the Liberal Democrats. Their image as the 'party of fairness' was shattered, while their subsequent efforts to invite identification by appealing this value would be greeted with cynicism.

CABLE AND WILLETTS ADDRESS THE UNIVERSITY SECTOR

Prior to the publication of the Browne Report, Cable favoured a graduate tax as a means of shifting the balance of funding away from the state and onto those who benefit from a university education. This change was necessitated, he believed, by the condition of the public finances and the weaknesses of the existing system, one of which was that a care worker or teacher is required to 'pay the same graduate contribution as a top commercial lawyer or surgeon ... whose graduate premium is so much bigger' (2010). For Cable this was clearly unfair, and he was eager to explore the possibility of a repayment system in which graduate contributions varied according to an individual's earnings. Here, he drew on the 'old' progressive definition of fairness to invite ideological identification, and he urged his listeners to 'help us think creatively about fairer mechanisms than the current one, recognizing that for students and their families a central issue is securing an equitable system of graduate contributions' (2010).

Cable then sought to foster instrumental identification by highlighting the benefits of a graduate tax for the sector, and he told Parliament that: 'a larger graduate contribution will help universities with their funding while maintaining their financial independence' (2010). Under these proposals the Government would no longer lend money to students, but instead would pay tuition fees directly to the universities. A graduate would begin repaying the state when they earned £15,000 or more (Shepherd 2010). Cable's identification strategies were ineffective, however, as they were subsequently rejected by representatives of the main university mission groups.[5] For instance, the then President of Universities UK (UUK), Steve Smith, described the proposed reduction in state funding as 'economically self-defeating', while the then chair of MillionPlus, Les Ebdon, asserted that the increased repayments associated with a graduate tax would have to be 'squared with the Coalition Government's commitment to social mobility' (both quoted in Shepherd 2010). As an alternative, Wendy Piatt, the then Director General of the Russell Group, endorsed higher fees and income-contingent loans as the 'fairest and most effective way of securing graduate contributions' (quoted in Shepherd 2010), an approach that would subsequently be adopted by the Coalition.

As we have seen, the Government's reforms were problematic for Cable, and he had to promote them to the university sector while justifying his change of heart. The storyline of the deficit was central to this strategy, and he told delegates at the 2011 UUK conference that: 'I inherited a situation in which my Department, much of whose spending is on universities, was due for a 25 per cent cut, and indeed we did then have a 25 per cent cut in the Spending Review' (2011).[6] For Cable, a reduction in funding on that scale was unthinkable, and on this basis the new model was by far the lesser of two evils. Not only that, but the Coalition's proposals would improve 'student choice and access, teaching and employability—as well as … putting the sector's finances on a sustainable footing' (2011). Cable thus invited his listeners to identify instrumentally with the Government's plans, on the grounds that they would enhance the undergraduate experience while ensuring the universities would be financially secure.

In a bid to establish a rapport with his audience, Cable repeatedly acknowledged the problems that these 'big changes' had created, saying, for instance: 'I appreciate that some people have had difficulties with [the new system]. It has been a difficult and sometimes traumatic process for us, but I can honestly say that I believe the alternatives would be worse' (2011). It is unclear whether 'us' referred to the Coalition or the Liberal Democrats, though the process was certainly challenging for the latter—not least for Cable himself. Cable's displays of empathy were reinforced by his cautious language, which was evident in his statement that 'I hope you will agree … that this [new system] is a good outcome for your sector' (2011). That the phrase 'I hope' recurred throughout the speech is perhaps indicative of Cable's awareness of the magnitude of the Coalition's reforms, and so constituted another appeal for interpersonal identification.

To show that the Coalition was in touch with, and responsive to, their views, Cable told delegates that:

> We have had powerful representations from the sector on the Stalinist system of student number controls, and so we are liberalizing student number controls to allow universities to recruit as many applicants achieving AAB at A-level as they choose to. (2011; for discussion see McGettigan 2013: Chap. 5).

This demonstration may have been a further attempt to build rapport, but it also created identification through antithesis. Cable's use of the adjective 'Stalinist' was clearly a gibe at Labour, whose top-down approach was implicitly contrasted with the drive towards liberalization that united university leaders and the Government. To reinforce this opposition, Cable invited ideological identification by explaining that the Coalition's decision to remove the restrictions on student numbers was about 'increasing competition, and supporting diversity within the sector' (2011), both of which are key neoliberal commitments.

Willetts also addressed the UUK conference in 2011. He began his speech by locating the Coalition's reforms in their historical context, telling his audience that 'it has been a consistent theme of the key enquiries into higher education that more funding should follow the decisions of learners'. After all, he continued, 'the Dearing review called for "at least 60 per cent of total public funding to institutions [to occur] according to student choice by 2003"' (2011). Here, Willetts used a terministic screen based on the principle of continuity to present the Coalition's reforms as a logical—and indeed necessary—extension of previous developments, which in turn implied that they were not as radical as many people (including Cable) believed. This portrayal may have been intended to establish rapport by offering reassurance, but equally it was consistent with the Conservatives' ideological commitment to gradual change and so provided a second basis for identification. However, Willetts later acknowledged that: 'Some people would have preferred the reforms to be less radical or phased in over time. But the reality is we have had to act quickly to address the fiscal deficit and to give universities time to prepare' (2011). Thus, like Cable, he drew on the storyline of the deficit to foster instrumental identification based on the interests of the nation and of the universities themselves.

Willetts then emphasized the financial advantages of the new system, namely that graduates would repay less each month due to the higher threshold and that investment in universities would increase by around 10 per cent by the end of the Parliament. This projected increase was based on the assumption that average fees would be £7,500, and Willetts exhorted delegates not to charge the maximum £9,000. After all, he explained, the Coalition was committed to keeping prices under control, but 'would rather do so through greater transparency, by freeing up student number controls and by encouraging new entrants. Greater competition is surely preferable to further regulation or funding changes' (2011). With these words, Willetts sought to foster instrumental identification with the Coalition's commitment by presenting competition as the best available option for the universities, while also making clear the potential consequences of a failure to comply.

In the event, however, the majority of universities set fees of £9,000, though these were offset by bursaries for poorer students as required by OFFA. Explaining this move, the Chair of Bradford University's ruling council said: 'The decision to charge a fee of £9,000 is one that has been made with great reluctance but is set against the context of the devastating cuts to the sector' (quoted in Paton and Prince 2011). This statement is a demonstration of instrumental division, whereby the Coalition's claim that the reforms would ensure the financial sustainability of universities was rejected in favour of the sector's own predefined interests. Among these may have been considerations of institutional prestige, and thus attractiveness to prospective students. As one vice chancellor suggested, '£9,000 fees have not been based on any calculation of cost but on perception of status' (quoted in Paton 2011); in other words, the fear of appearing 'substandard' mitigated against setting fees at anything below the maximum level.

The new fees regime came into effect in September 2012 and, again addressing the UUK conference, Willetts asserted that 'the financing changes, despite the controversy, are in the best interests of universities, students, and the nation' (2012a). To support this appeal for instrumental identification, he outlined three key objectives he believed were being met by the reforms. The first was that the Coalition had 'saved money for the Exchequer without reducing the cash flowing to our universities', and indeed more savings were expected the following year. Meanwhile, the second goal was increased competition and choice, both of which would be in the interest of students. Elaborating on this point in the wake of the decision of most universities to charge fees of £9,000 per year, Willetts reiterated the Coalition's commitment to 'relaxing [student number] controls for individual universities within an overall total, so that more students can go to whichever university wants to accept them' (2012a). The third objective was the increased amount of information available to prospective students, central to which was the new Key Information Set (KIS) data.[7] This data would enable students to compare institutions, and thus to make an informed choice.

According to Willetts, the Coalition's progress towards meeting the three objectives amounted to 'a revolution in teaching—the largest cultural change in our universities for a generation' (2012a; see also Willetts 2012b). After all, he continued, research had long been the primary focus, and it was now time for teaching to take centre stage. Willetts explained that students would be asking questions about the experience they received for their fees of up to £9,000 per annum and, while they are not simply consumers, 'they are certainly entitled to an excellent academic education for this funding' (2012b; see also McGettigan 2013: 58). With this in mind, he expressed the hope that 'applicants will make full use of the KIS data in figuring out which institutions can offer the most appropriate teaching environment for their individual needs—and that universities will adjust to student- and parent-power' (2012a). As such, it was clearly in the universities' interests to adapt to the new climate on pain of losing students (and therefore money), and on these grounds Willetts invited them to identify instrumentally with his case for change.

The Coalition's reforms also had an impact on participation, due to the requirements for improved access that accompanied higher fees. In discussing this aspect of policy, Willetts sought to foster ideological identification, and he demonstrated his consubstantiality with the sector by telling delegates that: 'What we all want to see is not social engineering—and certainly not quotas—but quite simply genuine meritocracy' (2012b). As he explained, the Coalition believed that widening participation was right because it ensured that talent did not go to waste. This in turn demanded that university admission procedures should be, 'as we say in the White Paper, "fair, transparent and evidence-based"' (2012a). For Willetts, the increase in spending of around £100 million between 2009–10 and 2012–13 showed that the Coalition's policies were having the desired effect, and indeed funding for widening participation activity had reached a record level. By claiming this was 'evidence of how much universities and the Government are committed to social mobility achieved, not by quotas, but by true equality of opportunity' (2012b), he demonstrated his consubstantiality with Cable. Here, Willetts also invited ideological identification by drawing on the 'new' progressive commitment to individual opportunity, and setting it against the 'old' belief in state-imposed quotas. This appeal to identification through antithesis was previously made by Cable, and it served to align the university sector with the Coalition while undermining the credibility of the 'statist' alternative and its advocates.

It is striking that Cable delivered relatively few speeches on higher education during his tenure at BIS. This may be attributable to his discomfort with the politics of the issue rather than with the policy itself (see Cowley and Kavanagh 2016: 106), which found expression in his frequent attempts to invite interpersonal identification through displays of empathy. He also drew on the storyline of the deficit to present the reforms as the least bad option, and so to foster instrumental identification. Appeals to the values of fairness and progressivity were conspicuous by their absence. Willetts, meanwhile, relied primarily on instrumental identification in his efforts to persuade the sector to accept the Coalition's approach, though with varying degrees of success. Once the fees regime was in place, he made more frequent use of ideological identification by invoking the neoliberal beliefs in meritocracy and limited government. Despite the ongoing criticism of the policy by students, academics and politicians, a number of vice chancellors subsequently called on the Government to remove the £9,000 cap on fees. For instance, in 2013, Sir Christopher Snowdon, the Vice Chancellor of Surrey University and President of UUK, described the cap as 'simply not sustainable' and asserted that fees 'can't remain frozen forever' (quoted in Paton 2014). He thus invited instrumental identification with his argument that fee restrictions were damaging the sector, though the toxicity of the issue ensured that such a change would not take place during the Coalition's term of office.

CLEGG'S PUBLIC APOLOGY, SEPTEMBER 2012

On 21 September 2012, Clegg issued a public apology for breaking his pledge not to increase tuition fees. This took the form of a party political broadcast (Laws 2016: 205) and, as Clegg later explained:

> I hoped that by apologizing, people might come to see that we'd tried our best in extremely difficult circumstances. Above all, I hoped that by doing so I might clear the air and get a fresh hearing for the bigger story … of the many successful changes we were making in government. (2016: 34)

The Liberal Democrats' opinion poll ratings had fallen following their decision to go into coalition with the Conservatives,[8] and it was therefore seen as vital for Clegg both to restore morale within the Party and to begin to rebuild its support well in advance of the general election (d'Ancona 2013: 291; Laws 2016: 205).

Clegg opened his apology by acknowledging the mixed public reaction to the Liberal Democrats' record in government. While many were glad that the Party had entered into coalition to provide the country with stable leadership at a time of uncertainty, others were 'disappointed and angry that we couldn't keep all our promises—above all our promise not to raise tuition fees'. Addressing the latter group directly, Clegg said:

> We made a promise before the election that we would vote against any rise in fees under any circumstances. But that was a mistake. It was a pledge made with the best of intentions—but we shouldn't have made a promise we weren't absolutely sure we could deliver. (2012)

Clegg's admission that the pledge was well intentioned, albeit mistaken, was an attempt to invite interpersonal identification; after all, nobody is infallible. With the same aim in mind, he then appealed to society's accepted standards of behaviour by stating that: 'When you've made a mistake you should apologize. But more importantly—most important of all—you've got to learn from your mistakes. And that's what we will do' (2012). These lessons resonate widely, and Clegg perhaps sought to align himself and the Liberal Democrats with such common norms. From that point, he could then seek to rebuild a rapport with the electorate.

There is an ambiguity within Clegg's apology, as he told his audience that: 'There's no easy way to say this: we made a pledge, we didn't stick to it—and for that I am sorry' (2012). Taking this sentence in conjunction with his statement that 'we shouldn't have made a promise we weren't absolutely sure we could deliver', it seems he was apologizing for making the pledge in the first place, rather than for breaking it while in government. Critically, there was no direct apology for the policy itself, which may have disappointed some listeners, but it is unsurprising given Clegg's view that the reforms represented a 'significant improvement on the old system' (2016: 33). However, the ambiguous wording of the above sentence left open this interpretation and so broadened its potential appeal. Clegg closed his address with a defence of his party's actions, asserting that:

> We were right to leave the comfort of opposition to face the realities of government. And I know we are fighting for the right things, day in, day out, too: rebuilding our economy to make it strong; changing the tax system to make it fair; defending the vulnerable in these tough times. (2012)

By acting on their core values and delivering in these areas, Clegg hoped, the Liberal Democrats could begin to regain the public's trust. In short, the message was 'judge us not on what we said two years ago, but on our subsequent achievements in government'.

Within hours of the broadcast, the satirical website The Poke had set Clegg's apology to music and posted it on YouTube.[9] The track, *Nick Clegg Says I'm Sorry*, quickly went viral and was subsequently released as a charity single on iTunes. While Clegg was aware that he would be ridiculed, his main concern was to 'reframe the way in which the voters perceived the Lib Dems'; how the message was put across was secondary (d'Ancona 2013: 291). To an extent the broadcast was a success, as it allowed Clegg to speak about such matters as the economy, civil liberties and mental health without being bombarded with questions about tuition fees at his every public appearance (Clegg 2016: 35). In consequence, the Liberal Democrats were able to regain a degree of respect before the 2015 general election, though trust would remain a significant challenge for the duration of the Coalition and beyond.

CONCLUSION

Cameron and Clegg's decision during the initial negotiations to defer the decision on higher education funding in England caused serious problems for the Liberal Democrats. During the 2010 general election campaign, Clegg explains, they had 'overstated what [they] could in practice deliver, and ... compounded [their] woes by advocating a policy that many people at the top of the party did not believe in' (2016: 32). In addition to this, all 57 Liberal Democrat MPs had opposed tuition fees in public. The intra-party divisions between backbenchers and the leadership came to the fore during the parliamentary debate of 9 December 2010. Here, Cable sought to foster ideological identification through appeals to 'progressivity', as opposed to the core Liberal Democrat value of fairness. While a number of Conservative MPs were ideologically consubstantial with the Coalition leadership based on the 'new' progressive conception of fairness as social mobility, Cable's strategy held less appeal for his own backbenchers, many of whom sought to preserve their Party's distinctive identity by distancing themselves from the Government. Consequently, the passage of the reforms through Parliament came at the cost of Liberal Democrat unity, as the Party was split three ways in the vote.

A consistent feature of Cable's rhetoric was his use of interpersonal identification. By admitting that the proposals had involved difficult choices and presented challenges to the universities, he sought to create a connection with his listeners through demonstrations of empathy. In the same vein, Clegg's apology in 2012 was intended to build rapport by calling attention to his own fallibility, while recognizing the disappointment his broken pledge had caused. Given that the tuition fees debacle had undermined public trust in the Liberal Democrats, senior party figures perhaps felt it necessary to supplicate themselves in a bid to make their audiences more receptive to their message. Lending support to this interpretation is the near-absence of interpersonal identification in Willetts's speeches to the sector. As the Conservatives had indicated their preparedness to increase tuition fees before the general election, no breach of trust had occurred and such strategies were therefore unnecessary.

This difference aside, once the Coalition had resolved to introduce the policy, 'Vince Cable showed complete loyalty in defending the decision, and David Willetts ... took his full share of responsibility for the policy' (Hazell and Yong 2012: 176). Indeed, this unity was evident in their speeches to the university sector, where they demonstrated consubstantiality on a reduced role for the state, as well as on a conception of the interests of students, the universities and the nation. Underpinning these points of agreement was the storyline of the deficit, which bound the partners together in opposition to the Labour Party. Crucially, the Liberal Democrats' partisan interest in ensuring the survival of the Coalition had taken precedence over other considerations, which was to their own detriment (see Stuart 2011: 52–53). As Clegg put it, 'the lingering feeling that we had sold ourselves short, and compromised on principle, remained right through till the election in 2015' (2016: 35). However, the rhetorical pattern established by the Coalition in this policy area would endure into the next parliament, as we will see later on.

NOTES

1. For criticisms of the Browne Report and the marketization of higher education more generally, see Collini (2010: 23–25) and Collini (2017: 97).
2. For an overview of the tuition fees regimes in Wales, Scotland and Northern Ireland, see McGettigan (2013: 26).
3. See, for instance, Gummer (HC Deb., 9 December 2010, vol. 520 col. 569), Sharma (HC Deb., 9 December 2010, vol. 520 col. 591), and Chishti (HC Deb., 9 December 2010, vol. 520 col. 599).
4. Likewise, the Conservative MP Andrew Percy noted that: 'Participation has been widening, but there is evidence that the poorest children are not going

to the best universities, and that remains a problem. The concern for many of us on the Government Benches—or some of us, certainly—is that increasing fees even further will mean they will be even less likely to go to the best universities' (HC Deb., 9 December 2010, vol. 520 col. 556).

5. Universities UK is composed of the vice chancellors (or principals) of universities in the UK. MillionPlus represents the UK's modern, or 'post-92', universities, while the Russell Group consists of 24 research-intensive universities.

6. The Comprehensive Spending Review took place on 20 October 2010. This exercise was intended to reduce the deficit by 'dramatically cutting public expenditure annually by 14.4 per cent and by 46.4 per cent over the next five years', while also curtailing the size and power of the state (Beech 2011: 267).

7. The KIS draws on a range of sources, such as the National Student Survey (NSS), the Destination of Leavers from Higher Education (DLHE) survey and the universities and colleges themselves. The information available includes the percentage of students satisfied with the quality of their course, the proportion in managerial/professional jobs six months after graduation and the financial support on offer from the institution (Unistats n.d.).

8. As David Cutts and Andrew Russell correctly point out, the Liberal Democrats' opinion poll rating fell by 8 per cent barely a month after their decision to enter into a coalition with the Conservatives. 'Three months on and three weeks before Lord Browne's report on Higher Education and Student Finance', they continue, 'it had more than halved to 11 per cent' (2015: 70). This observation challenges the widespread perception that support for the Liberal Democrats collapsed in the wake of their U-turn on tuition fees. See also Cowley and Kavanagh (2016: 17, 105).

9. See https://www.youtube.com/watch?v=KUDjRZ30SNo.

References

Beech, M. (2011). A Tale of Two Liberalisms. In S. Lee & M. Beech (Eds.), *The Cameron-Clegg Government: Coalition Politics in an Age of Austerity* (pp. 267–279). Basingstoke: Palgrave Macmillan.

Brown, R. with Carasso, H. (2013) *Everything for Sale? The Marketization of Higher Education* (London: Routledge).

Cable, V. (2010, July 15). *A New Era for Universities.* Retrieved from https://www.gov.uk/government/speeches/a-new-era-for-universities

Cable, V. (2011, September 8). *Speech to Universities UK Annual Conference 2011.* Retrievedfromhttps://www.gov.uk/government/speeches/universities-uk-annual-conference--2

Clegg, N. (2010, November 23). *Hugo Young Lecture*. Retrieved from http://www.theguardian.com/politics/2010/nov/23/nick-clegg-hugo-young-text

Clegg, N. (2012, September 20). *Nick Clegg's Tuition Fees Apology*. Retrieved from http://www.politics.co.uk/comment-analysis/2012/09/20/watch-nick-clegg-s-tuition-fees-apology

Clegg, N. (2016). *Politics: Between the Extremes*. London: The Bodley Head.

Collini, S. (2010). Browne's Gamble. *London Review of Books, 32*(21), 23–25. Retrieved from https://www.lrb.co.uk/v32/n21/stefan-collini/brownes-gamble

Collini, S. (2017). *Speaking of Universities*. London: Verso.

Cowley, P., & Kavanagh, D. (2016). *The British General Election of 2015*. Basingstoke: Palgrave Macmillan.

Cutts, D., & Russell, A. (2015). From Coalition to Catastrophe: The Electoral Meltdown of the Liberal Democrats. *Parliamentary Affairs, 68*(Suppl. 1), 70–87.

d'Ancona, M. (2013). *In It Together: The Inside Story of the Coalition Government*. London: Viking.

Griffiths, S. (2011). The Con-Lib Agenda in Education: Learning the Hard Way? In S. Lee & M. Beech (Eds.), *The Cameron-Clegg Government: Coalition Politics in an Age of Austerity* (pp. 75–88). Basingstoke: Palgrave Macmillan.

Griffiths, S. (2015). Education Policy: Consumerism and Competition. In M. Beech & S. Lee (Eds.), *The Conservative-Liberal Coalition: Examining the Cameron-Clegg Government* (pp. 36–49). Basingstoke: Palgrave Macmillan.

Hazell, R., & Yong, B. (2012). *The Politics of Coalition: How the Cameron-Clegg Government Works*. Oxford: Hart Publishing Ltd.

HC Deb., 9 December 2010, vol. 520 cols. 540–624.

Laws, D. (2016). *Coalition: The Inside Story of the Conservative-Liberal Democrat Coalition Government*. London: Biteback Publishing Ltd.

McGettigan, A. (2013). *The Great University Gamble: Money, Markets and the Future of Higher Education*. London: Pluto Press.

NUS. (2010, April 26). *1000 Candidates Sign Vote for Students Pledge to Oppose Tuition Fee Hike*. Retrieved from https://www.nus.org.uk/en/news/lib-dem-and-labour-mps-would-vote-together-to-oppose-tuition-fee-rise/

Paton, G. (2011, April 15). £9,000 Fees 'Seen as Status Symbols' for Top Universities. *Telegraph*. Retrieved from http://www.telegraph.co.uk/education/educationnews/8451517/9000-fees-seen-as-status-symbols-for-top-universities.html

Paton, G. (2014, June 19). Vice-Chancellor: Scrap £9,000 Cap on Student Tuition Fees. *Telegraph*. Retrieved from http://www.telegraph.co.uk/education/universityeducation/10911676/Vice-chancellor-scrap-9000-cap-on-student-tuition-fees.html

Paton, G., & Prince, R. (2011, April 19). Two-Thirds of Universities 'to Charge £9,000 Tuition Fees'. *Telegraph*. Retrieved from http://www.telegraph.co.

uk/education/universityeducation/8461112/Two-thirds-of-universities-to-charge-9000-tuition-fees.html

Shepherd, J. (2010, July 15). Graduate Tax Will Force Students to Pay Back More for Degrees. *Guardian*. Retrieved from https://www.theguardian.com/education/2010/jul/15/high-earners-pay-more-for-degrees

Stuart, M. (2011). The Formation of the Coalition. In S. Lee & M. Beech (Eds.), *The Cameron-Clegg Government: Coalition Politics in an Age of Austerity* (pp. 38–55). Basingstoke: Palgrave Macmillan.

Unistats. (n.d.) *About Unistats: The Key Information Set (KIS)*. Retrieved from https://unistats.direct.gov.uk/find-out-more/key-information-set

Walker, P., & Paige, J. (2010, December 9). Student Protests—As They Happened. *Guardian*. Retrieved from https://www.theguardian.com/education/blog/2010/dec/09/student-protests-live-coverage?INTCMP=SRCH

Watt, N. (2010, November 12). Secret Documents Show Liberal Democrats Drew Up Plans to Drop Flagship Student Pledge Before Election. *Guardian*. Retrieved from https://www.theguardian.com/politics/wintour-and-watt/2010/nov/12/nickclegg-danny-alexander

Willetts, D. (2011, February 25). *Speech to Universities UK Spring Conference 2011*. Retrieved from https://www.gov.uk/government/speeches/universities-uk-spring-conference-2011

Willetts, D. (2012a, September 13). *'A World Without Boundaries': Speech at UUK Conference*. Retrieved from https://www.gov.uk/government/speeches/uuk-conference-a-world-without-boundaries

Willetts, D. (2012b, April 18). *Speech to the HEFCE Annual Conference 2012*. Retrieved from https://www.gov.uk/government/speeches/hefce-annual-conference-2012

Wintour, P., & Watt, N. (2010, December 10). Prince Charles and Camilla Caught Up in London Violence After Student Fees Vote. *Guardian*. Retrieved from https://www.theguardian.com/education/2010/dec/09/charles-camilla-car-attacked-fees-protest

CHAPTER 4

Constitutional Reform

According to Philip Norton, the Coalition was formed 'despite the parties' views on constitutional reform and not because of them' (2011: 153). After all, the Conservatives wished to preserve the status quo, while the Liberal Democrats had long advocated a new constitutional settlement. Central to this was a change to the Single Transferable Vote (STV) form of proportional representation, which was one of the Liberal Democrats' flagship manifesto commitments in 2010. It was perhaps with this in mind that Nick Clegg famously described the Alternative Vote (AV)[1] as a 'miserable little compromise' (quoted in Bogdanor 2011: 91) during the general election campaign. As we saw in Chap. 2, however, the negotiations preceding the Coalition's formation would produce just such a deal. Although neither party truly favoured AV, it 'nevertheless offered the best chance for Liberal Democrats to achieve a change in a voting mechanism that bolstered the two-party system' (Loughlin and Viney 2015: 67).

On 22 July 2010, the Coalition introduced the Parliamentary Voting System and Constituencies (PVSC) Bill, which contained proposals for a referendum on AV and the redrawing of constituency boundaries. The first section of this chapter examines the strategies of identification and division employed in the debate on the Bill's Second Reading. This analysis reveals the predominance of ideological appeals based on various conceptions of fairness, though the 'national interest' supplied a secondary ground for instrumental identification. Next, the chapter considers the

© The Author(s) 2018
J. Atkins, *Conflict, Co-operation and the Rhetoric of Coalition Government*, Rhetoric, Politics and Society,
https://doi.org/10.1057/978-1-137-31796-4_4

arguments of Cameron and Clegg in the 2011 AV referendum campaign, highlighting how the debate on the PVSC Bill shaped their rhetorical strategies. It then turns to the inter-party dispute over House of Lords reform and shows that this conflict stemmed from the choice of terministic screen used to interpret the Coalition Agreement. Following the abandonment of Lords reform, the Liberal Democrats retaliated by voting to delay the proposed boundary changes, and this parliamentary debate is the focus of the final section. Throughout, the chapter argues that although the inter-party deliberations over constitutional reform were dominated by appeals to fairness, partisan interests had a strong—albeit covert—presence. These concerns afforded the parties a means of affirming their distinctiveness, but ultimately would prove detrimental to Coalition unity.

THE DEBATE ON THE PVSC BILL, 2010

The PVSC Bill received its Second Reading on 6 September 2010. This bill linked together two of the Coalition's key constitutional reforms, with Part I committing the Government to a binding referendum on the use of AV in Westminster elections and Part II setting out measures for the equalization of parliamentary constituencies. As a consequence of this linkage, 'AV would not become operational until the equalization measures had been introduced ... By contrast, the equalization measures could take effect even if the AV referendum failed' (Loughlin and Viney 2015: 68). The rationale for bringing together these reforms was to ensure that Conservative MPs would support the proposed referendum, and Liberal Democrats would vote for constituency equalization and a concomitant reduction in the size of the House of Commons. Both measures demanded a compromise from the parties' 2010 manifesto pledges, but the Conservatives regarded the AV referendum as 'a far bigger concession' (Hazell and Yong 2012: 159).

The Coalition's constitutional reforms came in the wake of the 2009 parliamentary expenses scandal, in which it was revealed that MPs had claimed reimbursement for items as varied as a chocolate bar, a bath plug and a duck house. This controversy led to numerous resignations and deselections, as well as several criminal prosecutions, and inflicted significant reputational harm on MPs (Grice 2009). Thus, in the run-up to the 2010 general election, the three main parties all pledged to work to rebuild public trust in Parliament. For Clegg, this demanded greater transparency and accountability, while showing the electorate 'we understand that they are in charge'. Given that the PVSC Bill was about 'the legitimacy of this House and restoring people's faith in how they elect their MPs', he believed it represented a significant step towards achieving these objectives (HC Deb., 6 September 2010, vol. 515 col. 34). Indeed, Clegg continued, boundary changes and a new voting system were 'the bare minimum that any Parliament serious about political renewal must deliver' and, from the public's standpoint, were 'long overdue' (HC Deb., 6 September 2010, vol. 515 col. 35).

Clegg then highlighted three problems with the existing constituency boundaries, namely that they created unequal electorates, the data on which they were based was obsolete and they produced too many MPs. Consequently, 'the will of the voters is not weighed equally', and he invited MPs to identify ideologically with his position by describing this unfairness as 'deeply damaging to our democracy' (HC Deb., 6 September 2010, vol. 515 col. 36). The PVSC Bill would rectify these flaws by redrawing the boundaries to ensure that every constituency contained around 76,000 voters, give or take 5 per cent.[2] If this requirement was met, the independent boundary commissions could then take into account 'local geography, local authority boundaries and local ties'. To ensure that constituencies remained more up to date, boundaries would be reviewed every five years (HC Deb., 6 September 2010, vol. 515 col. 37). Finally, the number of MPs would be reduced to 600. As Clegg explained, this move would not only save around £12 million per annum, but ensure that the Commons was 'sufficiently large to hold the Government to account while enabling us all to do our jobs of representing our constituencies' (HC Deb., 6 September 2010, vol. 515 col. 39). Taken together, he claimed, these boundary reforms would 'help to bolster the legitimacy of parliamentary elections' (HC Deb., 6 September 2010, vol. 515 col. 40).

With regard to the proposed referendum on AV, Clegg acknowledged that the Coalition was divided on the issue and that its members would campaign on opposing sides. However, he continued, the partners strongly agreed that the British people should make the final decision and, if they voted to replace the first-past-the-post system, AV would be introduced alongside the new constituency boundaries (HC Deb., 6 September 2010, vol. 515 col. 41). Clegg concluded his opening statement with the assertion that:

> Ensuring that people's votes are more equal and giving voters a say over their voting system are both important reforms. They are about correcting

unfairness in the way voters elect their representatives and putting power in the hands of people. (HC Deb., 6 September 2010, vol. 515 col. 44)

This appeal for ideological identification employed the equality conception of fairness—according to which every vote should carry the same weight—as well as the principle of individual empowerment, on which both party leaderships were consubstantial. As we will see below, the ambiguity inherent in the concept of 'fairness' permitted its use by MPs on both sides of the ensuing debate.

The Conservatives' 2010 manifesto contained a pledge to equalize constituencies, while the Liberal Democrats were committed to reducing the number of MPs following the introduction of the STV system for Westminster elections. As a result, there was considerable support for Part II of the Bill among backbenchers from both Coalition parties. For instance, the Liberal Democrat MP Roger Williams demonstrated consubstantiality with the leadership by expressing the belief that 'the equalization of constituencies will go some way towards restoring the British public's faith in the electoral system and, indeed, in this House' (HC Deb., 6 September 2010, vol. 515 col. 64), while Eleanor Laing (Conservative) described the measures as 'long overdue'. Utilizing the conception of fairness as equality, she then stated that 'a democratic system in which votes are not of equal value is an insult to democracy', and so expressed ideological identification with the proposed reforms (HC Deb., 6 September 2010, vol. 515 col. 64).

Other Coalition MPs supported constituency equalization on the ground that the existing boundaries gave Labour an unfair advantage. As the Conservative backbencher Jonathan Evans explained:

All the analyses carried out on the results of the past three general elections have shown that Labour would have had a disproportionate advantage had there just been a replication of votes between the Conservatives and Labour. In other words, if both parties had received exactly the same number of votes, the Labour Party would have had majorities in every one of those elections. (HC Deb., 6 September 2010, vol. 515 col. 67)

For Mark Williams (Liberal Democrat), this point called attention to the 'unfairness' present within the system, and thus to the need for change (HC Deb., 6 September 2010, vol. 515 col. 78). In short, both MPs were ideologically identified on this component of the Bill.

However, the Conservative MP Charles Walker observed that the proposed reduction in the number of constituencies would clearly benefit his own Party, and he warned that 'if this reform is to carry weight and legitimacy, it must be seen to be fair to all parties, not to the naked advantage of one party' (HC Deb., 6 September 2010, vol. 515 col. 99). These concerns are founded on the equality conception of fairness, which demands equal treatment for each party (Blau 2004: 167) and on which Evans, Williams and Walker were ideologically consubstantial. However, their value-based arguments were questioned by some on the Labour benches, who called attention to the electoral benefits of the changes. In the words of Phil Wilson MP, 'The only reason for the proposed reduction to 600 is partisan gain on the part of Coalition Members, especially those in the Conservative Party' (HC Deb., 6 September 2010, vol. 515 col. 108). Here, Wilson employed a terministic screen based on continuity to link the reforms to party interests, and so to challenge Clegg's claim that they were not 'an elaborate attempt to gerrymander the boundaries' (HC Deb., 6 September 2010, vol. 515 cols. 38–9). Although it is improbable that electoral considerations did not feature in Coalition MPs' support for boundary reform, an open declaration of these interests would have been indecorous and, moreover, would have reduced the likelihood of securing the cross-party backing necessary for the measures to pass through Parliament. Instead, MPs relied on strategies of ideological identification and division which, for the cynically minded, served to conceal their partisan interests behind a principled façade.

Turning now to Part I of the Bill, the debate on the proposed AV referendum was also dominated by appeals to fairness. Speaking in support of electoral reform, Mark Williams observed that:

> When we consider the ability of the current system to reflect the views of the people who elect us, we should remember that only 33 per cent of us were returned with more than 50 per cent of the vote. (HC Deb., 6 September 2010, vol. 515 col. 77)

This criticism of the winner-takes-all principle enshrined in the first-past-the-post system draws on the majority and equality notions of fairness. As Adrian Blau explains, 'Under the majority principle, it is unfair if a government [or an MP] lacks majority backing. Under the equality principle, an electoral system should put "everyone's hands on the levers of power" (Martin Linton, quoted in Wilson, *The Scotsman*, 27 December 1997)'

(2004: 171). While not ideal, Williams argued, AV 'will usually produce a more proportional outcome' (HC Deb., 6 September 2010, vol. 515 col. 78), and he sought to foster ideological identification with the Coalition's proposals on this basis.

A number of Conservatives rejected this attempt to invite identification, contending that AV may increase disproportionality and, as Bernard Jenkin put it, 'does not mean fair votes'.[3] Expanding on this point, he claimed that the system 'creates two classes of voter: one whose votes are counted once; and another, such as people who vote for the UK Independence Party, the British National Party or tiny parties, whose votes are counted again and again' (HC Deb., 6 September 2010, vol. 515 col. 85). In other words, it violates the principle of 'one person, one vote, one value' contained in the equality conception of fairness (Blau 2004: 167), on which ground Jenkin created ideological division between himself and the advocates of AV. Relatedly, Andrea Leadsom objected that AV 'introduces an element of lottery' because some individuals will only vote for one candidate, whereas others will cast all five of their preferences. 'If enough vote for five', she continued, 'a candidate can be elected to Parliament whom nobody really wanted but who was the lowest common denominator' (HC Deb., 6 September 2010, vol. 515 cols. 115–16). This objection also rests on the notion of fairness; in Blau's words, 'forcing voters to give their MP a majority is no fairer than having plurality winners' (2004: 171), and in turn raises questions concerning that Member's legitimacy. On these grounds, Conservatives differentiated themselves ideologically from the Coalition leadership, while reassuring their supporters of their continued opposition to a change in the electoral system.

As Norton points out, 'Conservatives were reluctant to concede that the political system was broken' (2011: 163), and indeed several reaffirmed their Party's longstanding commitment to keeping first-past-the-post. Gary Streeter, for instance, described it as 'the best system for electing people to the House', explaining that 'it is simple, everyone understands it, and by and large … it produces the right result' (HC Deb., 6 September 2010, vol. 515 col. 61). Implicit in this argument is the majority conception of fairness, according to which the party that wins the majority of parliamentary seats should form a government (Blau 2004: 167), and which supplied a starting point for fostering ideological identification with the preservation of the status quo. Similarly, Richard Shepherd endorsed first-past-the-post, but did so with reference to the opposite end of the parliamentary life cycle. Thus, he told MPs that this voting system 'best protects the sovereignty of the people', simply because 'you know how to get rid of the Member of Parliament' (HC Deb., 6 September 2010, vol. 515 col. 109). Shepherd's statement draws on a version of the populist notion of fairness, which demands that the electorate should choose—and indeed remove—governments, and so offered the defenders of first-past-the-post an alternative ideological basis for identification.

The populist conception of fairness also informed Walker's objection that, 'under the AV system, party negotiating teams will more often decide the outcome of a general election than will the public or the electorate' (HC Deb., 6 September 2010, vol. 515 col. 100; see Blau 2004: 167). This claim was perhaps intended to foster ideological division, while giving expression to many Conservative MPs' disquiet over their Party's membership of the Coalition. Thus, Jenkin described the PVSC Bill as 'the worst advertisement for the Coalition: a product of backroom party political horse-trading resulting in a measure—the Alternative Vote referendum—that neither Coalition party supported in its manifesto' (HC Deb., 6 September 2010, vol. 515 col. 84), an argument which built on Anne Main's earlier accusation of 'horse-trading'.[4] At root, these criticisms of AV and coalition politics are about transparency and accountability. As such, they constitute a rejection of Clegg's efforts to promote ideological identification with the proposed constitutional changes, as well as a wider unease with the circumstances surrounding the Coalition's formation.

In contrast, some Conservatives voted reluctantly for the referendum on AV because they believed it was 'crucial to maintaining the Coalition' (Norton 2011: 165; see also Norton and Thompson 2015: 132). As Eleanor Laing put it, 'I support the Coalition because we need the stability it provides, and I appreciate that a referendum is the price for that, but what a high price it is to pay' (HC Deb., 6 September 2010, vol. 515 col. 91). These MPs were instrumentally identified on the leadership's view that the Coalition was formed in the national interest, but they questioned whether the measures themselves were equally beneficial. Thus, Laing stressed that 'we must have [the referendum] not for the better welfare of the people or the general good of the country, but only for the perceived electoral advantage of the Liberal Democrats' (HC Deb., 6 September 2010, vol. 515 col. 92), while Jenkin stated that 'I believe that it is in the national interest to equalize constituencies, but I do not know whether it is in the national interest to combine that issue with a referendum on the Alternative Vote' (HC Deb., 6 September 2010, vol. 515 col. 84). For Laing and Jenkin, then, the national interest took precedence over partisan considerations, and they identified with the Coalition—though not its proposed reforms—purely for instrumental reasons.

Meanwhile, Conservative backbenchers such as Christopher Chope sought to foster instrumental division by noting that the AV referendum would cost between £80 million and £100 million, and describing it as an 'expensive and unnecessary distraction' from the Coalition's main task of deficit reduction (HC Deb., 6 September 2010, vol. 515 col. 102). Likewise, Iain Stewart MP drew on the storyline of the deficit to argue that: 'We do not need [the referendum]; there are far more important measures for the country that need to be taken to clear up the legacy we have inherited from the previous Labour Government' (HC Deb., 6 September 2010, vol. 515 col. 106). In other words, the referendum was contrary to the nation's financial interest; it was no more than an expensive concession to the Liberal Democrats, for whom it was a 'deal breaker' in the talks preceding the formation of the Coalition (Kawczynski, HC Deb., 6 September 2010, vol. 515 col. 94).

According to Robert Hazell and Ben Yong, the PVSC Bill was 'very tightly whipped: the Government could not afford any concessions, lest the combined package unravel' (2012: 160). The Bill eventually received Royal Assent on 16 February 2011, but the efforts of senior Government figures to ensure its passage through the Commons left Conservative backbenchers in particular feeling bruised by the experience. For the Coalition leadership, however, it was a different story, as a senior Cabinet Official explained:

> The passage of the PVSC Bill was a major piece of glue. Both sides know they could fight alongside each other under serious enemy fire and win, and win on something where neither side wanted the other bit of that Bill. That builds a very high level of trust. (Quoted in Hazell and Yong 2012: 161)

In rhetorical terms, it strengthened the bonds of interpersonal identification between the party leaders though, as we will see below, this was not to last.

INTER-PARTY DIVISION AND THE 2011 AV REFERENDUM CAMPAIGN

Given the depth of the divisions over electoral reform, the Coalition's *Programme for Government* allowed the parties to campaign on opposite sides of the argument (HM Government 2010: 27). Indeed, Matthew d'Ancona notes that, in summer 2010, Clegg was convinced he and

Cameron had an understanding that, although the latter would 'notionally oppose AV and make a few appearances in support of the "No" campaign, these would be token rather than passionate. Clegg would take a symmetrical step back, too' (2013: 76). However, with opinion polls indicating a victory for Yes in early 2011, and the No side struggling to raise funds, Conservative MPs urged Cameron to take a leading role in the campaign (Laws 2016: 89; Norton and Thompson 2015: 133). While the Prime Minister subsequently took a tough stand against AV, both he and Clegg were adamant that electoral reform was not a 'coalition breaker'. As Cameron explained: 'Far above our beliefs about how the voting system should work, we share a much more important belief—a belief in democracy and the voice of the people being heard' (2011a). Reinforcing this ideological consubstantiality was a commitment to 'continue to work together in the national interest' (Cameron 2011a; Clegg 2011a), on which the two leaders were instrumentally identified.

A core argument of the Yes camp was that the first-past-the-post system was outdated, whereas AV stood for 'confident modernity and common sense' (d'Ancona 2013: 77). Thus, Clegg employed a terministic screen based on the principle of discontinuity to portray the referendum campaign as a 'battle between reformers and conservatives', in which:

> The reformers propose a reasonable step towards greater representation or fairness in our political system. The conservatives defend the status quo, usually having come to terms with the last instalment of reform, but warning of disaster if another step is taken. (2011b)

Here, Clegg appealed for identification though antithesis, inviting his listeners to support the 'Yes' campaign in taking the necessary action to update Britain's democracy. After all, Clegg explained, first-past-the-post was 'designed for an age of political tribalism which no longer exists. AV suits the electoral conditions prevalent in Britain today—particularly the shift to multi-party politics' (Institute for Public Policy Research, quoted in Clegg 2011c).

Clegg then used a terministic screen based on continuity to link electoral reform to the widespread public disillusionment with politics, which had intensified following the MPs' expenses scandal (2011b, see also Curtice 2013: 221). To this end, he claimed that MPs in safe seats took their constituents' support for granted and, as a result, were more likely to abuse the expenses system (2011a). By contrast, AV 'puts people, rather than politicians, in charge', thereby reducing corruption while helping to cut the number of safe seats for life (2011b). Moreover, because AV preserves the positive aspects of first-past-the-post, such as constituency MPs, Clegg was able to present it as 'a very British reform; a perfect example of the British genius for constitutional evolution, rather than revolution' (2011b). Put differently, AV was a gradual change that would play a significant part in cleaning up British politics, and on this ground Clegg invited instrumental identification with the case for electoral reform.

To supplement this interest-based argument, the Yes side sought to foster ideological identification with their cause. In his first major speech of the campaign, for instance, Clegg asserted that AV would encourage parties to compete for votes not just in marginal seats but in every constituency and, furthermore, would compel politicians to reach out beyond their core supporters in order to reach the 50 per cent threshold. These changes would ensure that MPs 'will be more legitimate and will carry a stronger mandate from a broader range of people', which on Clegg's view 'can only be good for our democracy' (2011a). The concepts of legitimacy and democracy were, of course, central to Clegg's efforts to win parliamentary support for the PVSC Bill, and he again employed them to invite his audience to identify ideologically with the proposed adoption of AV. As John Curtice points out, however, the logic of Clegg's argument was open to question, as 'a switch to AV would likely alter the eventual outcome in relatively few seats' (2013: 221). In short, it seems the positive effects of AV on democracy and public trust in politics were overstated.

The Yes campaign also emphasized the apparent benefits of AV for the individual voter, specifically that, as compared with the first-past-the-post system, it 'both reduces the incentive to vote strategically and ensures that a larger proportion of votes cast contribute to the election of a winner' (Curtice 2013: 221). In other words, AV would make more people's votes count, and so give them:

> A bigger foothold in our democracy. A bigger stake in our country. And that will mean more people getting interested and involved in politics, knowing that their voices will be heard and that their actions can have a real impact. And that can only be good for our democracy. (Clegg 2011a)

Clegg's commitment to giving more people a voice is consistent with his party's belief in individual empowerment, as well as the equality conception of fairness. These values in turn supplied a starting point for ideological identification, though it is noteworthy that 'fairness'—as a core Liberal Democrat belief—was not more prominent in Clegg's argument for AV. Conversely, it had a strong presence in Cameron's case against electoral reform, which is considered next.

In the run-up to the referendum, Cameron restated three arguments made by Conservative backbenchers in the 2010 parliamentary debate, namely that AV produces unfair outcomes, it reduces accountability and its workings are unclear. Of these, the first two objections relied on ideological appeals, while the third was interest-based. Taking them in turn, Cameron asserted that AV 'won't make every vote count. The reality is it will make some votes count more than others' (2011a). As noted above, this issue arises because AV allows people to rank up to five candidates in order of preference which, for its critics, contravenes the equality conception of fairness. Consequently, it provided a basis for fostering ideological division with the Yes campaign; in Cameron's words, 'The principle of one person, one vote is what makes our democracy fair [and] AV flies in the face of that' (2011a). Under first-past-the-post, by contrast, a voter places a cross against the name of their chosen candidate, and the one who receives the most votes is declared the winner (Cameron 2011a).

A related concern was the 50 per cent threshold, which the Conservative MP Andrea Leadsom had raised during the debate on the PVSC Bill and, Cameron suggested, 'could mean a Parliament of second choices' (2011a). Thus, he asked delegates at his Party's Spring Conference to:

> Imagine it's the Olympics, London 2012. We're all watching the 100 metres. Usain Bolt powers first over the line. But then he gets to the podium, it's the guy who comes third who gets the gold. We wouldn't put up this in the Olympics; what on earth are we doing thinking about it for our politics? (2011b)

This scenario is based on the winner-takes-all notion of fairness, which has considerable intuitive appeal and so can provide a compelling ground for ideological identification. It also highlights the simplicity of the first-past-the-post system, which brings us to Cameron's second criticism of AV.

On Cameron's view, AV would 'make politics less accountable and make it much harder to kick out governments' (2011a). More specifically, he continued, it would increase the likelihood of hung parliaments and lead to horse-trading on both sides of a general election, as 'there will be gamesmanship between parties in different constituencies as they try to stitch up second preference votes. And there could well be an occasion where we have a genuine second-choice government' (2011a).[5] Here, Cameron sought to distance himself ideologically from the Yes campaign by appealing to the populist conception of fairness and the principle of democratic accountability—both of which, he contended, were upheld by first-past-the-post. After all, Cameron explained, the current system 'has risen to the demands of the time, often with a brutal decisiveness' (2011c), to remove unwanted governments and thereby ensure that the will of the people is respected.

According to Cameron, AV is unclear and, as such, 'I don't think we should replace a system that everyone gets with one that's only under-stood by a handful of elites' (2011a). This populist claim provided a start-ing point for the creation of instrumental division, with Cameron asserting that the complexity of AV gives rise to a variety of other problems. For instance, 'it increases the cost of politics. A whole machinery of bureau-cracy will have to be built to explain the system to people. A quango over-seeing the whole process. Consultants drafted in to construct a message'. In sum, the entire exercise would be 'a monumental waste of time, money and effort'. Cameron then speculated that a change to AV may require the introduction of 'unreliable' electronic voting machines, which would do nothing to restore the public's faith in politics (2011a). Indeed, the No campaign claimed that the new system 'would cost £250 million to imple-ment and suggested there were better uses of such money than enabling politicians to get elected' (Curtice 2013: 221). These claims were contest-able—David Laws, for instance, described the £250 million estimate as 'ludicrous' (2016: 90)—but they contributed to an overarching message that AV would increase the cost of politics (Curtice 2013: 221). At a time of austerity, Cameron believed, 'we need to protect those things that pro-vide our country with real value for money. Our current voting system does that—it's cheap to administer and comes with little bureaucracy' (2011c), and he thus invited his audience to identify instrumentally with his case for keeping first-past-the-post.

The referendum on AV took place on 5 May 2011 and, on a turnout of 42 per cent, the electorate voted to keep the first-past-the-post system by 67.9 per cent to 32.1 per cent. In his study of public opinion during the campaign, Curtice notes that support for the Yes side's main argu-ment—that AV would help to rebuild trust in politics—'fell markedly … such that by polling day far more people disagreed than agreed with the proposition'. Conversely, he continues, public backing for the No camp increased in the same period, as voters became convinced that 'AV would be costly, unfair and undermine Britain's tradition of "strong government"' (2013: 221). This finding suggests that Cameron's rhetorical strategies—founded on the values of fairness and accountability, as well as on the nation's economic interests—gained considerable traction with the public, who identified ideologically and/or instrumentally with his case against electoral reform. It is important to acknowledge, however, that 'there was dirty campaigning on both sides, with wild exaggerations of the positive or negative effects of AV' (Hazell and Yong 2012: 161). This is ironic given the Coalition's stated aim of restoring trust in politics and politicians, and indeed the bitterness of the campaign would cause considerable damage to relations between the governing parties, with significant long-term consequences.

Reflecting on the referendum, Clegg writes that: 'Conservative donors, MPs and activists fought a brutal and highly personalized campaign, taking advantage of my unpopularity over the Coalition compromise on tuition fees, all under the watchful eyes of David Cameron and George Osborne'. This ruthless approach was exemplified by a leaflet that showed Clegg holding the NUS pledge card, with the caption: 'AV leads to broken promises' (Clegg 2016: 132).[6] As a direct result of the No camp's efforts to create interpersonal division, 'the benefit of the doubt was replaced by a mood of wariness if not outright distrust' within the Coalition (Norton 2012: 193). In short, Clegg claimed, Cameron had wrecked their good relationship for the sake of Conservative Party unity, and so 'helped to provoke [his] right-wing backbenchers into disowning and seeking to undermine the Coalition for the remainder of the parliament' (2016: 134). A case in point was the conflict over House of Lords reform, which is examined in the following section.

The Conflict Over House of Lords Reform, Summer 2012

The House of Lords Reform Bill was introduced on 27 June 2012 and made provision for an elected Second Chamber. Many Conservatives opposed this bill, on the grounds that they disliked the proposed use of proportional representation and 'feared that an elected Lords would be able to challenge the mandate of an elected Commons' (Laws 2016: 146). Consequently, on 10 July 2012, 91 Conservative MPs voted against giving the bill a second reading and 19 abstained. The Liberal Democrats were furious at this perceived breach of the Coalition Agreement, and indeed Clegg believed that Cameron did not do enough to avert the rebellion (d'Ancona 2013: 286). Thus, he told the Prime Minister that, 'in the event of the House of Lords Reform Bill being stymied by Conservative MPs, I would withdraw Liberal Democrat support for the linked issue of reform to constituency boundaries' (Clegg 2016: 138). This was no great sacrifice for the junior partner, as it had become clear by 2012 that the Liberal Democrats were likely to lose the most from the boundary changes (Curtice 2015: 586; see also Laws 2016: 146–7). It also afforded Clegg a means of reasserting his Party's influence within the Coalition, while staving off the leadership challenge he believed would follow if he did not take 'substantial retaliatory action for the collapse of Lords reform' (d'Ancona 2013: 290).

At its heart, the inter-party dispute over constitutional reform turned on conflicting interpretations of the initial agreement. In Chap. 2 we saw that, during the coalition talks, Laws employed a terministic screen based on continuity to link the proposed AV referendum to boundary changes, and thereby attained consubstantiality with the Conservatives. This deal would shape subsequent bargains, as the two measures were put forward together in both the *Programme for Government* (see HM Government 2010: 27) and the PVSC Bill. On this basis, in summer 2012 the Conservatives claimed that constituency equalization had been agreed in exchange for the AV referendum, and that the Liberal Democrats were therefore obliged to deliver it (Laws 2016: 149). By means of the principle of discontinuity, they presented Lords reform as a wholly separate measure and so contested its linkage to the issue of constituency boundaries. Clegg, however, asserted that he 'was in favour of reducing the number of MPs as part of a package of political reforms to improve democratic account-ability, but not in isolation' (2016: 136).[7] He therefore used a terministic screen based on continuity to depict the reforms as an 'indivisible pro-gramme' that had to be enacted in full; in short, 'if Lords reform fell, so too could the boundaries plan' (d'Ancona 2013: 287).

On 6 August 2012, Clegg made a statement announcing that the Coalition's plans for House of Lords reform were to be abandoned. He opened his address by expressing his continued support for an elected Second Chamber, saying:

> I believe that those who make the laws of the land should be elected by those who have to obey the laws of the land. That is democracy—and it is what people rightly expect from their politics in the 21st century. (2012)

Through this strategy of ideological identification, Clegg perhaps sought to reassure Liberal Democrats and fellow reformers of his fealty to a core commitment, while affirming his Party's distinctive identity. He then reminded his listeners that Lords reform was a 'fundamental part' of the Coalition Agreement, a contract he defined not simply as a deal between the two parties, but as 'a set of commitments we have made, collectively, to the British people'. Despite the challenges they faced, Clegg continued, the Liberal Democrats had kept to their side of the bargain, and so had demonstrated that they were a 'mature and competent party of government' (2012). Here, he invited interpersonal and instrumental identification by portraying his Party both as honourable and as willing to subordinate its own interests to those of the nation. This in turn supplied grounds for fostering identification through antithesis, uniting his audience with the Liberal Democrats in opposition to the supposedly ignoble and self-serving Conservatives.

Unlike his own party, Clegg argued, the Conservatives had failed to honour the commitment to reform the Lords, and so had broken part of Coalition Agreement. Such behaviour was unacceptable, given that 'coalition works on mutual respect; it is a reciprocal arrangement, a two-way street', and he therefore called attention to the interpersonal division between the partners. Clegg then laid claim to the moral high ground by portraying himself as a principled politician and, at the same time, creating an implicit contrast with Cameron. To this end, he asserted that:

> Throughout this process my aim has always been to honour the Coalition Agreement in full—no more, no less. I stood ready—and stand ready—to deliver reforms that are controversial for my Party because that is part of a wider, reciprocal arrangement. (2012)

However, he continued, it was now necessary to 'restore balance to the Coalition Agreement', to 'amend that contract in order then to move on', and this was to be achieved through the withdrawal of Liberal Democrat support for constituency equalization (2012).

This episode is open to interpretation, which in turn is dependent on the terministic screen chosen to order reality. Either way, it is important to point out that the *Programme for Government* contained a commitment only to 'establish a committee to bring forward proposals for a wholly or mainly elected upper chamber' (HM Government 2010: 27); there was no promise actually to implement these reforms. For critics such as Mike

Finn, Clegg's statement of 6 August was 'simply tit-for-tat ... dressed up as a point of principle' (2015: 510), while his decision to take retaliatory action was 'based not simply on the impact of the Lords reform defeat but the cumulative defeats and humiliations the [Liberal Democrats] had faced over the previous two years' (2015: 511).[8] Ultimately, however, Lords reform and constituency equalization were 'crucial to the political interests of the parties' (Laws 2016: 146), which accounts for the intensity of feeling underlying their divergent understandings of the issue, along with their willingness to prioritize partisan concerns over coalition unity.

THE COMMONS DEBATE ON THE AMENDMENT TO THE ELECTORAL REGISTRATION AND ADMINISTRATION BILL, 2013

On 14 January 2013, the Labour peer Lord Hart of Chilton won cross-party support for an amendment to the Electoral Registration and Administration Bill, which would delay the boundary review and the reduction of parliamentary seats until 2018 (BBC 2013). Later that month, MPs voted on the motion 'That this House disagrees with Lords amendment 5', which was moved by the Conservative Leader of the House, Andrew Lansley. The crux of Lansley's argument was that 'there are major disparities in the size of constituencies', the result of which was that some votes count more than others. In addition to this, the postponement of the boundary review would mean that, in England, the 2015 general election 'would be based on the register of February 2000, with all the consequent disparities and inequalities which have been exacerbated since then' (HC Deb., 29 January 2013, vol. 557 col. 808). Here, Lansley sought to foster ideological division by appealing to the equality conception of fairness, on which ground MPs had previously supported Part II of the PVSC Bill, and he therefore urged them to reject the Lords amendment. To bolster his case, Lansley noted that the boundary review would reduce the number of MPs to 600, and so save £13.5 million a year. 'As we are cutting back on administration and costs across the whole of the public services', he argued, 'it is only right that we apply the same principles to ourselves' (HC Deb., 29 January 2013, vol. 557 col. 809), and he thus invited ideological identification with the motion based on the concept of social justice.

Several Conservative MPs were ideologically consubstantial with Lansley and echoed his criticisms of Lords amendment 5. For instance, Stewart Jackson observed that, by the time of the May 2020 general election, 'the enumeration data on which the electorates are based will be 20 years old', and asked whether this was 'appropriate, fair and equitable' (HC Deb., 29 January 2013, vol. 557 col. 816), while Sir Peter Bottomley claimed that 'to carry on having boundaries that are old and constituencies with unequal numbers of voters is ... an abuse' of the electoral process (HC Deb., 29 January 2013, vol. 557 col. 824). Likewise, Bill Wiggin reminded Conservatives that: 'In our last manifesto, we promised to champion a fairer system. It is only right that we try to make good that commitment' and redress the current imbalance that favours Labour (HC Deb., 29 January 2013, vol. 557 col. 837). He therefore made a second, instrumental appeal for identification with Lansley's position, which was founded on on his Party's electoral interests.

The Liberal Democrats, meanwhile, supported the Lords amendment in accordance with Clegg's statement of August 2012. As John Thurso explained, a delay of the boundary reforms would enable the Electoral Commission to improve the quality of the register, which at that time included only 82 per cent of those eligible to vote (HC Deb., 29 January 2013, vol. 557 col. 824). Implicit here is the notion that a more accurate register would enhance the legitimacy of elections, which in turn offers a ground for ideological identification. Thurso then pointed out that, as a consequence of constituency equalization, the boundary of his own seat—Caithness, Sutherland and Easter Ross—would '[go] all over the place, simply to squeeze in enough in respect of both the area and the numbers'. The proposed changes thus lacked 'any rationale of community' (HC Deb., 29 January 2013, vol. 557 col. 826), on which basis Greg Mulholland called for 'constituencies that do not cross county boundaries and major council boundaries, and ones that are geographically commonsensical' (HC Deb., 29 January 2013, vol. 557 col. 840). Here, both MPs echoed the Labour grandee Jack Straw's contention that the PVSC Bill was rooted in a flawed assumption, namely that 'arithmetic equals fairness and that ... human and natural factors should be cast aside' (HC Deb., 6 September 2010, vol. 515 col. 51).[9] The two Liberal Democrats thereby invited Labour MPs to identify with their cause, while distancing themselves from the Conservatives by rejecting their appeal to the equality conception of fairness. In so doing, they abandoned Clegg's primary ideological justification for boundary reform, a move that Thurso explained was necessitated by coalition politics.

Although he had supported the formation of the partnership, Thurso reiterated Clegg's view that 'the Coalition Agreement is not a pick-and-mix menu; it is an agreement', and he told the Commons that:

> I agreed to the boundary changes—in many respects with a heavy heart—but I did so in the knowledge that the rest of that agreement acted as a counterweight. To my mind, that would occur mainly through Lords reform. (HC Deb., 29 January 2013, vol. 557 col. 826)

In the absence of such reform, he believed, boundary equalization must be delayed. However, several Conservatives criticized Thurso's definition of the situation,[10] with Mark Spencer asking: 'whether it is honourable for someone to take a position and then move, frankly, to a different one when they see what is before them' (HC Deb., 29 January 2013, vol. 557 col. 832). In the same vein, Penny Mordaunt stated that 'the 54 Liberals who voted in favour last time must ask themselves why a boundary review is a less valid measure now than it was in 2010 or will be in 2018' (HC Deb., 29 January 2013, vol. 557 col. 834). For these MPs, the junior partner's support for amendment 5 was unprincipled and opportunistic, and on this basis they thus created interpersonal division between themselves and the Liberal Democrats.

Prior to the debate Clegg gave the Lords amendment his backing, and Conservative and Liberal Democrat MPs were 'whipped to vote in opposite lobbies'. As d'Ancona reports, Clegg had told Cameron that: 'I can't, under any circumstances, allow these boundary changes to take place before the next election … This is an existential threat. Sorry, you should have thought of this before the AV referendum' (2013: 289). In the event, 334 MPs supported the Lords amendment and 292 voted against; the boundary review was duly postponed until 2018. This outcome had the potential to cost the Conservatives up to 20 seats in the next general election, but it arguably ensured the survival of the Coalition (d'Ancona 2013: 290). In Laws's words, it would have been 'fatal to our party's interests, and indeed to Nick Clegg's leadership, if we risked losing seats in the House of Commons without getting anything else in return' (2016: 149). It also provided a much-needed demonstration of Liberal Democrat influence within the Coalition which, for the time being, served to appease the parliamentary party and the wider membership.

CONCLUSION

The preceding analysis highlights the importance of 'fairness' (broadly conceived) in the debate over constitutional reform. For both parties, the equality conception of fairness supplied a ground for ideological identification with the boundary reforms presented in the PVSC Bill, while later affording Cameron a basis for opposing AV during the referendum campaign. Here, the Prime Minister also invited identification with his case for keeping first-past-the-post by appealing to the equality, populist and winner-takes-all notions of fairness, and thereby demonstrated the versatility of this key political concept. In contrast, fairness was almost absent from Clegg's argument for AV, which instead centred on the ideals of democracy and individual empowerment. As Finn explains, 'AV was clearly a system that might benefit the Liberal Democrats electorally, but not one in line with their values and philosophical stance on electoral reform' (2015: 507); it was a compromise that—unlike the Party's preferred STV system—would not deliver 'fair votes'. This was reflected in the pro-AV campaign slogan 'Yes to Fairer Votes', which lacked both conviction and the intuitive appeal of Cameron's rhetorical strategies.

The predominance of fairness did not preclude the use of instrumental identification and division. After all, Conservative MPs appealed to the 'national interest' in a bid to win support for their position on the PVSC Bill, as indeed did Cameron and Clegg in the run-up to the AV referendum. However, partisan interests had a strong—if covert—presence in the parliamentary debates over constitutional reform. Thus, some Labour MPs accused Conservative supporters of boundary equalization of concealing electoral considerations behind appeals to fairness, while the governing partners' perceived interests would shape their interpretations of the Coalition Agreement in the conflict over Lords reform. Similarly, Liberal Democrat rebels invoked community interests to justify the (arguably politically motivated) withdrawal of their support for boundary changes and, by implication, the disavowal of their longstanding commitment to 'fair votes'. Although both parties' efforts to protect their interests and affirm their distinctiveness may have had short-term benefits, they created considerable interpersonal friction and so damaged Coalition unity. In the long run, the electoral consequences of this dispute are likely to be significant. As Curtice puts it: 'The Liberal Democrats' chances of winning seats have been diminished by the failure to introduce the Alternative Vote, while the Conservatives' task of winning an overall majority has been made markedly more difficult by the failure to redraw parliamentary boundaries' (2015: 594–595).

NOTES

1. Under the AV system, candidates are ranked in order of preference. Then, 'if no candidate is the first preference of a majority of voters, the candidate with the fewest number of first-preference rankings is eliminated and that candidate's votes are redistributed to the remaining candidates. This process is repeated until one candidate secures 50 per cent of the total vote' (d'Ancona 2013: 21). It is important to note that AV is not a form of proportional representation.
2. As Vernon Bogdanor (2011: 85, n. 10) points out, exceptions to the 5 per cent rule are the Isle of Wight, the Orkney and Shetland Islands and Comhairle na Eilean Siar (the Western Isles).
3. Similarly, David Davis noted that the Jenkins Commission on electoral reform rejected AV on the ground that 'in many cases it was actually less proportional—more disproportional—than our current system' (HC Deb., 6 September 2010, vol. 515 col. 70).
4. As Main put it, 'AV has been slipped into the Bill as a result of horse-trading—I can put it no other way—to make the Coalition work' (HC Deb., 6 September 2010, vol. 515 col. 81).
5. Compare the objections of Walker, Jenkin and Main, which were discussed in the previous section.
6. As d'Ancona points out, 'it had been the Labour members of the "No" team who had insisted on using Clegg's image in such leaflets. To energize the Labour vote, they argued, it had to be spelt out that the referendum was an opportunity to punish Clegg and the Lib Dems for letting the Tories in' (2013: 82).
7. This position is consistent with the Liberal Democrats' (2010) manifesto, which stated that: 'Our preferred Single Transferable Vote system gives people the choice between candidates as well as parties. Under the new system, we will be able to reduce the number of MPs by 150' (2010: 88).
8. Likewise, on 29 May 2012, the Conservative Chancellor George Osborne claimed that: 'Nick is just looking for excuses to torpedo boundary reform, because he is worried about losing MPs in 2015. This stuff about the House of Lords is just a smokescreen' (quoted in Laws 2016: 150).
9. Note that, in his opening statement on the PVSC Bill, Clegg said these factors would be taken into consideration once the numerical requirement had been met.
10. For instance, Peter Bone MP argued that the deal was 'a vote on AV in return for Liberal Democrat support on boundary reviews ... The Conservative Party kept to that deal but the Liberal Democrats have gone back on their part of it. They are a disgrace and should be on the Opposition Benches' (HC Deb., 29 January 2013, vol. 557 col. 839).

REFERENCES

BBC. (2013, January 14). *Peers Vote to Block MP Constituency Boundary Changes.* Retrieved from http://www.bbc.co.uk/news/uk-politics-21016025

Blau, A. (2004). Fairness and Electoral Reform. *British Journal of Politics and International Relations, 6*(2), 165–181.

Bogdanor, V. (2011). *The Coalition and the Constitution.* Oxford: Hart Publishing Ltd.

Cameron, D. (2011a, February 18). *Votes Referendum: Cameron's Speech in Full.* Retrieved from http://www.bbc.co.uk/news/uk-politics-12504935

Cameron, D. (2011b, March 6). *Speech to Conservative Spring Conference.* Retrieved from http://www.newstatesman.com/2011/03/enterprise-government-party

Cameron, D. (2011c, April 30). Why Keeping First Past the Post Is Vital for Democracy. *Telegraph.* Retrieved from http://www.telegraph.co.uk/news/politics/av-referendum/8485118/David-Cameron-why-keeping-first-past-the-post-is-vital-for-democracy.html

Clegg, N. (2011a, February 18). *Votes Referendum: Clegg Speech in Full.* Retrieved from http://www.bbc.co.uk/news/uk-politics-12504941

Clegg, N. (2011b, April 9). *AV is a Very British Reform.* Retrieved from http://www.libdemvoice.org/clegg-av-is-a-very-british-reform-23757.html

Clegg, N. (2011c, April 21). *AV Gives People More Power, More Choice.* Retrieved from http://www.libdemvoice.org/nick-cleggs-speech-at-the-ippr-on-political-reform-23865.html

Clegg, N. (2012, August 6). *Statement on House of Lords Reform.* Retrieved from http://www.bbc.co.uk/news/uk-politics-19146853

Clegg, N. (2016). *Politics: Between the Extremes.* London: The Bodley Head.

Curtice, J. (2013). Politicians, Voters and Democracy: The 2011 UK Referendum on the Alternative Vote. *Electoral Studies, 32*(2), 215–223.

Curtice, J. (2015). The Coalition, Elections and Referendums. In A. Seldon & M. Finn (Eds.), *The Coalition Effect 2010–2015* (pp. 577–597). Cambridge: Cambridge University Press.

d'Ancona, M. (2013). *In It Together: The Inside Story of the Coalition Government.* London: Viking.

Finn, M. (2015). The Coalition and the Liberal Democrats. In A. Seldon & M. Finn (Eds.), *The Coalition Effect 2010–2015* (pp. 492–519). Cambridge: Cambridge University Press.

Grice, A. (2009, December 23). Review of the Year 2009: Expenses Scandal. *Independent.* Retrieved from http://www.independent.co.uk/voices/commentators/andrew-grice/review-of-the-year-2009-expenses-scandal-1847865.html

Hazell, R., & Yong, B. (2012). *The Politics of Coalition: How the Conservative-Liberal Democrat Government Works*. Oxford: Hart Publishing Ltd.

HC Deb., 6 September 2010, vol. 515 cols. 34–116.

HC Deb., 29 January 2013, vol. 557 cols. 806–840.

HM Government. (2010). *The Coalition: Our Programme for Government*. London: Cabinet Office.

Laws, D. (2016). *Coalition: The Inside Story of the Conservative-Liberal Democrat Coalition Government*. London: Biteback Publishing Ltd.

Liberal Democrats. (2010). *Liberal Democrat Manifesto 2010*. London: Liberal Democrats.

Loughlin, M., & Viney, C. (2015). The Coalition and the Constitution. In A. Seldon & M. Finn (Eds.), *The Coalition Effect 2010–2015* (pp. 59–86). Cambridge: Cambridge University Press.

Norton, P. (2011). The Con-Lib Agenda for the 'New Politics' and Constitutional Reform. In S. Lee & M. Beech (Eds.), *The Cameron-Clegg Government: Coalition Politics in an Age of Austerity* (pp. 153–167). Basingstoke: Palgrave Macmillan.

Norton, P. (2012). Coalition Cohesion. In T. Heppell & D. Seawright (Eds.), *Cameron and the Conservatives: The Transition to Coalition Government* (pp. 181–193). Basingstoke: Palgrave Macmillan.

Norton, P., & Thompson, L. (2015). Parliament and the Constitution: The Coalition in Conflict. In M. Beech & S. Lee (Eds.), *The Conservative-Liberal Coalition: Examining the Cameron-Clegg Government* (pp. 129–144). Basingstoke: Palgrave Macmillan.

CHAPTER 5

The European Union

The issue of European integration is a major fault line in British politics. In 2010, this division was exemplified by the Conservative Party, whose MPs espouse varying degrees of Euroscepticism (see, for instance, Lynch 2015a; Heppell et al. 2017), and the pro-European Liberal Democrats. When the two parties formed a coalition following an inconclusive general election result, the pragmatic and constructive approach to Europe outlined in their *Programme for Government* took some commentators by surprise. At this time, 'there were reasons for believing that relations with the EU would be relatively quiescent during the Coalition's first months in office', given that the process of integration was slowing and there was no significant treaty revision in prospect (Lynch 2011: 222). However, by the end of the Coalition's parliamentary term, Cameron had promised an in/out referendum on Britain's membership of the European Union.

This chapter considers the Coalition's rhetorical strategies from 2010 to 2013, a period that can be viewed as a turning point in Britain's relationship with the EU (Gifford 2014: 512). It begins by outlining four narratives that have long featured in debates over Europe within British politics in general and the Conservative Party in particular (Fontana and Parsons 2015: 90), and it considers how they may be employed as bases for identification and division. Next, the chapter examines how senior Coalition figures argued for EU reform and demonstrates that the leadership relied on instrumental appeals based on Britain's economic prosperity, to the detri-

© The Author(s) 2018
J. Atkins, *Conflict, Co-operation and the Rhetoric of Coalition Government*, Rhetoric, Politics and Society,
https://doi.org/10.1057/978-1-137-31796-4_5

ment of values. The following section discusses the rhetoric of Coalition MPs in the parliamentary debates on the European Union Bill 2010–11 and the European Union (Referendum) Bill 2013–14. These debates were dominated by Conservative backbenchers, who relied on the ideological mode of identification and division to express their opposition to further European integration. The analysis reveals the presence of rhetorical path dependency in the arguments of the Coalition leadership, which would set a pattern for the subsequent debate on Britain's EU membership.

Rhetoric, Narratives and Identification

Cary Fontana and Craig Parsons identify four narratives that are present in the British debate over Europe. They are: Britain as a distinctively global—not European—nation; parliamentary sovereignty; incremental pragmatism; and liberalism, which originated in the 'postulates of market economics and the instrumental pursuit of individual interest' (2015: 92). The first narrative holds that Britain is an exceptional nation by virtue of the Empire/Commonwealth and its 'special relationship' with the United States, and that these global ties are threatened by European institutions (Fontana and Parsons 2015: 90). Buttressing this is the related narrative that Britain is unique among nations because it gave the world (or, specifically, its former colonies) principles such as liberty, parliamentary democracy and the rule of law (see Atkins 2016). These narratives provide the opponents of European integration a means of fostering division based on Britain's interests as a global nation, as well as on its self-understanding as the originator of fundamental rights and values. Equally, pro-Europeans may draw on the global power/exceptionalism narrative to invite instrumental identification with the claim that active involvement in the EU is vital to Britain's ability to exert influence on the international stage, and so to advance its national interest.

The second narrative is founded on the principle of parliamentary sovereignty and a concomitant rejection of shared or federal power. Here, supranationality is seen as having led to 'the ceding of power to unelected bodies, the erosion of the capacity of the state to represent the interests of "the People" and normative commitments enshrined in international law, particularly human rights, that lack any national constitutional basis' (Gifford 2014: 522). In short, European integration is incompatible with parliamentary sovereignty, a notion that is central to Eurosceptic efforts to invite their listeners to identify ideologically with their cause. The concept of sovereignty also features in pro-European arguments, where it is redefined as 'influence' and offered as a ground for ideological identification. Meanwhile, the third narrative states that 'Britain's stability and success since the 1600s were built on incremental reform rather than radical change, trusting to experience and practical compromise'. With this comes a 'hostility to utopian schemes' (Fontana and Parsons 2015: 91), of which the European project is arguably an exemplar, and membership of that organization is therefore viewed as inimical to Britain's interests.

The fourth, 'liberal', narrative emphasizes the economic impact of European integration. Also referred to as the 'technocratic/modernist' narrative, it 'portrays Britain's economic prosperity as based on its openness to free trade and liberalism' (Bevir et al. 2015: 9). This narrative is founded on the premise that the nation's economic interests are best served through its continued membership of the single market, and so affords pro-Europeans a means of inviting instrumental identification. The technocratic/modernist narrative is also open to a Eurosceptic interpretation, and so can be employed to foster division on instrumental grounds. As Mark Bevir, Oliver Daddow and Pauline Schnapper explain, it can be used to depict the EU as an impediment to free trade, on the ground that it 'restrict[s] access to global markets and impos[es] regulations which limit the competitiveness of European companies' (2015: 9). For some Conservative Eurosceptics, an alternative to EU membership is the 'Anglosphere', an alliance for economic and security co-operation with the USA and the Commonwealth that is based on shared values and institutions (Wellings and Baxendale 2015: 129). This vision brings together the technocratic/modernist and global power/exceptionalist narratives, with the latter adding a 'resonant historical, institutional and emotional dimension ... through evocation of imperial grandeur and global familial connections' (Bevir et al. 2015: 10). It thus enables Eurosceptics to invite instrumental identification while amplifying sentiments of national pride, and so to appeal to both the head and the heart of their audience.

According to Fontana and Parsons, the narratives of global power, parliamentary sovereignty and pragmatism are 'fundamentally populist', given that they are 'rooted in identity claims about what British people were like', while the fourth is technocratic (2015: 91). The remainder of this chapter examines how they were utilized to promote identification and division first by the Coalition leaders, and then by their parliamentary parties.

INTER-PARTY IDENTIFICATION: THE LEADERS

Whereas Clegg unequivocally asserted that 'I am a pro-European' (2013), Cameron described himself as a 'practical Eurosceptic'—one who knows 'there is a real benefit from being engaged but … [is] frustrated by some of the ways the relationship works' (2012). Nevertheless, they had a common commitment to economic liberalism and a shared understanding of Britain's national interest, and they were united in the belief that the EU was in need of reform. It is unsurprising, therefore, that speeches considered here focused on the importance of promoting economic growth, and so blended the technocratic/modernist narrative with appeals for instrumental identification.

Speaking at the 2011 World Economic Forum, Cameron made the case for EU reform, identifying as his top priority an 'aggressive, pan-continental drive to unleash enterprise'. This entailed deregulation and innovation and, of the former, Cameron stated that 'complex rules which restrict labour markets are not some naturally occurring phenomenon … All of these result from decisions we have taken—alone or together' (2011). Consequently, European leaders had the power to, for instance, introduce a 'one-in, one-out' rule for new regulations, remove small businesses from EU accounting rules and complete the single market. In this, Cameron claimed, he had the backing of Prime Ministers Fillon and Rutte among others, and thus invited his listeners to identify ideologically with their shared commitment to 'open markets and reform'. He also sought to establish instrumental identification, on the ground that the successful execution of these reforms 'could add up to 180 billion euros to Europe's economy' (2011).

Cameron then challenged the belief that liberal democracy was outdated, arguing that these values were a prerequisite for innovation. He urged his listeners to: 'Look at where the big ideas come from—the Facebooks and the Spotifys—and the vast majority are from open societies. That's because good ideas come through freedom—free thinking and the free association of like-minded people' (2011). Cameron's words echo Hayek's justification for an open society,[1] and so invited the European elite to identify ideologically with his case for reform. He then linked these ideals to economic interests, claiming that they 'create the right climate for business too'. After all, he asked:

> If you're looking to set up a headquarters abroad, are you going to invest where your premises can be taken away from you? Where contracts are routinely dishonoured? Where there's the threat of political upheaval? Or are

you going to invest where there are property rights, the rule of law, democratic accountability? (Cameron 2011)

For Cameron, then, liberal values and economic interests were inextricably linked, and both provided a basis for fostering identification through the technocratic/modernist narrative.

Later that year, Clegg addressed the European Parliament and—like Cameron—his main concern was with economic growth. Using a terministic screen based on the principle of continuity, Clegg defined the situation confronting Europe as a 'crisis of competitiveness' (2011) and demonstrated his consubstantiality with Cameron by attributing it to the same causes. These included demographic change, competition from the emerging markets and the 'low productivity or inflexible workforces or red tape' afflicting many European economies (2011). In effect, Clegg continued, the choice confronting Europe was 'reform now or regret it forever', and indeed the urgency of the situation precluded lengthy negotiations over treaty change. Clegg then invited his listeners to identify instrumentally with his proposals for reform, acknowledging that 'while our domestic situations vary, relaunching the European economy is our common endeavour' (2011). This undertaking would be guided by the principles of unity, growth and economic openness.

With regard to unity, Clegg demonstrated ideological identification with his audience by describing European co-operation as 'one of the most significant political and economic achievements of modern times'. He then explained that 'European nation states can deliver more prosperity and security for our citizens when we work together', on deepening the single market, for example, or tackling climate change (2011). This position was consistent with the Coalition's *Programme for Government* and reflected the partners' belief that the national interest was best promoted through international co-operation. Clegg then repeated Cameron's call for deregulation, arguing that the EU had 'gone beyond setting legitimate standards to protect workers, consumers and promote competition and, instead, has been too keen on imposing a straitjacket of uniformity on services and sectors, undermining our ability to compete internationally' (2011). Underpinning this claim is an appeal for ideological division based on a critique of centralized power and the 'one size fits all' approach associated with socialism, and an assertion of the liberal belief in individuality and flexibility as a ground for identification. Interestingly—given Clegg's pro-Europeanism—his case for reform drew on the Eurosceptic interpretation of the technocratic/modernist narrative espoused by many Conservatives, in which the EU is portrayed as an obstacle to economic competitiveness.

Building on this argument, Clegg urged Members of the European Parliament (MEPs) to prioritize growth. At present, he believed, European citizens were 'desperate for jobs and economic opportunity, yet too often those goals are lost somewhere in our processes as we draft and scrutinize legislation' (2011). To rectify this, the Commission needed to ensure that all new legislation contributed to economic growth, and not to the bureaucratic burden. Finally, Clegg expressed a commitment to economic openness, which demanded the completion of the single market. After all, he claimed, 'our long-term success depends on removing the remaining barriers between us' (2011), and he invited MEPs to identify instrumentally with the case for reform on this basis. Here, Clegg once more advanced the Eurosceptic form of the technocratic/modernist narrative, while demonstrating his ideological consubstantiality with Cameron on the values of economic liberalism. Eunice Goes attributes this shift in Clegg's position to electoral considerations. Although the Liberal Democrats' unpopularity was primarily a result of their participation in the Coalition, they also believed that 'their pro-European credentials adversely affected their electoral prospects' (Goes 2015: 97–98). Thus, in a bid to increase support, the Liberal Democrats downplayed their Europhilia, but this would come at the cost of their distinctive identity.

At a meeting of the European Council in December 2011, Cameron vetoed a proposed treaty amendment that would 'police the fiscal rules binding the Eurozone countries' (Goes 2014: 53; see also Lynch 2015a: 191). This move delighted Conservative MPs but angered the Liberal Democrats, and consequently Britain's influence in Europe was the central theme of both party leaders' speeches in 2012. Following the European Council of June 2012, Cameron set out Britain's three objectives, the first of which was action to address the Eurozone crisis. This would entail closer economic and fiscal integration but, for Cameron, it was vital that the single market was not distorted in the process, given that it was the 'biggest benefit that we get out of membership'. Although securing a commitment on this had been 'tough', Cameron had ensured that Britain's national interest would be protected (2012). The second objective was to boost economic growth, in pursuit of which Britain had united 12 countries behind a set of clear priorities. 'All of these', Cameron said, 'are included in the compact for growth and jobs which has been agreed today'

(2012). His final objective was to take a stand on the EU budget, and he 'made it absolutely clear that the British rebate is not up for renegotiation' (2012). As such, Cameron sought to demonstrate Britain's effectiveness in influencing the direction of EU policy to promote its own economic prosperity, and so invited instrumental identification with his position that the nation's interests were best served by its continued membership.

In his speech at Chatham House in November 2012, Clegg responded to calls for a renegotiation of Britain's relationship with the EU and the repatriation of powers from Brussels. While he recognized that the EU needed to do more to promote growth, and indeed described himself as 'a big advocate of EU reform', Clegg characterized his opponents' position as 'a false promise, wrapped in a Union Jack'. For many of these people, he continued, 'repatriation is pulling at a thread—and they want to unravel the whole thing ... And heading to the exit would be the surest way to diminish the UK' (2012; see also Clegg 2016: 199). It is noteworthy that Clegg described the idea that Britain could remain in the single market on a basis similar to that of Norway as a 'catastrophic loss of sovereignty'. This is not an invocation of the parliamentary sovereignty narrative, in which that concept is understood as national self-determination, but rather a redefinition of it in terms of influence. Supporting this interpretation is Clegg's statement that, for the US, 'the UK's leverage on the continent has always been part of our appeal' (2012; see also Clegg 2016: 203). However, his use of the term 'sovereignty' was perhaps intended to challenge the Eurosceptic position on its own terms, and to invite instrumental identification with his argument that a retreat from Europe would cause untold damage to Britain's standing in the world.

Clegg then set out an alternative approach that blended pragmatism with constructive co-operation (2012). In policy terms, this meant a tough stance on Britain's rebate, on which he and Cameron were 'absolutely united'. Although a deal would be difficult to negotiate, Clegg continued, it was the 'best way to protect British interests'. Once again, he urged the deepening of the single market, noting that the UK was among its architects. As such, its completion would happen only with the leadership of the UK, 'the most open, liberal economy in the EU', and in turn would boost trade and protect British jobs (2012). Finally, Clegg repeated his call for co-operation on law and order, noting that the UK had played a leading role in building 'the most advanced system for combating cross-border crime on the planet', and he expressed a wish that UK citizens would continue to reap the full benefits of this. Uniting these proposals is the pro-European understanding of the global power/exceptionalism narrative, according to which Britain is a leader within the EU and could use its influence to advance the national interest within that organization. Clegg thereby drew on the technocratic/modernist narrative to invite his audience to identify instrumentally with a strategy that would guarantee 'our security, our prosperity and our place in the world' (2012). In an appeal for identification through antithesis he then sought to unite his audience behind the case for Britain's EU membership, against the 'dogma-driven' Eurosceptics who advocated isolationism.

From late 2012, writes David Laws, the UK Independence Party (UKIP) were 'consistently polling ahead of the Liberal Democrats. UKIP support was also eating into the Conservative vote share, increasing the pressure for Cameron to adopt a more Eurosceptic position' (2016: 239; see also Copsey and Haughton 2014: 83–4). In a bid to neutralize UKIP and quell unrest within his parliamentary party, Cameron asserted 'a revised governing position on Europe' (Gifford 2014: 524) despite the grave reservations of senior Conservatives (Clegg 2016: 206). Thus, in a speech delivered at the London headquarters of Bloomberg in January 2013, Cameron set out his vision of a reformed EU and committed the Conservatives to offering an in/out referendum on Britain's membership. This move was in part a reassertion of the party's distinctive identity (Lynch 2015b: 251) but, in Chris Gifford's words, it also 'signalled a hardening of Euroscepticism on the part of a significant section of the political class and a new phase in the United Kingdom's relation with, and within, the EU' (2014: 513).

The starting point of Cameron's case for EU reform was a defence of British exceptionalism (Gifford 2014: 524). Drawing on that narrative, he explained that 'we have the character of an island nation—independent, forthright, passionate in defence of our sovereignty'—which entailed that Britain's approach to Europe was 'more practical than emotional'. As Cameron put it, 'For us, the European Union is a means to an end—prosperity, stability, the anchor of freedom and democracy both within Europe and beyond her shores—not an end in itself' (2013). Here, Cameron employed a terministic screen based on discontinuity to set Britain apart from Europe, both geographically and psychologically. This strategy of division is also evident in his characterization of Britain's 'practical' mindset, which drew on the narrative of incremental pragmatism and was implicitly contrasted with the Europeans' 'emotional' attachment to the EU project (see Clegg 2016: 196). Cameron thus closed off the possibility of using shared values to foster ideological identification in future debates over Britain's EU membership, so the argument for the remaining part of that organization would have to be made on primarily instrumental grounds.

In a rejection of isolationism, Cameron drew on the global power/exceptionalism narrative to identify openness as Britain's defining characteristic, saying: 'We have always been a country that reaches out. That turns its face to the world. That leads the charge in the fight for global trade and against protectionism' (2013). He was eager, therefore, for Britain to continue to play an active role in Europe, and to secure a better deal for both parties. With this in mind, Cameron identified three challenges that needed to be met, two of which had featured in the speeches considered above. Of these, the first was to ensure that the Eurozone had 'the right governance and structures to secure a successful currency for the long term' while safeguarding the interests of non-members. The second challenge was a 'crisis of European competitiveness', which Cameron again attributed to excessive regulation, and the third was the growing gulf between the EU and its citizens. Regarding this latter challenge, Cameron employed the principle of discontinuity to stress the distance between the 'remote, unaccountable' EU and 'the people', a populist strategy that had been absent from his 2011 and 2012 speeches and, as we will see below, reflected the concerns of his parliamentary party. In a bid to create ideological division, Cameron told his audience that the 'lack of democratic accountability and consent ... [was] felt particularly acutely in Britain' and that, without reform, there was a real possibility that 'Europe will fail and the British people will drift towards the exit' (2013).

Cameron then presented his vision of a reformed EU, which was founded on five principles. The first was competitiveness, which was to be promoted through the completion of the single market and a reduction in bureaucracy, while the second was flexibility. As in his previous addresses, Cameron espoused a 'flexible union of free member states who share treaties and institutions and pursue together the ideal of co-operation', and which accommodated the diversity of its members with regard to, say, their membership of Schengen or the Eurozone. This vision, he claimed, 'is not the same as those who want to build an ever closer political union— but it is just as valid' (2013). Implicit in the two principles is a division between Britain as a sovereign nation and the 'collectivism' of the EU (see Vail 2015: 106), the result of which was that Cameron reduced the likelihood of achieving ideological consubstantiality with European politicians.

Again, any identification with his case for reform would have to be for instrumental reasons.

The third principle was that 'power must be able to flow back to Member States, not just away from them', which once more demanded a rejection of uniformity, and the fourth was democratic accountability. As Cameron explained, 'There is not, in my view, a single European demos. It is national parliaments, which are, and will remain, the true source of real democratic legitimacy and accountability in the EU' (2013). These principles were rooted in the narrative of parliamentary sovereignty and its rejection of federal power which, for Gifford, indicates that Cameron had 'aligned himself with a harder Euroscepticism' (2014: 524) to appease his backbenchers. Moreover, by presenting the UK 'in quite fundamental respects as antithetical to the European project' (Gifford 2014: 525), Cameron once more ruled out the possibility of inviting ideological identification with his vision of a reformed EU.

Cameron's final principle—fairness—stated that 'whatever new arrangements are enacted for the Eurozone, they must work fairly for those inside it and out' (2013; see Lynch 2015a: 191). He explained that:

> Our participation in the single market, and our ability to help set its rules is the principal reason for our membership of the EU. So it is a vital interest for us to protect the integrity and fairness of the single market for all its members. (2013)

Here, Cameron made an argument about the national interest, but did so under the banner of 'fairness'. This move was perhaps intended to broaden support for his position by offering a second, seemingly value-based, ground for identification. However, the defence of 'fairness' was for the sole purpose of advancing the economic interests of member states, and of Britain in particular. Contrary to appearances, therefore, Cameron's appeal for identification was inherently instrumental.

In terms of what this meant for Britain, Cameron told his audience that 'public disillusionment with the EU is at an all-time high'. He attributed this to such issues as the EU's perceived interference in the nation's affairs and the drive towards closer political union, and claimed that 'democratic consent for the EU in Britain is now wafer thin'. To address this, he pledged that the 2015 Conservative Party manifesto would offer the public an in/out referendum following a renegotiation of the terms of Britain's membership. While he recognized the emotive appeal of 'charting our own course', Cameron cautioned that it would be 'a decision we will have to take with cool heads' after weighing up the consequences for the nation's prosperity, security and international standing (2013). His own view was clear—that 'Britain's national interest is best served in a flexible, adaptable and open European Union and that such a European Union is best with Britain in it', and he once again invited instrumental identification with his case for remaining in a reformed EU (2013).

Although Eurosceptics regarded Cameron's offer of a referendum as a clear victory (Gifford 2014: 513; Shipman 2016: 12), the Liberal Democrats were 'extremely alarmed ... not only because it was stretching Coalition policy but above all because of its potential political consequences. Britain's withdrawal from the EU was now a real possibility' (Goes 2014: 55). Thus, in October 2013, Clegg unambiguously stated that 'leaving the EU would be economic suicide. You cannot overstate the damage it would do to British livelihoods and prosperity'. After all, Britain's membership of the single market was linked to three million jobs and, moreover, afforded access to over 50 international trade agreements. He also drew on the pro-European version of the global power/exceptionalism narrative to warn that an exit would diminish Britain's global influence and, moreover, impede its efforts to address international crime and climate change. Therefore, claimed Clegg, 'Every way you look at it—jobs, influence, safety, the environment—the UK is infinitely better off in the EU' (2013) and, on these grounds, he fostered instrumental division with those who advocated Britain's departure while reasserting the Liberal Democrats' identity as a pro-European party.

Given these negative consequences, Clegg stated that: 'I'm not worried about how we make the case for membership to the British people—the argument is ours to win'. However, he continued, 'I am worried that we're not out there making it', and he proceeded to outline what the Coalition had achieved through a constructive engagement with the EU. Among these successes were a cap on the EU budget, the protection of Britain's rebate and the reform of EU accounting rules, and together they showed that 'the best way to represent our nation's interests is to stay and win the argument, showing leadership abroad for your citizens at home' (Clegg 2013). Clegg thus fused the technocratic/modernist and global power/exceptionalism narratives, and he urged his audience to: 'Stand up for a proud Britain leading in a better EU. Stand up for staying in Europe, for the sake of the national interest' (2013). In making the case for EU reform and Britain's continued membership, both Clegg and

Cameron drew primarily on the technocratic/modernist narrative that had also informed the position they adopted in the *Programme for Government*. However, whereas the party leaders relied on appeals for instrumental identification, the following section reveals that the arguments of Eurosceptic Conservative MPs were instead dominated by values.

COALITION MPS AND THE EU

On the issue of Europe, coalition relations were characterized by 'a reasonable degree of co-operation between the two parties at the leadership level, but also by a fair amount of conflict at the legislative level' (Goes 2015: 95). As previously noted, parliamentary debates enable MPs to convey to constituents their ongoing support for their party's traditional objectives in the face of coalition compromises (Martin and Vanberg 2008: 502), and thus afford the governing partners a means of managing the competing imperatives of unity and distinctiveness. At the same time, they provide a forum for backbenchers to vent their frustrations with coalition politics, and Eurosceptic Conservative MPs took full advantage of the opportunity to stress their ideological differences with both the Liberal Democrats and their own party leadership (Lynch 2015b: 243). These intra-party tensions were compounded by interpersonal division. As Matthew d'Ancona explains, some Conservatives distrusted Cameron following what they saw as 'an unforgivable broken promise [to hold a referendum] on the Lisbon Treaty' and, moreover, feared that Clegg was 'quietly nudging Cameron towards a weaker position on Europe' (2013: 242–243). This section examines the strategies of identification and division at play in two parliamentary debates, which highlighted the difficulty for Cameron in 'striking the right balance between pragmatism and Euroscepticism' (Lynch 2011: 232).

The European Union Bill 2010–11

The European Union Bill had its Second Reading on 7 December 2010. This proposed legislation sought to enact three pledges made in the *Programme for Government*, namely a referendum lock, 'additional controls on the use of the ratchet clauses in the EU treaties' and a reassertion of the sovereignty of the Westminster Parliament (Lynch 2011: 227; see also Vail 2015: 113). The referendum lock ensured that any future treaty which transferred competences from the UK to the EU would be subject to a binding referendum once it had received parliamentary approval. Given the lack of a clear definition of what constitutes a ratchet clause, the Bill 'lists the treaty articles and stipulates what action must be taken before the government can use them' (Lynch 2011: 227). Thus, a referendum would be required before the UK could join the Euro, for instance, but not on the accession of new Member States. Finally the Bill included a sovereignty clause, which stated that 'EU law only takes effect in the UK through the will of Parliament'. This clause was declaratory, so the relationship between UK and EU law remained unchanged (Lynch 2011: 228).

The debate opened with the Conservative Foreign Secretary, William Hague, outlining the case for the Bill. He noted that successive treaties had changed the EU considerably since the 1980s, the result of which was that it 'now has a greatly enlarged place in our national life, policy, and politics' (HC Deb., 7 December 2010, vol. 520 col. 191). At the same time, however, the democratic legitimacy of the EU was declining, and he presented the European Union Bill as a partial solution to this. So, to avoid a repeat of the Lisbon Treaty episode, the Bill would ensure that 'any future treaty change that transfers powers from Britain to the EU could be agreed only subject to the consent of the British people'. This 'radical change' was supported by both party leaders, who were instrumentally identified on the view that co-operation between EU member states was vital to 'our international economic competitiveness, sustainable low-carbon growth and the use of our collective weight in the world to advance our shared values and interests'. For Hague, 'Ensuring that our role is based on democratic consent is equally necessary' (HC Deb., 7 December 2010, vol. 520 col. 193), and he invited MPs to identify ideologically with the Coalition's proposals on this basis.

As Goes explains, 'the Liberal Democrats used the legislative process to support the Coalition's policies and to ensure that their influence was noticeable' (2014: 50). To this end, the party's President, Tim Farron, described the Bill as 'a fine example of a coalition product: it is a sensible compromise' (HC Deb., 7 December 2010, vol. 520 col. 217),[2] and he expressed the hope that, with the referendum lock giving the public the final say on the transfer of power to the EU, the Government had 'drawn a line—obviously—under the European constitutional question once and for all' (HC Deb., 7 December 2010, vol. 520 col. 219). Farron's support for this element of the Bill was consistent with his Party's values, on the ground that: 'We are ... fundamentally a democratic party and one that believes in devolving power to the lowest level possible and in reconnecting the public to politics through democratic reform' (HC Deb., 7 December 2010, vol. 520 col. 219). In this way, he demonstrated his ideological consubstantiality with the Coalition leadership.

Farron was the only Liberal Democrat to speak in the debate and, drawing on the pro-European version of the global power/exceptionalism narrative, he told Parliament that: 'British national interests are best served by playing an active and leading role in the European Union' (HC Deb., 7 December 2010, vol. 520 col. 219). After all, he explained, Britain and other EU member states face 'many major challenges' that can be addressed only through international co-operation. For Farron, these included 'delivering economic growth, completing the single market, delivering new free trade agreements, cracking down on cross-border crime, combating climate change, and fighting global poverty' (HC Deb., 7 December 2010, vol. 520 cols. 218–19). Here, he reiterated Clegg's argument that EU membership was in Britain's national interest, and likewise drew on the technocratic/modernist narrative to invite instrumental identification. Thus, Farron again displayed consubstantiality with the Coalition leadership and he, along with other Liberal Democrat backbenchers, supported the Government in the Commons vote (Hazell and Yong 2012: 166).

By contrast, Eurosceptic Conservatives sought to create division between themselves and the Coalition by criticizing aspects of the Bill. Richard Drax, for instance, advocated trade with Europe, but drew on the narrative of parliamentary sovereignty to argue that 'we should not be ruled and regulated by Europe, particularly by the unelected Commission' (HC Deb., 7 December 2010, vol. 520 col. 234). Although he welcomed the Coalition's commitment to increased democratic accountability, he dismissed the legislation as 'all smoke and mirrors', saying:

> The lock is entirely bogus. A referendum will be triggered only if Ministers believe what their civil servants tell them and agree that the subject is significant. If they do not consider it to be significant, there will be no referendum and the matter will become law.[3]

In short, Drax continued, 'we are asked to take the matter on trust' (HC Deb., 7 December 2010, vol. 520 col. 235; see also Redwood HC Deb., 7 December 2010, vol. 520 col. 212). This strategy of interpersonal division tapped into the suspicion with which some Eurosceptic Conservatives regarded their party leader. By calling Cameron's credibility into question, Drax urged MPs to support his call for strengthening the legislation, which in turn would reduce the possibility of its abuse by 'unscrupulous' Ministers.

Other Conservatives rejected Hague's attempts to invite instrumental identification. One such MP, Bernard Jenkin, dismissed the Bill as 'almost wholly irrelevant to the national interest' (HC Deb., 7 December 2010, vol. 520 col. 254; see also Gapes HC Deb., 7 December 2010, vol. 520 col. 228) and, as a supporter of the Anglosphere model,[4] he argued that Parliament ought to be discussing 'how we are going to do business with India'. Invoking the parliamentary sovereignty narrative to foster ideological division, Jenkin then explained that the legislation failed to enhance democratic legitimacy and halt the transfer of power to the EU. Instead, he claimed, it:

> Reflect[ed] the muddle that the Government have got themselves into because ... the prime purpose of this Bill is political; it was designed to appease sentiment in the absence of a referendum on all the treaties where we should have had referendums.[5]

As such, Jenkin continued, the Bill would neither reassure the public nor address the growing disconnect between them and their MPs, the latter of which was 'the real challenge that we face' (HC Deb., 7 December 2010, vol. 520 col. 254). Although consubstantial with the Coalition leadership on the principle of democratic accountability, Jenkin employed a terministic screen based on discontinuity to argue that the Bill would not realize its stated aim. He thus sought to distance himself from the Government's proposals, while reassuring his constituents that he remained true to his Eurosceptic beliefs. Moreover, by claiming that the Bill was politically motivated, Jenkin created interpersonal division between himself and the Coalition. Again, this was a legacy of the Lisbon Treaty episode, and it reflected the distrust between sections of the parliamentary party and the Prime Minister.

Another area of contention was the sovereignty clause (Clause 18), which some Conservative MPs criticized as weak. As Bill Cash memorably put it:

> The European Union claims sovereignty over our democratic Parliament, and this mouse of a Bill does little to preserve it ... Clause 18 is a judicial Trojan horse leaping out of Pandora's Box. It is not, as the Foreign Secretary claimed, an enlightened act of national self-interest. (Hansard HC Deb., 7 December 2010, vol. 520 cols. 224–5)[6]

Similarly, Drax claimed that 'toothless legislation that gives the impression of protecting our sovereignty while doing nothing of the sort will simply hide the rot a little longer', while Priti Patel contended that 'the sentiment behind the Bill is right, but it needs to be improved truly to reflect the sovereignty and primacy of this Parliament and the independence of our country, and, importantly, to put Britain's interests first' (HC Deb., 7 December 2010, vol. 520 cols. 236 and 264). These backbenchers used the narrative of parliamentary sovereignty to differentiate themselves ideologically from the Coalition, and to convey to constituents their rejection of a government compromise. They also sought to foster instrumental division based on the national interest, which they defined not in terms of constructive engagement with the EU, but as national self-determination. The Bill was passed in July 2011 but, as we will see next, it failed to appease Conservative Eurosceptics.

The European Union (Referendum) Bill 2013–14

According to Anthony Seldon and Peter Snowdon, Number 10 had hoped that the Bloomberg speech would 'substantially close down Eurosceptic rumbling'. However, they continue, these backbenchers had 'little confidence in [Cameron's] Bloomberg pledge on the referendum and pressure[d] him to bring forward legislation for an in/out referendum into the present parliament' (2015: 269). Thus, on 16 May 2013, the Conservative MP James Wharton introduced a Private Member's Bill requiring a referendum on Britain's EU membership to be held by the end of 2017. The Bill had its Second Reading on 5 July 2013, in advance of which Cameron stated that: 'I totally support it. It is my policy written into law. I would say to all MPs, turn up and vote' (quoted in Watt 2013; see also Vail 2015: 114). By contrast the Liberal Democrats were incensed, and they made it plain that they 'would not support a referendum on EU membership within this parliament' (Goes 2014: 56). Consequently they were largely silent in the debate and, together with a majority of Labour MPs, abstained in the vote.

After introducing the Bill, Wharton called attention to the changes that had taken place since Britain last voted on its membership of the European Community, observing that:

> Those who voted yes in 1975 believed that they had bought a ticket to a clear and certain destination—to a free trade area that would benefit Britain's

economy without undermining our sovereignty. They did not buy a ticket for a never-ending journey to ever-closer union, destination unknown. (HC Deb., 5 July 2013, vol. 565 col. 1172)

Following Cameron's renegotiation of Britain's relationship with the EU, he claimed, the electorate should have the opportunity to 'choose whether to renew their consent to membership or to withdraw it' (HC Deb., 5 July 2013, vol. 565 col. 1173). Wharton thus appealed to the principle of democracy to foster ideological identification, while the narrative of parliamentary sovereignty underpinned his critique of supranationality. On these grounds, he sought to win parliamentary backing for the Bill.

While Conservative MPs welcomed the proposals, some believed that they did not go far enough. Sir Richard Shepherd, for instance, urged that a referendum be held as soon as possible and affirmed that this was in Britain's interests (HC Deb., 5 July 2013, vol. 565 col. 1201; see also Henderson, HC Deb., 5 July 2013, vol. 565 col. 1232). Like Cash and Patel, he defined the national interest in terms of self-determination, and he drew on the narratives of parliamentary sovereignty and global power/ British exceptionalism to argue that:

This vote, what we decide and what people in the future decide will determine the character and strength of our national constitutional history, which is being threatened. Why should we defer in such an adventure, when this is the most remarkable and ancient of all the democratic communities within Western Europe? (HC Deb., 5 July 2013, vol. 565 cols. 1201–2)

This is an example of identification through antithesis, whereby 'we' are portrayed as a unique nation with a long tradition of self-government that is under threat from a supposedly undemocratic and overbearing EU. In conjunction with Shepherd's claim that 'the very story of liberty and freedom' lies within the history of the British Isles (HC Deb., 5 July 2013, vol. 565 col. 1201), this exceptionalist strategy of identification invokes fundamental values and sentiments of national pride, and so resonates on a primarily emotional level.

Once again, the narrative of parliamentary sovereignty featured heavily in the debate. For Andrew Bridgen MP, 'Sovereignty belongs to the people and their heirs and successors. It is not ours to take away: we must have a referendum' (HC Deb., 5 July 2013, vol. 565 col. 1209), while

Patel contended that: 'This Parliament's sovereignty has been eroded decade after decade just to satisfy the demands of Europe's political elite, who follow their dogmatic desire for ever-closer union, rather than putting the interests of our country and hard-pressed taxpayers first' (HC Deb., 5 July 2013, vol. 565 col. 1236). These populist invocations of parliamentary sovereignty, together with the rejection of supranationality as detrimental to the national interest, supplied both ideological and instrumental grounds for identification with the case for a referendum. As such, they constituted an effective appeal to the hearts and minds of Conservative MPs, who voted unanimously in favour of the Bill.

Only two Liberal Democrats contributed to the debate, and the entire parliamentary party abstained in the vote. Their Deputy Leader, Simon Hughes, sought to foster division by questioning the necessity of the Bill, given that the Coalition had already legislated for a referendum with the 2011 European Union Act (HC Deb., 5 July 2013, vol. 565 col. 1173), while Martin Horwood reiterated the Party's support for an in/out vote in the event of a major treaty change or transfer of power (HC Deb., 5 July 2013, vol. 565 col. 1225). Echoing Farron, he pointed out that the Liberal Democrats have consistently backed referendums, before noting that they would 'enthusiastically support much of the reform agenda' set out in Cameron's Bloomberg speech (HC Deb., 5 July 2013, vol. 565 cols. 1224 and 1226). However, Horwood continued, 'we can be in favour of reform, but not necessarily make that conditional on referendums'; a plebiscite should be held only in the circumstances specified in the European Union Act (HC Deb., 5 July 2013, vol. 565 cols. 1225 and 1227). So, although the Liberal Democrats were in favour of referendums on principle, they were unconvinced by the Conservatives' case for a vote before the end of 2017 and therefore refused to support the Bill.

On Horwood's view the Bill suffered from numerous problems, in particular that it 'condemns British business and British jobs to four years of uncertainty' and thus sends a negative message to investors (HC Deb., 5 July 2013, vol. 565 col. 1228). This situation would be deeply damaging to the nation's prosperity, and as such Horwood distanced himself from Wharton and his supporters on instrumental grounds. With the same aim in mind, he reiterated Clegg and Cameron's technocratic/modernist argument for remaining in the EU, telling Parliament that:

> UK businesses have access to free trade in the world's largest single market, worth nearly £11 trillion in gross domestic product, with over 500 million

consumers. One in 10 British jobs are linked to the single market. Some £495 billion-worth of British trade is with other EU member states. (HC Deb., 5 July 2013, vol. 565 col. 1228)

Horwood thus demonstrated his instrumental consubstantiality with the Coalition leadership and, with his assertion that 'the Liberal Democrats are not willing to risk millions of British jobs by voting no' in an in/out referendum (HC Deb., 5 July 2013, vol. 565 col. 1229), he rallied his Party in opposition to the Eurosceptic Conservatives.

CONCLUSION

The Coalition's *Programme for Government* demonstrates that Cameron and Clegg were instrumentally consubstantial on their approach to EU policy. Over the following three years, they consistently drew on the technocratic/modernist narrative to argue that membership of a reformed EU was in the national interest. This reliance on strategies of instrumental identification is indicative of rhetorical path dependency and, although Cameron had adopted a harder Eurosceptic position by 2013, he continued to assert that Britain's prosperity was inextricably linked to its EU membership. Also in his Bloomberg address, Cameron used the global power/exceptionalism and incremental pragmatism narratives to highlight the differences between Britain and Europe. He thus abandoned the possibility of using ideological appeals to win support for Britain's EU membership in a future referendum, and so locked himself in to an interest-based strategy of identification.

Meanwhile, the examination of the two parliamentary debates reveals that Eurosceptic Conservative MPs used ideological arguments to distance themselves from the Coalition leadership and reaffirm their Party's electoral distinctiveness. This strategy relied on the narrative of parliamentary sovereignty and a conception of the national interest as self-determination, both of which appeal to the heart, rather than to the brain. The few Liberal Democrats to participate in the debates expressed support only for the principle of referendums, which manifested their Party's ideological commitments to democratization and individual empowerment. They thus rejected the Conservative calls for a plebiscite before the end of 2017, and instead argued that it was in Britain's interests to remain in the EU. These arguments replicated Clegg's appeals for instrumental identification, based as they were on the nation's economic prosperity and the importance of international co-operation to tackle issues such as cross-border crime and climate change. That this broad rhetorical pattern—of instrumental arguments for EU membership and an ideological case against—endured beyond the lifetime of the Coalition is indicative of the 'stickiness' of these rhetorical formulations, the consequences of which are discussed in the concluding chapter.

NOTES

1. As Hayek explains, 'Wherever the barriers to the free exercise of human ingenuity were removed man became rapidly able to satisfy ever-widening ranges of desire. And while the rising standard soon led to the discovery of very dark spots in society ... there was probably no class that did not substantially benefit from the general advance' (2004: 16–17).
2. The primary responsibility for the Bill lay with William Hague and the Conservative Minister for Europe, David Lidington. However, the Liberal Democrats Nick Clegg and Chris Huhne (the deputy chair of the European Affairs Committee) were also actively involved in the process (Hazell and Yong 2012: 165).
3. Echoing this point, James Clappison (Conservative) asserted that: 'Whether we have a referendum under the circumstances detailed in the Bill depends on whether Ministers think they are significant enough. What a thing! Ministers are to decide whether something is significant enough, and the explanatory notes to the Bill then tell us that anyone who is aggrieved by such a decision should go off to the courts to seek a judicial review. What on earth is Parliament for?' (HC Deb., 7 December 2010, vol. 520 col. 251).
4. See Jenkin (2017).
5. Laura Sandys (Conservative) made a similar point, saying: 'had we discussed referendums—or had we had passed such a Bill six, seven or eight years ago—we would not face the level of distrust in the country that we are facing because of the Lisbon treaty' (HC Deb., 7 December 2010, vol. 520 col. 244).
6. Likewise, the Conservative MP Nick de Bois argued that: 'There is wiggle room in the Bill, and that is not good because we are attempting not just to pass a Bill, but to rebuild trust between the British people and the Government by challenging the transfer of powers in our relationship with Europe ... it is the little grey areas of wiggle room that are, in effect, a Trojan horse that can be exploited and undermine the genuine attempts of the Bill to protect any transfer of power' (HC Deb., 7 December 2010, vol. 520 col. 258).

REFERENCES

Atkins, J. (2016). (Re)imagining Magna Carta: Myth, Metaphor and the Rhetoric of Britishness. *Parliamentary Affairs, 69*(3), 603–620.

Bevir, M., Daddow, O., & Schnapper, P. (2015). Introduction: Interpreting British European Policy. *JCMS: Journal of Common Market Studies, 53*(1), 1–17.

Cameron, D. (2011, January 28). *Speech to the Davos World Economic Forum.* Retrieved from http://www.politics.co.uk/comment-analysis/2011/01/28/david-cameron-s-davos-speech-in-full

Cameron, D. (2012, June 29). *Prime Minister's Speech in Brussels.* Retrieved from https://www.gov.uk/government/speeches/prime-ministers-speech-in-brussels

Cameron, D. (2013, January 23). *EU Speech at Bloomberg.* Retrieved from http://www.newstatesman.com/politics/2013/01/david-camerons-speech-eu-full-text

Clegg, N. (2011, November 9). *Reform or Wither: A Vision for a Prosperous, Competitive Europe.* Retrieved from https://www.gov.uk/government/speeches/deputy-prime-ministers-speech-at-the-european-parliament

Clegg, N. (2012, November 1). *Nick Clegg Speech on His Vision for the UK in Europe.* Retrieved from http://www.libdems.org.uk/nick_clegg_speech_on_his_vision_for_the_uk_in_europe#

Clegg, N. (2013, October 8). *In Europe for the National Interest.* Retrieved from http://www.libdems.org.uk/nick_clegg_speech_on_a_richer_stronger_safer_greener_europe

Clegg, N. (2016). *Politics: Between the Extremes.* London: The Bodley Head.

Copsey, N., & Haughton, T. (2014). Farewell Britannia? 'Issue Capture' and the Politics of David Cameron's 2013 EU Referendum Pledge. *JCMS: Journal of Common Market Studies, 52*(Annual Review), 74–89.

d'Ancona, M. (2013). *In It Together: The Inside Story of the Coalition Government.* London: Viking.

Fontana, C., & Parsons, P. (2015). 'One Woman's Prejudice': Did Margaret Thatcher Cause Britain's Anti-Europeanism? *JCMS: Journal of Common Market Studies, 53*(1), 89–105.

Gifford, C. (2014). The People Against Europe: The Eurosceptic Challenge to the United Kingdom's Coalition Government. *JCMS: Journal of Common Market Studies, 52*(3), 512–528.

Goes, E. (2014). The Coalition and Europe: A Tale of Reckless Drivers, Steady Navigators and Imperfect Roadmaps. *Parliamentary Affairs, 67*(1), 45–63.

Goes, E. (2015). The Liberal Democrats and the Coalition: Driven to the Edge of Europe. *The Political Quarterly, 86*(1), 93–100.

Hayek, F. A. (2004). *The Road to Serfdom.* Abingdon: Routledge Classics.

Hazell, R., & Yong, B. (2012). *The Politics of Coalition: How the Cameron-Clegg Government Works.* Oxford: Hart Publishing Ltd.

HC Deb., 7 December 2010, vol. 520 cols. 191–264.

HC Deb., 5 July 2013, vol. 565 cols. 1172–1236.

Heppell, T., Crines, A., & Jeffery, D. (2017). The United Kingdom Referendum on European Union Membership: The Voting of Conservative Parliamentarians. *JCMS: Journal of Common Market Studies,* 1–17. https://doi.org/10.1111/jcms.12529

Jenkin, B. (2017, January 30). Westminster Reflections: Bernard Jenkin MP Says President Trump Could Be Yet Another Huge Challenge for the EU. *Diplomat.* Retrieved from http://www.diplomatmagazine.com/westminster-reflections-bernard-jenkin-mp-says-president-trump-could-be-yet-another-huge-challenge-for-the-eu/

Laws, D. (2016). *Coalition: The Inside Story of the Conservative-Liberal Democrat Coalition Government.* London: Biteback Publishing Ltd.

Lynch, P. (2011). The Con-Lib Agenda for Europe. In S. Lee & M. Beech (Eds.), *The Cameron-Clegg Government: Coalition Politics in an Age of Austerity* (pp. 218–233). Basingstoke: Palgrave Macmillan.

Lynch, P. (2015a). Conservative Modernization and European Integration: From Silence to Salience and Schism. *British Politics, 10*(2), 185–203.

Lynch, P. (2015b). The Coalition and the European Union. In M. Beech & S. Lee (Eds.), *The Conservative-Liberal Coalition: Examining the Cameron-Clegg Government* (pp. 243–258). Basingstoke: Palgrave Macmillan.

Martin, L. W., & Vanberg, G. (2008). Coalition Government and Political Communication. *Political Research Quarterly, 61*(3), 502–516.

Seldon, A., & Snowdon, P. (2015). *Cameron at 10: The Inside Story 2010–2015.* London: William Collins.

Shipman, T. (2016). *All Out War: The Full Story of How Brexit Sank Britain's Political Class.* London: William Collins.

Vail, M. I. (2015). Between One-Nation Toryism and Neoliberalism: The Dilemmas of British Conservatism and Britain's Evolving Place in Europe. *JCMS: Journal of Common Market Studies, 53*(1), 106–122.

Watt, N. (2013, June 30). David Cameron Challenges Nick Clegg Over EU Referendum. *Guardian.* Retrieved from https://www.theguardian.com/politics/2013/jun/30/david-cameron-nick-clegg-eu-referendum

Wellings, B., & Baxendale, H. (2015). Euroscepticism and the Anglosphere: Traditions and Dilemmas in Contemporary English Nationalism. *JCMS: Journal of Common Market Studies, 53*(1), 123–139.

CHAPTER 6

Foreign Policy

In December 2010, public demonstrations in Tunisia marked the beginning of a series of uprisings across North Africa and the Middle East that became known as the 'Arab Spring'. The Coalition subsequently sought to undertake humanitarian intervention in three states, and it twice won parliamentary support for such action (Oliver 2015: 114). This chapter focuses on the rhetoric of identification and division used in relation to the proposed missions in Libya and Syria. The intervention in Iraq in 2014 is not considered for reasons of space. For each case study, the chapter examines the strategies employed first by senior Coalition figures and second by MPs in the debate preceding any military operation. It shows that, on both occasions, the leadership sought to foster ideological identification based on the principle of humanitarian intervention, and used the storyline of the 2003 Iraq war to create an antithesis with the proposed action. While these strategies proved effective in the debate on Libya, they failed to gain traction with regard to Syria, where the contrast with Iraq was less clear. As a result, MPs rejected Cameron's efforts to invite ideological identification with a broader conception of 'legitimate authority', and drew on a pragmatic definition of the 'national interest' to distance themselves instrumentally from the Government.

© The Author(s) 2018
J. Atkins, *Conflict, Co-operation and the Rhetoric of Coalition Government*, Rhetoric, Politics and Society,
https://doi.org/10.1057/978-1-137-31796-4_6

THE ARAB SPRING AND THE COALITION LEADERSHIP'S
CASE FOR INTERVENTION IN LIBYA

By February 2011, the Arab Spring had reached Libya. Here, Muammar Gaddafi's regime sought to violently suppress the uprising, and within days hundreds of protestors had been killed by security forces (Vickers 2015: 231). In response to this crackdown, Britain joined with France and Lebanon to propose Resolution 1973 to the United Nations Security Council (UNSC). The resolution was passed on 17 March 2011 and accused the Libyan government of systematically violating the human rights of its population. To halt the attacks, Resolution 1973 authorized the use of 'all necessary means to protect civilians and civilian areas, except for a foreign intervention force (i.e. a ground invasion)'. Alongside this, it imposed a 'no-fly zone' over Libya and demanded an immediate ceasefire, and on 19 March the UN initiated air strikes targeting Libyan air defence systems. Thus, within 12 months of becoming Prime Minister, Cameron had committed Britain to 'a humanitarian intervention which basically had regime change as its end goal' (Vickers 2015: 232).

Addressing business leaders in March 2011, William Hague offered a narrative in which he identified 11 September 2001 and the global financial crisis of 2008 as two pivotal events of the early twenty-first century. The Arab Spring was the third such event, and for Hague it represented an 'historic shift of massive importance, presenting the international community as a whole with an immense opportunity' (2011a). This moment would then act as a catalyst for change across the world; after all, he argued, 'the desire for freedom is a universal aspiration, and governments that attempt to isolate their people from the spread of information and ideas around the globe will fight a losing battle over time' (2011a). Indeed, Hague claimed, those governments that hindered the development of democracy and oppressed their people would be held to account either by their own population or by the international community. The Gaddafi regime was a case in point, given that it had 'responded to legitimate demands for change with military force', and this situation could not be allowed to continue (2011a).

In response to the Arab Spring, Hague explained that he and Cameron were working to transform the EU's neighbourhood policy 'so that it can act as a magnet for positive change, providing clearer incentives for the creation of free, democratic and just societies that respect human rights'. At the same time, he continued, the EU should 'hold out the prospect of deeper economic integration with Europe so that the people of the region can see a clear path to a more prosperous future' (2011a). Implicit here is the suggestion that the expansion of free trade would also promote the economic interests of EU member states by opening up new markets, which in turn offered a ground for instrumental identification with the Coalition's Middle East policy. However, Hague then warned that if the Arab Spring did not advance freedom and democracy in the region, 'we could see a collapse back into more authoritarian regimes, conflict and increased terrorism in North Africa on Europe's very doorstep', and he pointed out that Britain and its allies had intervened in Libya to prevent this outcome (2011b). Hague's understanding of the Arab Spring and its consequences drew on his conception of 'enlightened self-interest', according to which 'Britain's national interest is more than its own physical defence, but ties into the upholding of international laws and norms' (Beech and Oliver 2014: 113). Thus, his case for military action brought together the instrumental and ideological modes of identification, and so increased the likelihood of attaining consubstantiality with his audience.

Meanwhile, Clegg employed a terministic screen based on continuity to portray the years following 11 September 2001 as a 'dark decade for multilateralism', in which 'the Iraq war and its aftermath; the disappointment of the climate change talks in Copenhagen; and the profound crisis in the financial system ... all eroded faith in the institutions and spirit of global co-operation' (2011a). In this Whig-like narrative of history, the main events all posed a direct challenge to key Liberal Democrat commitments—namely opposition to the Iraq war, environmentalism and economic liberalism. Using the principle of discontinuity, Clegg then claimed that 2011 marked a revival of the ideals of multilateralism, and he told his listeners that 'our aim should be to seize this moment, and "lock in" the [recent] progress' towards greater openness in societies across the Middle East (2011a). International co-operation and the open society are also important Liberal Democrat values, and as such Clegg's narrative provided grounds for fostering ideological identification with his interpretation of the Arab Spring.

Clegg expanded on this theme by contrasting open societies with closed societies. He explained that 'open societies are those which choose democracy and freedom at home, and engagement and responsibility abroad', whereas closed societies 'turn inwards, favouring protectionism in economic policy and detachment from foreign affairs' (2011a). This definition of an open society corresponds to the view of Britain and its international role outlined in the *Programme for Government* and, in a demonstration of ideological consubstantiality with Hague, Clegg asserted that 'the values of open societies are ... human values. And they are shared around the world' (2011a). In turn, Clegg's juxtaposition of the two types of societies supplied a starting point for identification through antithesis, from which he argued that:

> We need international institutions for openness. Institutions that are seen in the eyes of the world as both legitimate and effective: for global security, finance, trade, law and the environment. In all these cases, our goal must be to shift from a 'Western' model of multilateralism to a truly global model. (2011a)

Here, Clegg invited his audience to unite behind the Coalition and its commitment to multilateralism. After all, he continued, it was vital that the UN and other international organizations took the lead in both the Libya mission and post-conflict reconstruction, and the UK would be co-operating with them at all stages of this process (2011a, b).

Echoing his governing partner's conception of a liberal conservative foreign policy, Clegg contended that 'our idealism must be tempered by realism ... We need to know our limits. We need to be humble about the extent to which we can interfere in the business of any nation state'. This blend of idealism and pragmatism was clearly evident in relation to Libya, where the UK made a strong case for humanitarian intervention but had acted only with the support of the international community (2011a). Clegg then created an antithesis between the mission in Libya and the 2003 Iraq war, on which ground he proceeded to offer a defence of liberal interventionism:

> It would be a terrible tragedy if the mistakes of Iraq led to a retreat from the principle of liberal interventionism ... The lesson of Iraq is not that intervention in support of liberal aims is always wrong. The lesson of Iraq is that any such action must only—and must always—be multilaterally sanctioned and driven by humanitarian concerns.

In short, he concluded, 'Liberal vigilantism is dead. Law-abiding liberal interventionism is not' (2011a), and thus created a contrast between the 'recklessness' of New Labour's foreign policy and the Coalition's 'responsible' approach.

To augment this appeal for identification through antitheses, Clegg used a terministic screen based on the principle of discontinuity to highlight five differences between Libya and Iraq. The first was that the former mission was sanctioned by the UN and so was 'unambiguously legal', whereas the latter was undertaken without a Security Council resolution. Second, he claimed, 'there is a clear humanitarian case for intervention in Libya. In Iraq the case rested solely on the danger posed by weapons of mass destruction, a case which turned out to be illusory' (2011a). Third, the intervention in Libya had strong regional support, while many neighbouring countries had opposed the Iraq war. Fourth, he continued, 'there is today a strong emphasis on post-conflict stabilization and aid, led by the UN—compared to the chaotic aftermath of Iraq' and, fifth, the action in Libya was limited and guided by clear objectives, unlike the 'all-encompassing military action in Iraq' (2011a).

It is important to note that Clegg's interpretation of the Iraq war was not strictly accurate. Contrary to his second point, for instance, Tony Blair consistently offered a secondary humanitarian argument for military action (see Atkins 2011: Chap. 9), and—against Clegg's fourth distinction—an assessment undertaken by US experts of the post-conflict reconstruction effort in Iraq found that 'significant progress' had been made by late June–early July 2003, though with the caveat that there were 'huge challenges ahead' (Hamre et al. 2003). This simplified account suggests that the Iraq war functions as a storyline, a narrative combining elements from domains such as law, politics and international relations, and which, through repetition, has become the received interpretation of the conflict. As well as reducing discursive complexity, storylines facilitate 'the creation of a social and moral order in a given domain', and so permit both the positioning of actors and the assignment of moral judgements (Hajer 1997: 64–65). The storyline of Iraq certainly performs this role, with Blair being widely condemned as a 'war criminal'[1] or, in Clegg's words, as a perpetrator of 'liberal vigilantism'. The moral dimension of this storyline is also evident in Clegg's assertion that 'the action in Libya does not signal a return to the trigger-happy policies of the past. It represents a responsible, collective decision to intervene on clear legal and moral grounds' (2011a). In turn, this use of antithesis afforded the Liberal Democrat leader grounds for inviting identification with the Coalition's handling of the situation in Libya.

In their 2010 manifestos, both governing partners used the storyline of the Iraq war to differentiate their foreign policy agendas from that of New

Labour. Their shared values and common conception of the national interest informed the *Programme for Government* and, moreover, were present in the speeches considered above. As we will see in the next section, Clegg's reasons why military action in Libya was 'both necessary and distinct from the Iraq war' echoed strongly the argument made by Cameron in the House of Commons. For Timothy J. Oliver this overlap is unsurprising, and indeed 'one could hardly expect otherwise in the early phase of the Coalition when the focus was firmly on showing that partnership government could work' (2015: 114). It also indicates that not only were the two leaders ideologically consubstantial on the principle of humanitarian intervention, but that their acceptance of the storyline of the Iraq war enabled them to construct an antithesis with the mission in Libya.

The Commons Debate on UNSC Resolution 1973, 2011

In his statement opening the debate, Cameron claimed that military intervention in Libya was justified on both legal and humanitarian grounds. Taking these themes in turn, he asserted that 'the action has the full, unambiguous legal authority of the United Nations', and reminded MPs that the Government had taken the unusual step of providing them with a summary of the legal advice received from the Attorney General.[2] Indeed, not only was the mission authorized by Resolution 1973, Cameron continued, but 'the Arab world has asked us to act with it to stop the slaughter'. By highlighting the broad international and regional backing for military action in Libya, Cameron sought to demonstrate that 'this is not another Iraq' (HC Deb., 21 March 2011, vol. 524 col. 709). He thus employed the storyline of the Iraq war to create identification through antithesis, and he invited MPs to support the operation in Libya on the basis of its comparative legitimacy.

Whereas New Labour had 'been prepared to go into a country, knock over its Government and put something else in place' (HC Deb., 21 March 2011, vol. 524 col. 706), Cameron pointed out that Resolution 1973 excluded 'an occupation force in any form on any part of Libyan territory' (HC Deb., 21 March 2011, vol. 524 col. 709). Here, he reinforced the contrast with the Iraq war and explained that, in the present case, the UN was concerned only with 'protecting civilians and protecting life, and giving the Libyan people a chance to determine their own future'

(HC Deb., 21 March 2011, vol. 524 col. 710). In short, Libya would not be 'a step on the same dangerous path of democracy promotion through the use of force that characterised the post-11 September Blair era' (Daddow 2013: 114). Moreover, given that Gaddafi had murdered and systematically brutalized innocent people, Cameron believed there was a compelling humanitarian case for intervening, and this in turn supplied him with a starting point for fostering ideological identification with his cause.

Using a terministic screen based on the principle of continuity, Cameron linked inaction in Libya to terrorism and mass immigration, and he warned MPs that:

> If Gaddafi's attacks on his own people succeed, Libya will become once again a pariah state, festering on Europe's border, and a source of instability exporting terror beyond its borders. It will be a state from which literally hundreds of thousands of citizens could try to escape, putting huge pressure on us in Europe. (HC Deb., 21 March 2011, vol. 524 col. 708)

In the light of Gaddafi's 'track record of violence and support for terrorism against our country', the dangers of leaving him in place were clear. Therefore, Cameron claimed, it was in Britain's interests to participate in the international action (HC Deb., 21 March 2011, vol. 524 col. 708), and he invited his audience to identify instrumentally with this conclusion. The 'national interest' is ambiguous, and so is vulnerable to abuse by unscrupulous politicians (Atkins 2006: 281). Equally, however, and as we will see below, its openness to interpretation means this concept has the potential for widespread appeal, and thus holds considerable rhetorical value.

Several backbenchers from both Coalition parties accepted the antithesis between military action in Libya and the Iraq war, and so united behind the Government. One such MP was the Liberal Democrat Sir Menzies Campbell, who proceeded to describe the former intervention as 'necessary, legal and legitimate'. This language is almost identical to that of Cameron, for whom the Libya mission was 'necessary, legal and right' (HC Deb., 21 March 2011, vol. 524 col. 704),[3] and indeed Campbell followed the Prime Minister in citing Gaddafi's brutal treatment of the Libyan people, Resolution 1973, and the broad base of international and regional support as justification for his claim (HC Deb., 21 March 2011, vol. 524 cols. 727–8). A number of other parliamentarians, including the Conservatives Dan Byles and William Hague (HC Deb., 21 March 2011, vol. 524 cols. 754–5 and 801) and the Liberal Democrat Jo Swinson (HC Deb., 21 March 2011, vol. 524 cols. 744–6), put forward similar versions of this argument, and thereby aligned themselves with Cameron in support of the intervention.

The humanitarian case for the mission in Libya also attracted considerable backing from MPs. As David Morris (Conservative) put it:

> We cannot stand by and watch people who are not that far away from us, geographically—on the shores of Europe—suffer as they are suffering. We are dealing with a man who, time and again, has violated human rights … People have been killed through his orders, indirectly, and by his regime, certainly. (HC Deb., 21 March 2011, vol. 524 col. 775)[4]

Although he voted reluctantly with the Government, citing the moral burden of war, Morris's appeal to the principle of humanitarian intervention showed that he identified with the Coalition on ideological grounds. The Liberal Democrats were particularly receptive to this strand of Cameron's argument, due to their longstanding commitment to human rights. Thus, both Campbell (HC Deb., 21 March 2011, vol. 524 cols. 727–8) and Swinson invited ideological identification by invoking the doctrine of the Responsibility to Protect (R2P), which was 'codified by the UN World Summit in 2005 … [and] mandated the "collective use of force" by other nations where necessary, in order to prevent genocide and the slaughter of non-combatants' (d'Ancona 2013: 172). Indeed, for Swinson, the UN's willingness to take action in Libya under the R2P reinforced the contrast with Iraq, where it 'would not have applied in any way' (HC Deb., 21 March 2011, vol. 524 col. 744), and so augmented Cameron's appeal for identification through antithesis.

According to the Liberal Democrat MP Stephen Gilbert, Britain's values and national interest were inextricably linked. He explained that:

> Our values demand our active support for people who will no longer tolerate a corrupt regime that keeps them in ignorance, poverty and conformity. In the long term … our national interest will be best served by standing with those who share our values and against those who seek to suppress self-determination. (HC Deb., 21 March 2011, vol. 524 cols. 763–4)

Gilbert's primary concern was with the defence of freedom, which of course is the core concept of liberalism. Implicit in his claim is the suggestion that, by supporting those engaged in the struggle for liberty, Britain will facilitate its promulgation and so advance the national interest. This is consistent not only with the universalist element of liberalism endorsed by Clegg and Hague (above), but with the liberal interventionism of Blair's famous Chicago speech.[5] Here, Blair asserted that: 'If we can establish and spread the values of liberty, the rule of law, human rights and an open society then that is in our national interests ... The spread of our values makes us safer'. For Blair, therefore, 'values and interests merge' (1999), a conclusion that later would provide Gilbert with both ideological and instrumental grounds for inviting identification with the case for military action in Libya.

Meanwhile, Conservative parliamentarians employed a different conception of the 'national interest', with Hague, for instance, claiming that:

> If many of the countries of the Middle East turn into stable democracies and more open economies, the gains for our security and prosperity will be enormous. If they do not, the potential breeding grounds for terrorism and extremism will prosper. (HC Deb., 21 March 2011, vol. 524 col. 797)

Here, he added economic considerations to Cameron's definition, and so offered parliamentarians a wider basis for instrumental identification while reiterating the Prime Minister's security-focused argument. A further modification came from James Morris MP, whose addition of humanitarian issues created a tripartite account of Britain's 'new modern national interest' on which ground he backed the mission in Libya (HC Deb., 21 March 2011, vol. 524 col. 783). The versatility of the 'national interest' also enabled some backbenchers to distance themselves from the Coalition. Thus, Sir Edward Leigh (Conservative) asked: 'Where is our strategic interest in Libya, which after all is 1500 miles away? What are Egypt and Tunisia doing? They are its neighbours. Why is there not a single Arab plane in action at this moment?' (HC Deb., 21 March 2011, vol. 524 col. 772). In so doing, he defined the 'national interest' narrowly, in terms of geographical proximity, and thus distanced himself instrumentally from the Government.

Considerations of the national interest led some MPs to raise questions about the possible consequences of intervention. As the Conservative backbencher Richard Drax put it:

> We should be concerned about a pariah state festering on Europe's southern boundary; wounded, Gaddafi's regime would be even more dangerous ... What if Gaddafi holds out in his western stronghold while menacing

Benghazi? What happens then? Will that test the West's resolve? I suspect it will. (HC Deb., 21 March 2011, vol. 524 col. 785)

Similarly, Swinson warned that, unless the action reached a swift conclusion, the UK's existing commitments in Afghanistan meant it 'may not be able to react easily with military might to developments that would require a further response' (HC Deb., 21 March 2011, vol. 524 col. 745). Underlying these scenarios was a concern that the conflict would become protracted and potentially destabilize the Middle East. Such an outcome would be deeply damaging to both the region and the UK in human, economic and security terms, and the two MPs appealed for caution on this basis.

The national interest also featured in arguments about the consequences of inaction in Libya. One Conservative MP, Rory Stewart, demonstrated consubstantiality with the Coalition by affirming that intervention was justified on humanitarian and national security grounds, but then claimed it was driven primarily by 'the kind of message that we are trying to pass to people in Egypt or Tunisia'. He explained that:

If we had allowed Gaddafi simply to hammer Benghazi—people in Egypt, Tunisia and Syria would have concluded that we were on the side of oil-rich regimes against their people. We would have no progressive narrative with which we could engage with that region over the next three decades. (HC Deb., 21 March 2011, vol. 524 col. 741; see also Swinson HC Deb., 21 March 2011, vol. 524 col. 745)

Here, the 'national interest' is understood in terms of Britain's moral leadership and influence in the world, a definition rooted in the global power/exceptionalist narrative examined in the previous chapter. For Stewart, a failure to act would harm Britain's reputation, and he thus sought to foster instrumental identification with the mission in Libya.

When the House divided after the debate, MPs backed the Government by 557 votes to 13. This outcome reflects the efficacy of the Coalition leadership's strategies of identification, which centred on humanitarian principles, definitions of the 'national interest' and the antithesis with Iraq. The military action lasted for seven months and, following Gaddafi's death at the hands of Libyan rebels on 20 October 2011, power shifted to the National Transitional Council (Beech and Oliver 2014: 112). Initially, this development was seen as the conclusion to a successful mission and

Cameron, like many others, hoped for 'a new dawn of democracy sweeping across the Arab world' (Seldon and Snowdon 2015: 541). However, Libya since became a 'fragile country, dominated by rival militias', in which 'women's rights have been suppressed, politicians and activists have been kidnapped and assassinated. The governing body, the General National Congress, has collapsed'. A low-level civil war has been ongoing since May 2014 and, by the end of the Coalition's term of office, Libya resembled 'post-invasion Iraq at its worst, but without Western troops on the ground' (Vickers 2015: 233).

Cameron and Clegg's Case for Action Against Syria in 2013

In spring 2011 the Arab Spring reached Syria, as protests erupted against the government of Bashar al-Assad. The regime responded with violence, and the insurgency descended into a civil war involving disparate state and non-state groups (Vickers 2015: 233). On 21 August 2013, it was reported that a chemical weapons attack had taken place on the outskirts of the capital city Damascus, killing hundreds of civilians (Seldon and Snowdon 2015: 325). Cameron and the US President Barack Obama concurred that the attack demanded a robust international response and, in an effort to ensure the legitimacy of any action, the UK sought a UNSC resolution. However, it soon became apparent that support from China and Russia was not forthcoming, while regional actors including Iran opposed any military intervention (Kaarbo and Kenealy 2016: 29). In spite of this lack of consensus Cameron recalled Parliament, and a vote on UK involvement in the US-led mission in Syria took place on 29 August 2013. Two days prior to the debate, Cameron and Clegg gave interviews in which they made the case for action, and their chosen strategies of identification and division are considered below.

The starting point of Cameron's argument was the Assad regime's alleged violation of the Geneva Protocol (1925), which prohibited the use of chemical and biological weapons. Using the assumed 'we', he then asserted that: 'I don't believe we can let that stand' (2013). As an appeal to identification, 'use of the pronoun "we" (along with surrogate forms) often goes unnoticed', and indeed the common bond it takes for granted tends to be ill-defined (Cheney 1983: 148–149). However, Cameron's next sentence suggests he was referring to 'Britain'—as opposed to 'the international community'—as he reassured his listeners that:

> Any action we take or others take would have to be legal, would have to be proportionate. It would have to be specifically to deter and degrade the future use of chemical weapons ... this is not about getting involved in a Middle Eastern war. (2013)

Instead, Cameron explained, the question was whether intervention in Syria was likely to deter the future use of chemical weapons. After all, a failure to act may send a signal that regimes can deploy these weapons with impunity, and so inflict untold suffering on innocent civilians. Cameron thus drew on the principle of humanitarian intervention to invite ideological identification, and he buttressed it with a reference to Britain's moral leadership role, arguing that: 'It must be right to have some rules in our world, and to try to enforce those rules' (2013).

Clegg's reasons for supporting a possible intervention overlapped considerably with those given by Cameron, and he also sought to foster ideological identification on humanitarian grounds. To this end, he told his listeners that 'the murder of innocent men, women and children through the use of chemical weapons is a repugnant crime and a flagrant abuse of international law', and he warned them that inaction would 'set a very dangerous precedent indeed' (2013a). Again like Cameron, Clegg was eager to stress that any measures taken would be legal, proportionate and 'specific to stopping the use of chemical weapons' (2013b; see also Clegg 2013a), and he reassured his audience that 'we are not considering an open-ended military intervention with boots on the ground like we saw in Iraq' (2013a). By doing so, Clegg used the storyline of the Iraq war to create identification through antithesis, and so to persuade the public to support the Coalition's case for military involvement in Syria.

While Clegg was adamant that any action should be multilateral, he felt that Cameron had been slow to grasp the importance of UN involvement and confided to David Laws that: 'I think he saw it initially as some sort of sop to the Liberal Democrats. But now he can see it is important to his own side too' (quoted in Laws 2016: 320). By the eve of the Commons debate, however, both leaders had made strenuous efforts to secure an international and cross-party consensus on Syria. As Clegg wrote in an email to party members:

We have listened to EU countries and the Arab League ... we are taking this to the UN and ... we are ensuring the House of Commons has the final say before any direct British involvement—one vote tomorrow, and another one if and when we are asked to participate directly. (2013b)

Clegg's position was consistent with the Liberal Democrats' belief in international co-operation, on which ground he invited ideological identification with the Coalition's approach to Syria. However, it also reflected a concern—which Cameron shared—that any action must be distinguished clearly from Iraq, and with this aim in mind he once again set out five points of differentiation.

The first of Clegg's reasons was that the deployment of chemical weapons is a war crime and there was no doubt that they had been used. However, it is unclear exactly how Syria is distinguished from Iraq in this statement, and it is notable that the question of culpability is unaddressed. Clegg's second point was that Britain was co-operating with international partners including the Arab League. The implication here is that, unlike with Iraq, there was regional involvement in determining the response to Syria. Third, proportionate military action against a regime that had used chemical weapons was legal under humanitarian law, although Clegg omitted to mention the lack of a UNSC resolution. His fourth reason offered the only explicit contrast with Iraq, namely that:

This is not about boots on the ground. This is not about regime change. This is about upholding international and humanitarian law and deterring the use of chemical weapons to protect innocent people from being murdered in future by brutal dictators. (2013b)

Finally, Clegg wrote, the Government had taken the case for action to the UN and 'the Attorney General is publishing unedited advice based on evidence'. A Commons vote would take place the following day (2013b). Again, this distinction lacks clarity, as the Blair government also went to the UNSC and held a parliamentary vote before embarking on military action in Iraq. Nonetheless, Clegg concluded his email with an appeal for ideological identification based on his Party's commitments to internationalism and humanitarian principles, saying: 'I don't believe anyone who shares these values can stand back and watch what is currently happening in Syria' (2013b).

As Oliver points out, the two leaders once more employed similar language to justify military action, 'formulating their arguments around overlapping themes even when addressing them to different audiences' (2015: 115). Indeed, Clegg's statement to Laws that 'I cannot remember a time in the last year when Cameron and I have been so aligned' (quoted in Laws 2016: 320) provides further evidence of their consubstantiality on the need to intervene in Syria. However, their parties were divided on the matter. Among the Conservatives, Hague and George Osborne supported Cameron, but the Defence Secretary, Philip Hammond, called attention to the size and power of Syria's air force and warned, 'This is no Libya' (quoted in Laws 2016: 317). Meanwhile, the Liberal Democrats Paddy Ashdown and Shirley Williams backed any intervention, but Lorely Burt and Tim Farron were opposed (Laws 2016: 326–327). The next section examines how these divisions were manifested in the parliamentary debate.

THE COMMONS DEBATE ON SYRIA AND THE USE OF CHEMICAL WEAPONS, 2013

As with Libya, Cameron's primary justification for military action in Syria was the alleviation of human suffering. After acknowledging that intervention should be undertaken only in exceptional circumstances, he told MPs that: 'this is a humanitarian catastrophe and if there are no consequences, there will be nothing to stop Assad and other dictators using these weapons again and again' (HC Deb., 29 August 2013, vol. 566 col. 1434). Furthermore, a failure to act would fatally undermine the international taboo against the use of chemical weapons, which had been in place for almost a century. On Cameron's view, it was clearly in the national interest that the rules on chemical weapons were upheld (HC Deb., 29 August 2013, vol. 566 cols. 1434–5), which suggests he believed the demonstration of moral leadership was advantageous to Britain's international standing. This instrumental argument thus supplemented Cameron's appeal for ideological identification on humanitarian grounds.

In the absence of UN authorization, the principle of humanitarian intervention was employed as a legal basis for military action (Oliver 2015: 115). As Cameron explained, the Attorney General had confirmed that 'the use of chemical weapons in Syria constitutes both a war crime and a crime against humanity' and, moreover, his legal advice had been placed in the Library of the House of Commons (HC Deb., 29 August 2013, vol. 566 col. 1435). While the Prime Minister conceded that the best approach was to secure a UNSC resolution, he denied it was the only source of legitimate authority and urged MPs to:

> Consider for a moment what the consequences would be if that were the case. We could have a situation where a country's Government were literally annihilating half the people in that country, but because of one veto on the Security Council we would be hampered in taking any action. (HC Deb., 29 August 2013, vol. 566 cols. 1429–30)

The broadening of the conception of legitimate authority to incorporate the R2P is contestable, but—in theory at least—it increased the likelihood of creating ideological identification with the case for the proposed action (see also Clegg 2013b). This was important for Cameron, as the absence of explicit UN backing differentiated Syria from the mission in Libya, and arguably positioned it closer to the invasion of Iraq. In consequence, it is unsurprising that he again used the storyline of the Iraq war, which had proved highly effective in 2011, in a bid to invite identification through antitheses and secure support for the proposed intervention.

Echoing Clegg (2013a), Cameron identified a number of reasons why the situation in Syria was 'fundamentally different' from that in Iraq:

> We are not invading a country. We are not searching for chemical or biological weapons. The case for ultimately supporting action … is not based on a specific piece or pieces of intelligence. The fact that the Syrian Government have, and have used, chemical weapons is beyond doubt. The fact that the most recent attack took place is not seriously doubted. (HC Deb., 29 August 2013, vol. 566 col. 1427)

In addition, he claimed, NATO, Europe, and the Arab League were united in the belief that the Assad regime should be held to account, and that action therefore was necessary (cf. Clegg 2013a). Here, Cameron glossed over the concerns of regional actors such as Iran and Jordan to convey a unity of purpose that had been lacking in the run-up to the Iraq war. Through this antithesis, Cameron invited MPs to join with the Government and the international community—though critically not the UNSC—in backing the proposed mission. After all, he argued, 'we must not let the spectre of previous mistakes paralyze our ability to stand up for what is right' (HC Deb., 29 August 2013, vol. 566 col. 1440).

Although the majority of parliamentarians were ideologically consubstantial with Cameron on the principle of humanitarian intervention (see Oliver 2015: 115), few accepted his argument that the R2P supplied a legal basis for military action. One of these latter MPs, Andrew Mitchell asserted that 'it is hard to think of a situation which more rightly triggers the Responsibility to Protect that has been referred to this afternoon' (HC Deb., 29 August 2013, vol. 566 col. 1474), while Brooks Newmark similarly claimed the UN 'is failing to live up to its mandate to protect. We therefore need to find a coalition of the willing' (HC Deb., 29 August 2013, vol. 566 col. 1504). Both Conservative MPs also concurred that action was necessary in order to deter others from using chemical weapons against civilians. The only Liberal Democrat to echo Clegg's support for intervention under the R2P was Campbell, though he noted that 'it is a fundamental of that doctrine that every possible political and diplomatic alternative will have been explored and found not to be capable' (HC Deb., 29 August 2013, vol. 566 col. 1456). These MPs thus identified ideologically with Cameron's broader understanding of the concept of 'legitimate authority'.

However, the Conservative backbencher Richard Ottaway questioned whether the R2P was working as intended, on the ground that it effectively means 'the UN is now redundant and that the humanitarian doctrine has legs of its own and can be interpreted virtually any way the parties wish' (HC Deb., 29 August 2013, vol. 566 col. 1460).[6] As with the 'national interest', the ambiguity of 'legitimate authority' means it can be defined to suit the needs and goals of political actors. Thus, John Baron (Conservative) employed a terministic screen based on discontinuity to argue that, contra Cameron, R2P 'is not linked to chemical weapons ... [and] could have been invoked 100,000 lives ago. Therefore, the idea that it becomes relevant because chemical weapons have been used is a nonstarter' (HC Deb., 29 August 2013, vol. 566 col. 1496). In rejecting Cameron's redefinition of legitimate authority, these rebels sought to distance themselves ideologically from the Coalition leadership, while aligning themselves with a sceptical public in opposition to the proposed intervention.[7]

According to Cameron, 'the evidence that the Syrian regime has used these weapons, in the early hours of 21 August, is right in front of our eyes' (HC Deb., 29 August 2013, vol. 566 col. 1427). Some MPs took this assertion on trust, and so displayed interpersonal identification with the Prime Minister. As Newmark argued, the evidence 'puts the blame squarely on the shoulders of Bashar al-Assad and his brother, Maher', while the Liberal Democrat Andrew George accepted Cameron's claim 'on the balance of probability' (HC Deb., 29 August 2013, vol. 566 cols. 1504 and 1519). However, other Conservatives were dubious, with Julian Lewis, for example, contending that 'it is very far from certain that the evidence stacks up' (HC Deb., 29 August 2013, vol. 566 col. 1519; see also Strong 2015: 1132). To varying degrees, such cynicism can be attributed to the ongoing tensions between Conservative parliamentarians and the leadership. As one MP put it, 'It all comes down to loyalty ... backbenchers know that ... [Cameron] wouldn't die in a ditch for them, so why should they die in a ditch for him?' (quoted in Hardman 2013; see Kaarbo and Kenealy 2016: 39–40).

While interpersonal division may have played a part in creating mistrust, a further contributing factor was the legacy of Iraq. After all, Parliament was once again being asked to give its support to a proposed intervention in the absence of a UN resolution and on the basis of classified intelligence (Strong 2015: 1131; Kaarbo and Kenealy 2016: 41). In Ottaway's words, the Attorney General's conclusion that military action was legal even without UN authorization 'poses more questions than it answers' (HC Deb., 29 August 2013, vol. 566 col. 1460). Regarding the intelligence, David Davis (Conservative) alluded to the Iraq war and argued that 'we must have clear evidence to show the House that, if there is a casus belli, it is real, not confected or constructed. That may mean more aggressive disclosure of intelligence than we would normally have' (HC Deb., 29 August 2013, vol. 566 col. 1470).[8] Both backbenchers therefore questioned the leadership's use of the principle of discontinuity to distinguish the two missions, and in consequence rejected Cameron and Clegg's efforts to establish identification through antithesis.

Some parliamentarians rebuffed the Prime Minister's appeal for instrumental identification based on the national interest. Thus, the Liberal Democrat Sir Malcolm Bruce claimed that the Government needed to determine 'the extent to which our involvement matters and our position in the world is enhanced', on the ground that this matter had not been adequately addressed (HC Deb., 29 August 2013, vol. 566 col. 1483). In other words, he rejected on its own terms Cameron's implicit argument that it was in Britain's interest to provide moral leadership to the world by intervening in Syria. Others drew on a more parochial conception of the national interest to distance themselves from the Coalition, with Leigh, for instance, asking: 'Has Syria ever been a colony? Has it ever been in our sphere of interest? Has it ever posed the remotest threat to the British people?' These questions mattered because 'our economy is not in very good shape. Neither are our social services, schools or hospitals' (HC Deb., 29 August 2013, vol. 566 col. 1521). Here, Leigh created an antithesis between Syria and Britain and, drawing on the storyline of the deficit, sought to foster instrumental identification with his view that the nation's interest was best served by looking after its own citizens before others.

Following the experience in Libya, several MPs worried about the unintended consequences of intervention. In a reversal of Cameron's argument for that mission, Andrew Turner (Conservative) used a terministic screen based on continuity to link military action in Syria to the threat of terrorism, saying: 'I fear that missile strikes may ... provoke more terrorist attacks on British streets or those of our territories and allies abroad' (HC Deb., 29 August 2013, vol. 566 col. 1510). However, their main fear was 'mission creep'; in Julian Lewis's words, the Middle East was 'a powder keg, and we should not be lobbing weapons into the heart of such combustible material' (HC Deb., 29 August 2013, vol. 566 col. 1468). Although shared by MPs from both Coalition parties, this concern was raised repeatedly by Liberal Democrats (Kaarbo and Kenealy 2016: 38–39), despite Clegg's reassurance that the proposed action was limited in scope (2013b). As Burt put it: 'I still worry that we might be embarking on a slippery slope: that what we agree today will pave the way to further action' (HC Deb., 29 August 2013, vol. 566 col. 1499). Common to these objections to British involvement in Syria was a broad understanding of the national interest, which encompassed human, financial and security considerations. This conception was also employed in the debate on Libya, and it once again enabled critics to distance themselves instrumentally from the Coalition by rejecting its narrow definition of Britain's interests.

The motion was defeated by 285 votes to 272, with 30 Conservative and nine Liberal Democrat MPs rebelling against the Government. Reflecting on the defeat, Clegg noted that Syria had brought him and Cameron together after a 'long period of bruising coalition disputes' (quoted in Laws 2016: 328). In contrast, sections of the two parliamentary parties were united by a belief that the proposed action was unjustified, and thus aligned themselves in opposition to their respective leaderships. While Liberal Democrat rebels were concerned about the absence of a UN resolution and the consequences of intervening in Syria, many Conservative backbenchers lacked confidence in Cameron's approach. As Juliet Kaarbo and Daniel Kenealy explain:

> Recalling Parliament in such a haphazard manner, attempting to rush through a vote before the UN inspectors completed their work, and refusing to disclose comprehensively the legal advice received by the UK Government, were all signs that Cameron underestimated the degree of opposition. (2016: 39–40)

Moreover, Cameron and his Cabinet colleagues did not meet with many of the Conservative doubters to explain the case for military action before the vote, which aggravated existing intra-party tensions caused by the Prime Minister's style of leadership. As one backbencher put it, the impression conveyed was that the party whips just 'couldn't be bothered' (quoted in Kaarbo and Kenealy 2016: 40).

CONCLUSION

The rhetorical strategies employed by senior Coalition figures in their efforts to win support for military action in Libya and Syria are strikingly similar. After all, the leaders were ideologically consubstantial on the principle of humanitarian intervention, and both employed identification through antithesis to distinguish the proposed interventions from Iraq. To this end, they selectively emphasized elements of each situation and, drawing on the storyline of the 2003 Iraq war, sought to create contrasts between present and past actions. Their efforts proved highly effective in the debate on Libya, as there was an immediate humanitarian emergency and the mission was backed by the UN. Indeed, several MPs broadened Cameron's definition of the 'national interest' in their efforts to foster instrumental identification with the case for military intervention. Despite the efforts of some backbenchers to distance themselves from the leadership by means of a narrow understanding of this contested concept, the Government won a decisive victory in the vote.

As regards Syria, the antithesis with Iraq was less clear-cut. Given the lack of a UN resolution, Cameron invoked the R2P as an alternative legal basis for humanitarian intervention. In so doing, he used a wider interpretation of the concept of 'legitimate authority' as a starting point for creating ideological identification, but met with little success. Cameron also invited MPs to identify instrumentally with the case for action, implying that it was in Britain's interest to provide moral leadership to the world. Again, this definition failed to gain traction, and backbenchers utilized pragmatic conceptions of the 'national interest' to demonstrate instrumental division. Unlike in 2011, interpersonal friction between the Parliamentary Conservative Party and the leadership was evident in the debate on Syria. This is partially attributable to previous conflicts over issues such as constitutional reform and Europe, but it also reflected dissatisfaction with Cameron's management of his Party. These factors combined to produce a humiliating defeat for the Prime Minister.

The loss of the vote on Syria had repercussions beyond Westminster. The proposed military action was called off, and a precarious diplomatic solution to disarm the Syrian regime was engineered by Russia. In effect, writes Michael Clarke, the defeat had 'scuppered the US operation and damaged the UK's reputation around the world as a resolute power, a firm ally of the US and a country that was skilled in the political exercise of military leadership' (2015: 366; see also Seldon and Snowdon 2015: 342–345). This diminution in status was the exact outcome that Cameron had hoped would be avoided by British involvement in the mission. As a consequence he became more circumspect with regard to foreign intervention, though he won parliamentary backing for air strikes against the so-called Islamic State in Iraq in 2014. Overall, however, Cameron's ability to offer overt military support to the USA was considerably weakened (Seldon and Snowdon 2015: 345).

NOTES

1. See, for instance, the website http://www.arrestblair.org and the Channel 4 drama *The Trial of Tony Blair* (2007).
2. For the full text of the Government's note on the legal basis for intervention in Libya, see BBC (2011).
3. In his opening statement, Cameron argued that: 'This action was necessary because, with others, we should be trying to prevent this dictator from using military violence against his own people; it was legal because … it had the backing of the UN Security Council; and it was right … because we should not stand aside while he murders his own people—and the Arab League and many others agreed' (HC Deb., 21 March 2011, vol. 524 col. 704).
4. Likewise, William Hague said: 'The Arab world and the Western world care about the civilians of Libya, but their Government do not. We are determined to stop violence, bloodshed and suffering—the very things that the

Gaddafi regime is happy to unleash' (HC Deb., 21 March 2011, vol. 524 col. 801).

5. For discussion of Blair's 'doctrine of the international community', see inter alia Atkins (2006), Ralph (2011) and Daddow and Schnapper (2013).

6. Likewise, the Conservative MP John Baron asked: 'Is military intervention without a UN resolution legitimate? International law is terribly subjective—there are no hard and fast rules, but the best we have is the UN' (HC Deb., 29 August 2013, vol. 566 col. 1496). Meanwhile, Lorely Burt (Liberal Democrat) contended that: 'In order to ensure that we act with maximum legitimacy, we must have transparent international law on our side and make sure that the actions that we take have wide international approval' (HC Deb., 29 August 2013, vol. 566 col. 1500).

7. As James Strong points out, 'just 22 per cent of opinion poll respondents favoured British intervention' in Syria (2015: 1133).

8. Echoing this point, Ottaway explained that, in 2003, 'Parliament was briefed on the intelligence, but we were given only part of the story and, in some cases, an inaccurate story. A summary of the intelligence [on Syria] has been published, but it is the bare bones' (HC Deb., 29 August 2013, vol. 566 col. 1460).

References

Atkins, J. (2006). A New Approach to Humanitarian Intervention? Tony Blair's 'Doctrine of the International Community'. *British Politics, 1*(2), 274–283.

Atkins, J. (2011). *Justifying New Labour Policy*. Basingstoke: Palgrave Macmillan.

BBC. (2011, March 21). *In Full: UK Government's Legal Note on Libya*. Retrieved from http://www.bbc.co.uk/news/uk-politics-12810050

Beech, M., & Oliver, T. J. (2014). Humanitarian Intervention and Foreign Policy in the Conservative-Led Coalition. *Parliamentary Affairs, 67*(1), 102–118.

Blair, T. (1999, April 24). *Doctrine of the International Community*. Retrieved from http://www.britishpoliticalspeech.org/speech-archive.htm?speech=279

Cameron, D. (2013, August 27). *Syria: Transcript of PM's Interview*. Retrieved from https://www.gov.uk/government/speeches/syria-transcript-of-pms-interview

Cheney, G. (1983). The Rhetoric of Identification and the Study of Organizational Communication. *Quarterly Journal of Speech, 69*(2), 143–158.

Clarke, M. (2015). The Coalition and Foreign Affairs. In A. Seldon & M. Finn (Eds.), *The Coalition Effect 2010–2015* (pp. 345–369). Cambridge: Cambridge University Press.

Clegg, N. (2011a, March 29). *An Axis of Openness: Renewing Multilateralism for the 21st Century*. Retrieved from https://www.gov.uk/government/speeches/an-axis-of-openness-renewing-multilateralism-for-the-21st-century

Clegg, N. (2011b, August 22). *Arab Spring Speech.* Retrieved from http://www.politics.co.uk/comment-analysis/2011/08/22/nick-clegg-arab-spring-speech-in-fulll

Clegg, N. (2013a, August 27). *Syria: Transcript of Nick Clegg's Interview.* Retrieved fromhttps://www.gov.uk/government/speeches/syria-transcript-of-nick-cleggs-interview

Clegg, N. (2013b, August 28). *'This Is Not Iraq': Nick Clegg's Email to Party Members on Syria.* Retrieved from https://www.markpack.org.uk/45141/this-is-not-iraq-nick-cleggs-email-to-party-members-on-syria/

Daddow, O. (2013). The Use of Force in British Foreign Policy: From New Labour to the Coalition. *The Political Quarterly, 84*(1), 110–118.

Daddow, O., & Schnapper, P. (2013). Liberal Intervention in the Foreign Policy Thinking of Tony Blair and David Cameron. *Cambridge Review of International Affairs, 26*(2), 330–349.

d'Ancona, M. (2013). *In It Together: The Inside Story of the Coalition Government.* London: Viking.

Hague, W. (2011a, March 22). *A Turning Point for Africa?* Retrieved from https://www.gov.uk/government/speeches/a-turning-point-for-africa

Hague, W. (2011b, May 4). *We Will Continue to Fight Against Terrorism Wherever It Rears Its Head.* Retrieved from https://www.gov.uk/government/speeches/we-will-continue-to-fight-against-terrorism-wherever-it-rears-its-head

Hajer, M. A. (1997). *The Politics of Environmental Discourse: Ecological Modernization and the Policy Process.* Oxford: Oxford University Press.

Hamre, J., Barton, F., Crocker, B., Mendelson-Forman, J., and Orr, R. (2003, July 17). *Iraq's Post-Conflict Reconstruction: A Field Review and Recommendations.* Retrieved from https://www.cfr.org/content/publications/attachments/Iraq_Trip_Report.pdf

Hardman, I. (2013, August 29). Syria Defeat: What Happened to the Whips? *The Spectator.* Retrievedfromhttps://blogs.spectator.co.uk/2013/08/syria-defeat-what-happened-to-the-whips/

HC Deb., 21 March 2011, vol. 524 cols. 704–801.

HC Deb., 29 August 2013, vol. 566 cols. 1427–1521.

Kaarbo, J., & Kenealy, D. (2016). No, Prime Minister: Explaining the House of Commons' Vote on Intervention in Syria. *European Security, 25*(1), 28–48.

Laws, D. (2016). *Coalition: The Inside Story of the Conservative-Liberal Democrat Coalition Government.* London: Biteback Publishing Ltd.

Oliver, T. J. (2015). Intervention by Design or Failure: The Coalition and Humanitarian Intervention. *The Political Quarterly, 86*(1), 110–117.

Ralph, J. (2011). After Chilcot: The 'Doctrine of International Community' and the UK Decision to Invade Iraq. *British Journal of Politics and International Relations, 13*(3), 304–325.

Seldon, A., & Snowdon, P. (2015). *Cameron at 10: The Inside Story 2010–2015.* London: William Collins.

Strong, J. (2015). Interpreting the Syria Vote: Parliament and British Foreign Policy. *International Affairs, 91*(5), 1123–1139.

Vickers, R. (2015). Foreign Policy and International Development. In M. Beech & S. Lee (Eds.), *The Conservative-Liberal Coalition: Examining the Cameron-Clegg Government* (pp. 227–242). Basingstoke: Palgrave Macmillan.

CHAPTER 7

Coalition Termination: The 2015 General Election Campaign

This chapter focuses on the 'short' period of the 2015 campaign, which began on 30 March and ended with the general election on 7 May. Its main concern is to consider how the former partners in the Coalition defended their record in government and, at the same time, reasserted their distinctive identities. This process requires considerable rhetorical skill—especially for the smaller party, whose influence and achievements are often less visible to the public. The chapter begins by examining the pledges made in the four policy areas considered in this book, first in the Conservative Party manifesto and then in that of the Liberal Democrats. Next, it discusses the strategies of unity and division employed by Cameron and Clegg, concentrating firstly on their manifesto launch speeches and then on the two televised debates in which both participated, namely *The ITV Leaders' Debate* and the BBC *Question Time Special*. In so doing, it argues that while the Conservatives' ownership of economic policy enabled them to claim the recovery as their own, differentiation was problematic for the Liberal Democrats, whose strategic options were significantly curtailed by previous bargaining outcomes and rhetorical choices.

THE CONSERVATIVE PARTY MANIFESTO

Cameron's *Foreword* to the Conservatives' 2015 manifesto drew on the storyline of the deficit and placed the economy centre stage. Having inherited an economic 'mess' from Labour, he claimed his government was

© The Author(s) 2018

J. Atkins, *Conflict, Co-operation and the Rhetoric of Coalition Government*, Rhetoric, Politics and Society,
https://doi.org/10.1057/978-1-137-31796-4_7

'getting our national finances back under control ... Britain is back on its feet, strong and growing stronger every day' (2015: 5). This process had demanded patience and difficult decisions, and for Cameron it was 'the product of a supreme national effort'. He explained that:

> It is a profound Conservative belief that our country is made great not through the action of government alone, but through the flair, the ingenuity and hard work of the British people—and so it has proved the last five years. (2015: 5)

Here, Cameron depicted the 'British people' as uniquely hard working and inventive, and so utilized the exceptionalism narrative to arouse feelings of national pride. Furthermore, by portraying his government and the population as partners in a collective endeavour, he invited the electorate to identify with the Conservatives as 'the party of the British people'.

However, Cameron warned that the economy was still fragile, and he asserted that the fundamental questions at the election were how to maintain the recovery, and how to ensure that it benefited all citizens throughout their lives. The latter primarily entailed the provision of public services, which was dependent on a strong economy, and Cameron asked the electorate to consider:

> Which party is best placed to keep our economy strong? The team which has delivered the growing economy we have today, which created more jobs since 2010 than the rest of the European Union put together; or the party which left behind a ruined economy just five short years ago? Now is a time to build on the progress we have made, not to put it all at risk. (2015: 5)

This is an example of identification through antitheses, whereby listeners were invited to identify with the 'economically competent' Conservatives and reject the 'irresponsible' Labour Party. To broaden the appeal of his argument, Cameron also invited instrumental identification with his claim that the Conservatives had restored economic growth, and that they were the party who would safeguard the nation's long-term prosperity.

Turning now to the four policy areas, the section of the Conservative manifesto dealing with higher education promised that 'we will ensure that if you want to go to university, you can' (2015: 35). This involved building on the Coalition's reforms which, in 2014–15, had seen student numbers rise to over 500,000, with a record proportion of students from disadvantaged backgrounds entering university. Thus, the Conservatives committed themselves to 'abolishing the cap on higher education student numbers and removing an arbitrary ceiling on ambition' from September 2015, and ensuring the 'continuing success and stability of [the tuition fees regime], so that the interests of both students and taxpayers are fairly represented' (2015: 35). As they had in coalition, the Conservatives sought to foster ideological identification on the basis of the principle of liberalization, while contrasting their approach with the 'arbitrary' controls associated with top-down government in a bid to create identification through antithesis. They also invited students and taxpayers (university employees are notably absent here) to identify instrumentally with the Party, on the ground that it alone would defend their interests 'against those who threaten to obstruct or deny them' (Collini 2017: 159–160).

With regard to policy, the Conservatives pledged to give students the best possible value for money. This entailed introducing a framework 'to recognize universities offering the highest teaching quality'; encouraging the universities to provide more two-year degree courses; and increasing the amount of data available to potential students 'so that they can make decisions informed by the career paths of past graduates' (2015: 35). These proposals would realize Willetts's vision of a 'revolution in teaching' (2012) by placing it on a par with research and improving the student experience, while diversifying existing provision and increasing choice. At the same time, the Conservatives demonstrated their commitment to widening participation by calling attention to rising student numbers and their decision to abolish upfront fees, and once again invited ideological identification with the 'new' progressive definition of fairness as social mobility. All of these measures were a continuation of the policy programme enacted by the Coalition, and indeed there is clear evidence of rhetorical path dependency in the Conservatives' chosen identification strategies.

In contrast, the passages on constitutional reform emphasized the Conservatives' discontinuity with the Coalition, and so served to reassert their unique identity. This was unsurprising given that the formation of the partnership had demanded a number of concessions in this area of policy—especially on the referendum on the Alternative Vote—and that their proposed boundary reforms had been delayed until after the 2015 general election. Thus, the manifesto reprised the Conservatives' 2010 pledge to redraw constituency boundaries, which would cut the number of MPs to 600 and ensure that the value of each ballot was more equal (2015: 49). Again, these proposals were consistent with the conception of fairness as equality, which in turn supplied a basis for fostering ideological identification. Additionally, the Conservatives promised to 'respect the will of the British people, as expressed in the 2011 referendum, and keep First Past the Post for elections to the House of Commons' (2015: 49). Of course, this was an easy promise to make, given the Party's long-held belief that the existing system best advanced its electoral interests. However, it also allowed them to draw a line under their time in coalition, and thus to reaffirm their electoral distinctiveness.

Meanwhile, the section on Europe opened with a summary of the Coalition's successes, among which were the withdrawal of Britain from Eurozone bailouts and Cameron's vetoing of the proposed amendment to the Lisbon Treaty in December 2011. Echoing the technocratic/modernist arguments of both Cameron and Clegg, the Conservatives endorsed the single market, free trade and 'working together where we are stronger together than alone' (2015: 72), and thereby invited instrumental identification with their conception of the national interest. However, they continued, EU was 'too big, too bossy and too bureaucratic' and, in a bid to foster ideological identification, they said: 'No to "ever closer union". No to a constant flow of power to Brussels. No to unnecessary interference' (2015: 72). This appeal drew on the narrative of parliamentary sovereignty, which had a strong presence in the two parliamentary debates examined in Chap. 5. By bringing together these two strategies of identification, the Conservatives sought to appeal to voters across the spectrum of opinion on Europe, and so to maximize their potential support on this issue.

Although the European Union (Referendum) Bill 2013–14 was rejected by the House of Lords, its primary objective was at the heart of the Conservative manifesto. Here, the Party reiterated Cameron's claim at Bloomberg that 'consent [for Britain's continued membership] has worn wafer-thin', a concern for democratic legitimacy that Eurosceptic backbenchers had also utilized as a basis for ideological identification. To address this issue, the Conservatives pledged to:

Negotiate a new settlement for Britain in Europe, and then ask the British people whether they want to stay in the EU on this reformed basis or leave … We will hold that in/out referendum before the end of 2017 and respect the outcome. (2015: 72)

This commitment gave expression to Cameron's shift towards a harder Euroscepticism, which had occurred in response to pressure from the UK Independence Party (UKIP) and his own MPs (Cowley and Kavanagh 2016: 52). As such, it represented a departure from the 2010 Conservative manifesto, while simultaneously distancing the Party from the pragmatic approach set out in the *Programme for Government.*

Using a terministic screen based on continuity, the Conservatives presented economic security and national security as interdependent. From this starting point, they invited instrumental identification with their approach to foreign policy, explaining that: 'Our prosperity depends upon Britain remaining an active, outward-looking nation, one that is engaged with the world, not looking in on itself' (2015: 75). Thus, the Conservatives pledged to maintain Britain's global influence and to co-operate with its allies to tackle such challenges as nuclear proliferation, Islamist extremism and Russian aggression. In particular, they would use Britain's membership of international organizations, the 'special relationship' with the USA, and institutions like the British Council and the BBC World Service to 'achieve the best for Britain' (2015: 75). These efforts would be supported by a strong military and a commitment to international aid. Here, the Conservatives claimed that their economic strategy would enable them to 'maintain our world-class Armed Forces, to uphold our national security and project power globally', while aid would promote global prosperity and so boost Britain's international trade (2015: 75).

Through the principle of continuity, the Conservatives then depicted Britain's prosperity and security as dependent on 'a stable international system that upholds our values'. To support this understanding of the situation, they cited the intervention in Libya and the government's support for Syrian refugees, and they promised to continue to provide global leadership. This was to be achieved by, for instance, defending religious freedom across the world, supporting human rights and strengthening the Commonwealth's concern with 'promoting democratic values and development' (2015: 75). All of these pledges offered grounds for ideological identification, while affirming Britain's status as a leading player on the world stage as per the global power/exceptionalism narrative. With regard to policy, specific commitments included maintaining the 'special relationship', strengthening ties with Britain's 'close Commonwealth allies' as well as with India and China, and working towards peace and stability in the Middle East (2015: 76–77). Although this approach was no longer portrayed as a 'liberal Conservative foreign policy' (2010: 109) and the Party identified a number of new challenges facing the international community, their approach was very much a continuation of that which they set out in the 2010 manifesto and later agreed in the Coalition's *Programme for Government*.

THE LIBERAL DEMOCRAT MANIFESTO

According to Clegg, three-quarters of the Liberal Democrats' 2010 manifesto pledges were included in the *Programme for Government*. Indeed, he continued, 'front-page commitments like raising the Income Tax threshold and investing in the poorest schoolchildren through the Pupil Premium became flagship Coalition policies', and the Liberal Democrats delivered them in government (2015: 9). It is noteworthy that, unlike Cameron, Clegg directly referred to the Coalition in his *Foreword*. This perhaps reflects the importance that the Party attached to multi-party government, together with a desire to show that it can be made to work in Britain. Equally, it may have been intended to demonstrate that, contrary to their critics, the Liberal Democrats had exerted considerable influence over the Coalition's agenda and so preserved their electoral distinctiveness. Thus, Clegg claimed that, despite the difficult economic conditions, his Party's policies were 'making a difference to people's lives and helping make Britain a freer, greener, more liberal country' (2015: 9), and he invited the electorate to identify ideologically with these core Liberal Democrat values.

These changes were only the beginning, and the manifesto was intended to build on the Party's achievements in office. On this basis, wrote Clegg:

> We can say we will finish the job of balancing the books, but do so fairly, because we have started that job in this Parliament … And we can say we will protect our environment because we have almost trebled the amount of electricity from renewable energy in this Parliament. (2015: 9–10)

However, he believed, there was a fundamental question confronting political parties, namely: 'Do we want to continue to be an open society, confident and optimistic about our place in the world, or do we want to become a closed one, increasingly insular and backward-looking?' (2015: 10). For the Liberal Democrats there was only one response, and they invited ideological identification based on their long-held commitment to internationalism. There was also an implicit attempt to create identification through antithesis, whereby the Party opposed their outward-looking approach to the 'isolationism' of those who wanted Britain to leave the EU, and they appealed to those who shared their view to support them.

As we saw in Chap. 3, higher education was a particularly challenging area for the Liberal Democrats. Nonetheless, they continued to defend the policy as they had in government, claiming the Party had:

> Ensured that no undergraduate student in England has to pay a penny up front of their tuition fees. Students in England do not have to pay anything until they are earning over £21,000 per year ... This means only high-earning graduates pay their tuition fees in full. (2015: 62)

Here, the Liberal Democrats employed a terministic screen based on continuity to present the Coalition's reforms not as a deviation from, but as a means towards realizing, their 2010 goal of enabling everyone to obtain a degree 'regardless of their parents' income' (Liberal Democrats 2010: 33). To support this redefinition of the situation while inviting ideological identification with the 'new' progressive belief in opportunity and social mobility, they followed the Conservatives in citing the record number of university applications, including from disadvantaged students. However, the Party recognized that more work was needed to promote access to higher education, and to this end they pledged to improve the Key Information Set (KIS) and 'establish a review of higher education finance within the next Parliament'. This review would 'consider any necessary reforms, in the light of the latest evidence of the impact of the existing financing system on access, participation (including of low-income groups), and quality' (Liberal Democrats 2015: 62). As such, it opened up the possibility that the policy may be amended, which was perhaps intended to mollify those who still felt betrayed after the Party's U-turn on tuition fees. Nevertheless, this section of the manifesto demonstrates a continuation of the rhetorical strategies employed by the Coalition, while highlighting the extent to which the Liberal Democrats' policy in 2015 was constrained by their earlier bargain with the Conservatives.

On the contentious issue of constitutional reform, the Liberal Democrats returned to their 2010 theme of better politics, identifying overcentralized decision-making and the influence of powerful corporations as key obstacles to the empowerment of individual citizens (2015: 131; see also Liberal Democrats 2010: 87). However, they claimed, 'we were thwarted in some of our attempts to reform politics', notably through fair votes, and they pledged to continue their efforts to deliver these 'essential changes' (2015: 130). In particular, the Liberal Democrats would introduce the Single Transferable Vote for elections to Westminster and to local government in England, a promise that had featured in their 2010 manifesto and which supplied a ground for ideological identification based on the 'equality' conception of fairness. This proposal may have been designed to reassure voters that they remained faithful to their core commitments despite the traumas of coalition, though it is undeniable that partisan interests would also have been a consideration here.

Alongside their pledge to introduce proportional representation, the Liberal Democrats promised to cancel the boundary review that had been initiated by the Coalition and was due to report in 2018. While they acknowledged that 'new constituencies would need to be established for a new voting system', they expressed the belief that 'constituency boundary reviews should respect natural geographical communities, with greater flexibility for the Boundary Commission to deviate from exact equality to take account of community ties and continuity of representation' (2015: 132). The Liberal Democrats thus revived their totemic policy of voting reform, while rejecting the 'artificial' boundary changes espoused by the Conservatives—both of which were important for re-establishing the Party as a distinct political force after five years as the junior coalition partner.

As they had throughout their time in government, the Liberal Democrats drew on the technocratic/modernist narrative to foster instrumental identification with their case for Britain's continued membership of the EU. This, they claimed, was 'essential for creating a stronger economy and for projecting influence in the world', and the manifesto explained that 'a modernized EU is crucial to responding to the global challenges Britain faces, whether they are climate change, cross-border crime and terrorism, or conflict' (2015: 147). While a vote to leave the EU would leave the UK weaker and poorer, the Liberal Democrats stressed that this 'does not mean that the institutions and policies of the European Union are perfect and do not need reform' (2015: 147). They then called attention to the reforms they had secured in government, among which were a £30 billion reduction in the EU budget, changes to the Common Fisheries Policy and a rebalancing of EU spending towards innovation, jobs and economic growth (2015: 149).

For the Liberal Democrats, it was only by 'remaining fully engaged in the EU … [that we can] deliver the further reforms that are urgently needed not only for the UK, but also for the rest of the EU' (2015: 149). Thus, they reiterated their 2010 manifesto promises to work with other Member States to deepen the single market, as well as to offer an in/out referendum in the event of 'any Treaty change involving a material transfer of sovereignty from the UK to the EU' (2015: 149). This latter pledge was enshrined in the European Union Act (2011), and its presence in the manifesto is indicative of the consistency of the Liberal Democrats' position. However, the Party also adopted commitments made by Cameron under the Coalition, promising to work to make the EU more efficient and to 'continue to reduce the burden of EU legislation on business by curbing unnecessary red tape [and] exempting small businesses from EU rules where possible' (2015: 149; see Cameron 2011).

Although this commitment was congruent with the Liberal Democrat belief in limited government, which in turn provided a ground for ideological identification, their promise to increase EU accountability was distinctly Conservative. As the manifesto explained, this objective was to be achieved by 'enhancing the role of national Parliaments in scrutinizing EU decision-making and by giving a combined majority of national Parliaments the automatic ability to block unwanted legislation' (2015: 149). These proposals were present in Cameron's Bloomberg speech and were underpinned by the narrative of parliamentary sovereignty, which had featured heavily in Conservative MPs' contributions to the Commons debates on Europe. As such, their appearance in the Liberal Democrats' programme may indicate that a degree of ideological identification, based on the concept of parliamentary sovereignty, had developed between the partners during the Coalition's term of office.

Like the Conservatives, the Liberal Democrats recognized that 'this is a challenging time for peace and security across the world' (2015: 143). In response, they argued, the UK needed to intensify its diplomatic efforts and co-operate with the EU and NATO to 'promote an active, rights-based foreign policy for our mutual defence'. More broadly, the UK should continue to play a leading role in international organizations and, where possible, work to uphold the values of liberty and opportunity for all (2015: 143). Here, the Liberal Democrats invited ideological identification with their approach, at the core of which was conflict prevention. This commitment was an afterthought in the Party's 2010 manifesto, which emphasized the values of fairness and the rule of law (2010: 67), and its primacy five years later may be a reaction to the military interventions undertaken by the Coalition. In practical terms, a focus on conflict prevention would demand co-operation across several government departments, including the Foreign and Commonwealth Office and the Ministry of Defence, as well as the strengthening of multilateral institutions and support for the UN's Responsibility to Protect doctrine, which centres on 'the security of individuals, rather than states' (2015: 144). As we have seen, this doctrine was put forward as an alternative justification for intervention in Syria, and its presence in the Liberal Democrat manifesto demonstrates continuity with the Coalition's approach. Moreover, the shift away from state security is consistent with the principle of liberal individualism, and so offers a ground for ideological identification.

If these conflict prevention measures failed, the Liberal Democrats acknowledged that military action may be required. In such situations, they asserted that 'the UK should intervene only when there is a clear legal and/or humanitarian case, endorsed by a vote in Parliament, working within the remit of international institutions wherever and whenever possible' (2015: 144). The issue of humanitarian intervention was neglected in the *Programme for Government*, though it later became a key strand in the Coalition's foreign policy. Indeed, the Liberal Democrats' assertion encapsulates the two main rhetorical strategies used in the arguments for action in Libya and Syria, namely an invitation to identify ideologically with the principle of humanitarian identification and the use of antithesis to distinguish these missions from the 2003 Iraq war. In short, this is a further example of rhetorical path dependency. Finally, the Liberal Democrat manifesto repeated policy pledges from its 2010 programme, including support for a two-state solution to the Israel-Palestine conflict as well as for global nuclear non-proliferation efforts (2015: 145; see Liberal Democrats 2010: 68).

The discussion so far reveals that both manifestos display continuities with, and departures from, the ideas and policies of the Coalition. Interestingly, the area where continuity is most strongly evident is higher education, as the Liberal Democrats presented the tuition fees regime as consistent with their goal of widening participation while the Conservatives pledged to build on the government's reforms. There are also overlaps between the parties' approach to foreign policy and that which developed during the Coalition's term of office, though the Liberal Democrats sought to distinguish themselves by placing a new emphasis on conflict prevention. However, clear differences are evident in the sections of the manifestos dealing with constitutional reform and Europe. On the former, the two parties simply restated their 2010 pledges on the electoral system and boundary reform, while on latter the Conservatives adopted an overtly Eurosceptic tone and the Liberal Democrats again positioned themselves as pro-European party (albeit with qualifications). These areas of policy had proved extremely divisive for the Coalition, and so offered a potentially effective tool for party differentiation during the government's termination phase.

THE PARTY LEADERS' MANIFESTO LAUNCH SPEECHES

Although in 2010 the Conservatives had won the argument concerning the 'inevitability' of austerity, Andrew Cooper notes that 'the perception of "cuts" dominated voters' views of the government, and the Tories needed people to believe there was a greater purpose to the government's actions than merely cutting the deficit for its own sake' (2017: 125). With this in mind, the Party accepted the suggestion of their campaign manager, Lynton Crosby, and presented their strategy for the economy as a 'long-term economic plan'. Thus, deficit reduction was not an end in itself, but a precondition for delivering improved living standards and better public services (Cowley and Kavanagh 2016: 63–64). A second theme of the campaign was leadership, whereby the 'prime ministerial' Cameron was contrasted with the 'weak, ineffective' Ed Miliband, and voters were offered a straight choice between Conservative 'competence' and Labour 'chaos'. As the campaign went on and the opinion polls appeared to indicate that there would be another hung parliament, a third theme was added, namely the threat of a Labour government supported by the Scottish Nationalist Party (SNP), who would then, it was claimed, hold the English electorate to ransom (Bale and Webb 2015: 47; Wring and Ward 2015: 225).

Speaking at the launch of the Conservative manifesto, Cameron described the previous five years as a 'critical period', in which 'we have drawn on all the resources of our nation to turn a great recession into a great recovery' (2015a). Through these efforts the Conservatives—in partnership with the British people—had laid the foundations of a strong economy, and the focus of the manifesto was on 'seeing through our clear long-term economic plan'. Cameron then invited voters to identify instrumentally with his party's approach by asserting that 'the next five years are about turning the good news in our economy into a good life for you and your family'. This vision of a good life entailed 'families secure, the peace of mind that comes with a proper job and a career, the security of knowing your children are getting a great education'. Based on the assumption that a majority of voters would share at least one of these ambitions, Cameron then positioned the Conservatives as 'the party of working people' (2015a).

To reinforce his strategy of instrumental identification, Cameron drew on the global power/exceptionalism narrative to inspire feelings of optimism and national pride, saying:

> Britain has lived its long life as an exemplary country. The small island with a massive impact. The bright light in the North Sea that has exceeded expectations decade after decade, century after century ... In Britain we've always shown we have the ingredients, the will—above all the people—to overturn what's inevitable and with a strengthening economy behind us—this buccaneering, world-beating, can-do country—we can do it all over again. (2015a)

In making this populist argument, Cameron utilized the assumed 'we' to unite his party and the electorate in a shared venture, and he urged his listeners to 'let us finish what we have begun' (2015a). Strong leadership was vital here and, Cameron claimed, only the Conservatives could offer this.

At the launch of his Party's Scottish manifesto, Cameron employed a terministic screen based on the principle of continuity to bring Labour and the SNP together as a 'clear threat to the future of our United Kingdom' (2015b). In this 'coalition of chaos', he warned, the SNP would act as 'the chain to Labour's wrecking ball, running right through our economic recovery—and it will be you who pays the price. With jobs losses, massive tax rises and an economy back on brink of bankruptcy' (2015b). Using identification through antithesis, Cameron sought to unify his audience in opposition to this 'threat', and to win their support for the Conservatives as the defenders of the Union and the party of economic competence. There is also an appeal to instrumental identification here, as—unlike their 'reckless' opponents—the Conservative Party had a plan to strengthen the economy and would offer a good life to those willing to 'work hard and do the right thing' (Cameron 2015b).

Whereas the Liberal Democrats had positioned themselves as a 'party of protest' in previous elections, this strategy was unavailable to them in 2015. As Olly Grender, the Deputy Chair of the Liberal Democrats' General Election Committee in 2015, explains, the SNP and UKIP had already taken that message and, moreover, it 'lacked credibility for a party in power' (2017: 153). With this in mind, Clegg opened his manifesto launch speech by reflecting on the decision to enter into coalition with the Conservatives. Here, he sought to create a rapport with the electorate by noting that, instead of taking the easy option:

> We did the responsible thing. We did the fair thing. We did the gutsy thing. We stepped up to the plate and put the good of the country first even though it meant working with people we disagreed with. Even though we knew we would have to make some compromises. Even though we knew we would take a hit to our popularity. (2015)

Because of the Liberal Democrats' preparedness to subordinate partisan concerns to the national interest, Britain now had a 'stronger economy and a fairer society'. In Clegg's words: 'We brought stability. We turned round the economy. We stopped the Conservatives from putting people like them above people like you' (2015). Thus, he projected an image of governing competence by claiming the Coalition's successes for the Liberal Democrats, while using identification through antithesis to unite his Party and his audience in opposition to the Conservatives who, he implied, would work only for the wealthy minority.

Given that the opinion polls were pointing towards another hung parliament, the Liberal Democrats believed their messaging 'needed to reflect what we would bring to a coalition government' (Grender 2017: 154). For senior figures, the Liberal Democrats' distinctiveness lay in their capacity to correct the perceived deficiencies of the two main parties; as David Laws put it: 'We don't have confidence that Labour is serious on economic policy, or that the Conservatives have a strong enough policy commitment to creating a fairer society' (quoted in Grender 2017: 154). On this basis, Clegg invited instrumental identification with the Liberal Democrats as a moderating force that would ensure a future multi-party government acted in the national interest:

> The Liberal Democrats will add a heart to a Conservative government and a brain to a Labour one. We won't allow the Conservatives to cut too much and jeopardize our schools and hospitals and we won't allow Labour to borrow too much and risk our economy again. (2015)

Indeed, he continued, 'the Liberal Democrats will always act responsibly. We will always act fairly. And we will always act in the best interests of the whole United Kingdom' (2015).

In a bid to distinguish his party's approach from that of its rivals, Clegg combined his instrumental appeals to the national interest with a strategy of ideological identification. The concept of fairness was central here, and he described the Liberal Democrat manifesto as 'a blueprint for a stronger economy and a fairer society', a plan with a commitment to opportunity at its heart (2015). To realize this vision, the Party identified as its top priorities 'prosperity for all, with the budget balanced fairly and investment in a high-skill, low-carbon economy'; fair taxes; educational opportunity for every child; high-quality healthcare for all citizens; and the protection of the environment (2015). These commitments were to be the Liberal Democrats' main negotiating points in any subsequent coalition talks (Grender 2017: 154) and, with this in mind, Clegg stressed that 'this is a programme for government, not opposition … that builds on our record' in office (2015).

THE TELEVISED DEBATES

The themes and rhetorical strategies identified above were also present in the two televised debates that featured both Cameron and Clegg. In a departure from the 2010 format,[1] *The ITV Leaders' Debate* of 2 April included the Green Party, Plaid Cymru, the SNP and the UKIP alongside the three main parties. Meanwhile, the BBC *Question Time Special* involved the Conservative, Liberal Democrat and Labour leaders and was broadcast on 30 April (Wring and Ward 2015: 229). Although these occasions offered few opportunities for the leaders to interact with each other, members of the studio audience were able to question them directly about a range of issues.[2] Of these, public spending and the deficit was the most popular (Beckett 2016: 288–289), enabling the former coalition partners to claim credit for the economic recovery while affording the Liberal Democrats an opportunity to reassert their electoral distinctiveness. Given the high levels of message discipline, and therefore repetition, the two debates are considered together.

In his opening statement to *The ITV Leaders' Debate*, Cameron drew on the storyline of the deficit to assert that: 'five years ago, this country was on the brink' (ITV 2015). Since that time, he continued, 'we've been working with the British people through a long-term economic plan', which entailed cutting the deficit while investing in the NHS and reducing income tax. There is ambiguity here, as 'we' could equally refer to the Conservatives or to the Coalition; after all, the raising of the income tax threshold was a key Liberal Democrat policy. Nonetheless, Cameron subsequently combined the assumed 'we' with an appeal for interpersonal identification, acknowledging 'all the shared sacrifice that we've been through' but expressing the belief that this was 'the right thing to do' (BBC 2015). A Conservative government would build on these economic foundations by investing in public services, so for Cameron the choice facing the electorate was: 'Stick with the plan and with the team who brought that plan because it's working, or put it all at risk by the people who gave us the spending, the debt, the taxes and the waste' (ITV 2015). He thus invited the audience to identify instrumentally with the Conservatives, whose long-term plan was about 'security for you, for your family, for our country' (ITV 2015), in opposition to the Labour Party that had 'wrecked' the economy.

Clegg also employed the storyline of the deficit, but as justification for the Liberal Democrats' decision to enter into coalition with the Conservatives. Echoing his manifesto launch speech, Clegg sought to foster interpersonal identification by describing this move as 'difficult' and 'brave' in the light of its political costs for his party (BBC 2015). However, he continued:

> The only way we could create a stable government at a time of an economic firestorm, which could've engulfed this country—we could've been the next domino to fall after Greece and Portugal and Spain—was the Conservatives and the Liberal Democrats. (BBC 2015)

This appeal for instrumental identification was prominent in the early days of the Coalition, particularly among senior Liberal Democrats who may have used the emerging crisis in Greece as an alibi for their decision to form a government with the Conservatives (Stuart 2011: 48). Its reappearance five years later is curious, given that it did nothing to halt the sharp decline in the Party's popularity in the summer of 2010, but Clegg's dramatic portrayal of the economic situation at the time of the Coalition's formation supplied a basis for inviting identification with the Liberal Democrats as a party prepared to place the national interest above its own.

During the 2015 campaign, Clegg's main concern was that:

> Having got this far over five years and millions of people across the country having made huge sacrifices ... we undo it all by lurching off to the right with ideological hard-line cuts or lurching off to the left borrowing pots of money we can't afford. (ITV 2015)

Here, he used a terministic screen based on discontinuity to present the economic plans of the Conservatives and Labour as detrimental to the individual and the national interest, while simultaneously distancing the Liberal Democrats from their opponents. Indeed, Clegg continued, 'we need to remain anchored in the centre ground so that we can finish the job of balancing the books, but do it fairly' (ITV 2015). This statement is a rephrasing of the Party's election slogan, 'a stronger economy and a fairer society', which invited both instrumental and ideological identification and—it was hoped—would therefore have widespread appeal. After the election, however, 'some critics in the Party ... said this was too "middle of the road" as a message and lacked identity' (Grender 2017: 154). In other words, the Liberal Democrats' strategy of equidistance was ineffective as a means of reasserting their distinctiveness, which is vital for the electoral success of the smaller party following the termination of a coalition partnership.

As we have seen, the governing parties were instrumentally consubstantial on the proposition that deficit reduction was in the national interest. Consequently, any Liberal Democrat criticisms of the Conservatives' economic policy had to be ideological and directed at the means, rather than at the end itself; a strategy of instrumental division was precluded by the parties' previous bargains and rhetorical formulations. Thus, in *The ITV Leaders' Debate*, Clegg attacked the Conservatives' 'ideologically driven cuts' to the education budget, telling Cameron that:

> I remember vividly when your party wanted to cut spending for schools at the beginning of the last Parliament, and I said 'No' because you don't make society fairer by cutting the money that goes to nurseries, colleges and schools (ITV 2015).

This attempt to create ideological division based on fairness (defined as social mobility) was swiftly dismissed by Cameron, who reminded Clegg that 'we sat in the Cabinet room together, we took difficult decisions together. Nick, I defend all of the decisions we took, and I think your ... pick-n-mix approach really is not going to convince anyone' (ITV 2015). Indeed, the Liberal Democrats' broad support for most of the Coalition's welfare reforms—including 'those identified as causing hardship', notably the benefit cap and the 'bedroom tax' (McEnhill 2015: 108)—made this appeal to fairness appear opportunistic, irrespective of whether it was defined in 'old' or 'new' progressive terms.

Not surprisingly, the issue of university funding proved difficult for Clegg in the televised debates. On the *Question Time Special*, for instance, his first questioner asked: 'Your promise on student fees has destroyed your reputation. Why would we believe anything you said?' (quoted in Muir 2015). As he had previously, Clegg responded by seeking to create interpersonal identification through empathy and humour:

> I got it wrong, I said sorry—musically, no less. When you make a mistake ... in politics just as in life, sometimes you can't do exactly what you want. I was absolutely between a rock and a hard place five years ago on that particular policy. (BBC 2015)

Again using a tried and tested strategy, he acknowledged that some people would be unable to forgive or forget. However, he was hopeful that 'there are plenty of other fair-minded folk who will accept that nonetheless there were many, many, many other good policies that I did put into practice' (BBC 2015). These included the Pupil Premium and raising the income tax threshold, and Clegg thus utilized a terministic screen based on discontinuity in an attempt to direct his audience's attention away from the tuition fees disaster and onto the Liberal Democrats' achievements in government.

Another questioner asked Clegg why he voted in favour of increasing tuition fees, even though the Liberal Democrats were permitted to abstain. After pointing out that the New Labour governments introduced—and then raised—student fees, Clegg employed the storyline of the deficit to remind his listeners that 'When we came into government there was no money left ... and both the larger parties ... wanted fees to go up very, very considerably'. He then sought to invite ideological identification, claiming that his party secured 'the fairest deal we could in those circumstances, and thankfully now got more young people at university than ever before' (BBC 2015). By means of a terministic screen based on the principle of continuity, Clegg linked the Coalition's reforms to their positive outcome, which in turn was consistent with the Liberal Democrats' 'new' progressive belief in fairness as opportunity and social mobility.

The issue of Europe provided both parties with opportunities for differentiation. On this matter, Cameron reiterated the Conservatives' commitment to hold a referendum on whether the UK should remain in a reformed EU, and he told his audience that:

> I've been very clear that I will not lead a government that does not deliver that pledge ... And I want everyone ... to know that, if you get me as Prime Minister, you get that chance to have that in/out referendum. (BBC 2015)

Although Cameron described this as a 'red line', Clegg reminded the Prime Minister that the European Union Act (2011) provided for a referendum if any future treaty transferred powers from the UK to the EU, and he proceeded to criticize the Conservatives' 'inconsistency':

> Sometimes they say 2016 [for an in/out referendum], sometimes they say they're going to leave the European Union if they don't get what they want, sometimes they say they'll stay. I don't know what they're going to think on Europe next Tuesday, let alone on May the 8th. (BBC 2015)

Clegg, meanwhile, expressed his continued support for the Coalition's policy, and so took the opportunity to present himself as a moderate politician who, unlike Cameron, was anchored firmly in the centre ground and would act in the national interest.

In the event of a referendum, Clegg was clear that he would argue for Britain remaining a member of the EU. While he admitted that the EU was not perfect, he deployed the technocratic/modernist narrative to foster instrumental identification, saying: 'I cannot envisage circumstances where I think it is sensible for the United Kingdom to leave what is the world's largest borderless marketplace of 500 million shoppers, who buy our manufactured products, our services, our goods'. After all, Clegg explained, an exit would mean that 'we become poorer, unemployment goes up, and investment goes down' (BBC 2015). This argument, in conjunction with his claim that co-operation to address global challenges was in the national interest, constituted Clegg's case for Britain's EU membership during the Coalition's term of office, and so is a further demonstration of rhetorical path dependency. An ideological justification for staying in an 'excessively bureaucratic' supranational organization like the EU would have made little sense in the light of the Liberal Democrats' commitment to the decentralization of power, so a strategy of instrumental identification was Clegg's only real rhetorical option.

Another questioner asked what the leaders would do if the election produced a second hung parliament. Clegg's reply was unequivocal, and he ruled out a coalition partnership with either of the main parties if they 'insist on those cuts to our education system' (BBC 2015). This 'red line' was a further attempt to position the Liberal Democrats as the 'party of fairness', and so to foster ideological identification. Cameron, meanwhile, appealed to the national interest, saying that 'if we fall short [of an outright majority], I will do the right thing for the country. I did last time and

I would again' (BBC 2015). However, a coalition would involve compromising on policies such as apprenticeships and the EU referendum, and Cameron was reluctant to do so. He thus urged: 'Let's have a decisive outcome and these things don't have to be compromised on and we can have a really decisive government, a more accountable government for you as a citizen' (BBC 2015). In short, a majority Conservative government would be advantageous to individuals and the nation alike and, on this basis, Cameron invited his listeners to identify instrumentally with his position and to vote for his Party on 8 May.

CONCLUSION

The 2015 general election produced a decisive outcome, with the Conservatives winning a parliamentary majority of 12. Post-election polling by the Conservative peer, Lord Ashcroft, showed the economy was a key factor in this victory, as 46 per cent of participants (a plurality) agreed that '"the national economy is not yet fully fixed, so we will need to continue with austerity and cuts in government spending over the next five years", including 84 per cent of those who voted Conservative' (Bale and Webb 2015: 50). This demonstrates the efficacy of the Conservatives' economic narrative, in which the storyline of the deficit served to remind the electorate of how far the country had come, and the assumed 'we' depicted austerity as a collective endeavour. The Party also drew on the global power/exceptionalism narrative to offer a vision of the future, and sought to invite identification through appeals to both the individual and the national interest. Meanwhile, identification through antithesis enabled the Conservatives to unite voters in opposition to the 'threat' of a Labour-SNP coalition, and to claim that they alone would defend the Union and ensure the nation's economic security. They thus combined instrumental identification with the language of fear, and so appealed to both the head and the heart of the electorate.

In contrast, the Liberal Democrats finished with only eight MPs, a loss of 49 seats. Their inability to repair the reputational damage inflicted by their U-turn on tuition fees was pivotal, as voters focused not on their plans for the future but on the bargains they had made in the past. As Hugh Muir notes of the leaders' performances on the *Question Time Special*, 'Cameron and Miliband face partisan probing and disbelief, but Clegg meets disdain. The two other leaders saw their policies pulled apart. Once Clegg stepped out, the target was him' (2015). Given the limited rhetorical resources he had available, Clegg had little choice but to defend the Coalition's policy on university funding, as a second about-face would have irretrievably damaged his party's credibility. However, it is debatable whether there was anything the Liberal Democrats could have done to rebuild public trust at this time. After all, trust was an important theme in their 2010 campaign[3] and, as Grender suggests, 'had it not been tuition fees, it is possible something else totemic would have been used, such as the health reforms, with the same outcome' (2017: 159). The Liberal Democrats' early commitment to preserving coalition unity at all costs increased the likelihood that they would face accusations of 'betrayal', so ensuring that their chances of emerging from the Coalition with their reputation intact were slim at best.

Whereas the Conservatives' ownership of economic policy enabled them to claim credit for the Coalition's success in securing the recovery, the Liberal Democrats struggled to differentiate themselves. Central to their strategy was the concept of fairness, which had also played a prominent role in their 2010 campaign. Five years later, however, their efforts to invite ideological identification lacked plausibility. As Mark Stuart explains, 'no amount of effort on the part of Liberal Democrat ministers to bolt "fairness" onto each and every cut in public expenditure [seemed to work] with the electorate' (2011: 53) during the governance phase of the Coalition—not least because of the perception that austerity was hitting the most vulnerable members of society hardest. Adding to the Party's difficulties was the legacy of previous bargains and rhetorical approaches, which acted as a constraint at the termination stage. They could not backtrack on unpopular policies or revert to portraying themselves as a 'party of protest', so they opted to focus on what they would contribute to a second coalition government. For senior Liberal Democrats, this would be achieved by adopting an equidistant stance, whereby the Party defined itself as the midpoint between Labour and the Conservatives. Instead of projecting governing competence, this approach only seemed to 'confirm that the Party had lost its radical, distinctive edge' (Cutts and Russell 2015: 83) and their electoral appeal was substantially diminished as a result.

NOTES

1. On the negotiations preceding the 2015 televised debates, see, for instance, Beckett (2016: 279–283) and Bailey (2017).

2. For a discussion of voters' engagement with, and reaction to, the televised debates, see inter alia Beckett (2016: 284–289) and Emes and Keith (2017: 237–242).
3. Matthew d'Ancona explains that 'One of Clegg's campaign slogans [in 2010] had been: "No more broken promises"'. As a consequence of the decision to increase tuition fees, he continues, 'the Deputy PM faced a crisis of trust' (2013: 63).

References

Bailey, R. (2017). Election Debates: The Less Than Smooth Path to TV's Big Campaign Events. In D. Wring, R. Mortimore, & S. Atkinson (Eds.), *Political Communication in Britain: Polling, Campaigning and Media in the 2015 General Election* (pp. 221–234). Basingstoke: Palgrave Macmillan.

Bale, T., & Webb, P. (2015). The Conservatives: Their Sweetest Victory? *Parliamentary Affairs, 68*(Suppl. 1), 41–53.

BBC. (2015, April 30). *Question Time—Election Leaders Special.* Retrieved from https://www.youtube.com/watch?v=VE5HFj-qCdg

Beckett, C. (2016). The Battle for the Stage: Broadcasting. In P. Cowley & D. Kavanagh (Eds.), *The British General Election of 2015* (pp. 278–301). Basingstoke: Palgrave Macmillan.

Cameron, D. (2011, January 28). *Speech to the Davos World Economic Forum.* Retrieved from http://www.politics.co.uk/comment-analysis/2011/01/28/david-cameron-s-davos-speech-in-full

Cameron, D. (2015a, April 14). *David Cameron Speech: Conservative Party Manifesto Launch.* Retrieved from http://press.conservatives.com/post/116374071635/david-cameron-speech-conservative-party-manifesto

Cameron, D. (2015b, April 16). *Speech Launching Scottish Manifesto.* Retrieved from http://press.conservatives.com/post/116558056605/david-cameron-speech-launching-scottish-manifesto

Clegg, N. (2015, April 15). *Speech Launching the Liberal Democrat Manifesto.* Retrieved from http://www.politics.co.uk/comment-analysis/2015/04/15/nick-clegg-manifesto-speech-in-full

Collini, S. (2017). *Speaking of Universities.* London: Verso.

Conservative Party. (2010). *Invitation to Join the Government of Britain: The Conservative Manifesto 2010.* London: The Conservative Party.

Conservative Party. (2015). *The Conservative Party Manifesto 2015.* London: The Conservative Party.

Cooper, A. (2017). The Conservative Campaign. In D. Wring, R. Mortimore, & S. Atkinson (Eds.), *Political Communication in Britain: Polling, Campaigning and Media in the 2015 General Election* (pp. 123–131). Basingstoke: Palgrave Macmillan.

Cowley, P., & Kavanagh, D. (2016). *The British General Election of 2015*. Basingstoke: Palgrave Macmillan.

Cutts, D., & Russell, A. (2015). From Coalition to Catastrophe: The Electoral Meltdown of the Liberal Democrats. *Parliamentary Affairs, 68*(Suppl. 1), 70–87.

d'Ancona, M. (2013). *In It Together: The Inside Story of the Coalition Government*. London: Viking.

Emes, C., & Keith, J. (2017). The Election Debates in 2015: The View from the Living Room. In D. Wring, R. Mortimore, & S. Atkinson (Eds.), *Political Communication in Britain: Polling, Campaigning and Media in the 2015 General Election* (pp. 235–245). Basingstoke: Palgrave Macmillan.

Grender, O. (2017). Chill Wind: The Liberal Democrat Campaign. In D. Wring, R. Mortimore, & S. Atkinson (Eds.), *Political Communication in Britain: Polling, Campaigning and Media in the 2015 General Election* (pp. 151–160). Basingstoke: Palgrave Macmillan.

ITV. (2015, April 2). *The ITV Leaders' Debate (UK General Election 2015)*. Retrieved from https://www.youtube.com/watch?v=2oLlD2WXsYY

Liberal Democrats. (2010). *Liberal Democrat Manifesto 2010*. London: Liberal Democrats.

Liberal Democrats. (2015). *Manifesto 2015: Stronger Economy. Fairer Society. Opportunity for Everyone*. London: The Liberal Democrats.

McEnhill, L. (2015). Unity and Distinctiveness in UK Coalition Government: Lessons for Junior Partners. *The Political Quarterly, 86*(1), 101–109.

Muir, H. (2015, April 30). Nick Clegg Makes the Best of a Bad Job. In G. Hinsliff, A. Perkins and H. Muir, Question Time Leaders' Performances: Guardian Columnists Give Their Verdict. *Guardian*. Retrieved from https://www.theguardian.com/politics/2015/apr/30/camerons-question-time-performance-smooth-smiley-but-unconvincing

Stuart, M. (2011). The Formation of the Coalition. In S. Lee & M. Beech (Eds.), *The Cameron-Clegg Government: Coalition Politics in an Age of Austerity* (pp. 38–55). Basingstoke: Palgrave Macmillan.

Willetts, D. (2012, September 13). 'A World Without Boundaries': Speech at UUK Conference. Retrieved from https://www.gov.uk/government/speeches/uuk-conference-a-world-without-boundaries

Wring, D., & Ward, S. (2015). Exit Velocity: The Media Election. *Parliamentary Affairs, 68*(Suppl. 1), 224–240.

CHAPTER 8

The Legacy of the Coalition and Its Lessons for the Future

As Michael Laver and Norman Schofield observe, it has become common in coalition scholarship to conceive of policy bargaining as an attempt to 'minimize the policy distance between a party's ideal policy point and the policy point of the government' (1998: 187). A rhetorical analysis builds on this understanding by illuminating how, through strategies of identification and division, such compromises are reached, and how considerations of unity and distinctiveness influence both the choice of governing partner and subsequent policy outcomes. This book has explored these themes throughout the life cycle of the Conservative-Liberal Democrat coalition, and the present chapter begins with a summary of its main findings. Next, it considers the legacy of the Coalition for the 2015–16 majority government of David Cameron, focusing on higher education policy and the referendum on the UK's membership of the EU. The following section discusses the rhetoric of identification employed by the Conservatives and the Democratic Unionist Party (DUP) in the wake of their confidence and supply agreement in June 2017, and compares them with the strategies of the 2010–15 Coalition. After identifying lessons for future multi-party governments, the chapter concludes by highlighting potential areas for further research.

© The Author(s) 2018
J. Atkins, *Conflict, Co-operation and the Rhetoric of Coalition Government*, Rhetoric, Politics and Society,
https://doi.org/10.1057/978-1-137-31796-4_8

The Coalition's Rhetoric
of Identification and Division

During the formation stage, the Conservatives and the Liberal Democrats achieved identification in all three dimensions. The negotiating teams soon established a rapport which, together with their ideological proximity and a common conception of the 'national interest', facilitated agreement even in contentious areas such as constitutional reform. In their early press conferences, senior Coalition figures invited party members and the wider electorate to identify ideologically with the new administration, to which end they mobilized its guiding principles of freedom, fairness and responsibility, as well as their shared belief in limited government. The partners also appealed to the 'national interest' in a bid to foster instrumental identification and quell intra-party dissent. Alongside these appeals, the Coalition drew on the storyline of the deficit to create identification through antithesis. Here, listeners were encouraged to unite with the Government behind the cause of deficit reduction, in opposition to the 'fiscally irresponsible' Labour Party. These multiple grounds for identification would contribute to the Coalition's survival for a full parliamentary term.

Higher education funding was a difficult issue for the Liberal Democrats, due to their pre-election pledge to oppose any increase in tuition fees. In seeking to justify their change of position following the Coalition's adoption of key recommendations from the Browne Report, the Party used interpersonal identification to foster understanding and win back trust. Although this reflected their consensual approach to politics, it perhaps was perceived as ingratiating by a public accustomed to strong, decisive government (see Diamond 2014: 34); what the Liberal Democrats saw as a necessary compromise to ensure the survival of the Coalition was viewed as a betrayal by the electorate. Meanwhile, the parliamentary debate on the reforms was dominated by ideological appeals to the 'old' and 'new' progressive conceptions of fairness, which were virtually absent from the speeches of Cable and Willetts to the university sector. Instead, both relied on instrumental identification, invoking the interests of students, the universities and the nation as a whole. This strategy proved effective in the main, though the sector's predefined interests would, on occasion, take precedence over other considerations.

As in the initial negotiations, the concept of fairness (broadly conceived) played a central role in the parliamentary debate on the

Parliamentary Voting System and Constituencies (PVSC) Bill, where both sides employed different definitions in a bid to foster ideological identification with their cause. This value subsequently had a strong presence in Cameron's arguments against the Alternative Vote (AV) in the 2011 referendum campaign, which attracted considerable public support and contributed to a decisive victory for the No side. However, the bitterness of the campaign generated interpersonal friction between Cameron and Clegg, which was manifested in an inter-party dispute over House of Lords reform in the summer of 2012. The framework enabled us to identify the cause of this conflict as the parties' use of different terministic screens to interpret the Coalition Agreement, which in turn was shaped by their own perceived interests. As a consequence, Liberal Democrat MPs could justify their decision to vote for the postponement of the constituency boundary review, a move that angered the Conservatives but allowed the junior partner to reassert its distinctive identity.

By contrast, there was a reasonable degree of co-operation between the two leaders on Europe. After all, both had adopted a pragmatic approach to EU and were united in the belief that it was in need of reform. Most of the conflict instead took place between Cameron and sections of his own parliamentary party, a division that was manifested in their choice of identification strategies. The analysis shows that the Coalition leadership relied heavily on appeals for instrumental identification, which drew on the technocratic/modernist narrative and stressed the link between EU membership and Britain's economic prosperity. To a lesser extent, Clegg sought to invite identification by means of the concept of sovereignty (redefined as 'influence') and a pro-European understanding of the exceptionalism narrative, in which Britain was depicted as a leading player within the EU. Contrariwise, Eurosceptic Conservative MPs primarily employed the parliamentary sovereignty and global power/exceptionalism narratives to distance themselves from the Coalition. This strategy of ideological division was supplemented by a modified conception of the national interest, understood in terms of self-determination. The irreconcilability of these two positions contributed to growing unrest among Conservative Eurosceptics which, in conjunction with the rise of UKIP, pushed Cameron into offering an in/out referendum on Britain's EU membership in his Party's 2015 manifesto.

As regards foreign policy, the Coalition's arguments for intervention in Libya and Syria centred on the storyline of the 2003 Iraq war. This enabled senior government figures to contrast their 'responsible, collective' approach with New Labour's 'reckless liberal vigilantism', and so to foster identification through antithesis. In both parliamentary debates, the Coalition leadership buttressed this strategy with appeals for ideological and instrumental identification, which respectively were founded on the principle of humanitarian intervention and conceptions of the 'national interest'. While MPs overwhelmingly supported the mission in Libya, they refused to back military action against Syria. Here, the Coalition's case for intervention resembled that of Tony Blair in a number of important respects—specifically, the claim that action was necessary to alleviate human suffering and deter other regimes from using chemical weapons; the emphasis on classified intelligence; the bypassing of the UN; and the suggestion that Britain should provide moral leadership to the world (Richards 2013; see Atkins 2011: Chap. 9). It is unsurprising, then, that the Coalition failed to create a clear contrast between Syria and Iraq, and so to establish identification through antithesis.

Turning now to the termination phase of the coalition life cycle, the application of the framework reveals that the Liberal Democrats struggled to differentiate themselves in the run-up to the 2015 general election. The campaign was dominated by the economy, and the Conservatives' ownership of this policy area gave them a significant advantage. Here, Cameron urged the electorate to support his Party in delivering its long-term economic plan and, using the storyline of the deficit, he invited them to align themselves with the 'competent' Conservatives in opposition to Labour, who had 'wrecked' the economy. To supplement this strategy of instrumental identification, Cameron employed the global power/exceptionalism narrative to create a positive vision of the future, and thus to appeal to hearts as well as minds. Meanwhile, the Liberal Democrats based their campaign on the concept of fairness, which had served them well in 2010 but lacked conviction after five years of austerity. Compounding this difficulty was their U-turn on tuition fees, which had seriously damaged their reputation and undermined public trust. As they could no longer present themselves as a 'party of protest', the Liberal Democrats instead sought to demonstrate governing competence through a strategy of equidistance. However, this decision would cost them their electoral distinctiveness, and so further diminished their appeal.

THE LEGACY OF THE COALITION

As noted in the previous chapter, the 2015 general election produced a majority Conservative government. This section provides an overview of developments in two of the four policy areas under the Cameron administration of 2015–16. There were no new military interventions undertaken during this period, and the constitution remained unchanged, so the discussion focuses on higher education policy in England and the UK's membership of the EU. Taking these areas in turn, the Conservatives built on the Coalition's reforms by implementing their manifesto pledges to introduce a Teaching Excellence Framework (TEF) and to improve access for students from disadvantaged backgrounds. They also legislated for a referendum on Britain's membership of the EU, which followed Cameron's promised renegotiation and took place on 23 June 2016. The section examines the strategies of identification and division employed in the two areas, calling attention to the 'stickiness' of previous rhetorical formulations where appropriate.

Higher Education Policy in England, 2015–16

In a speech at Universities UK (UUK) on 1 July 2015, the Minister of State for Universities and Science, Jo Johnson, paid tribute to the success of the Coalition's policies. However, he continued, there was 'vital unfinished business from the reforms of the last Parliament' and, to rectify this, he promised to implement three of the Conservatives' key manifesto commitments (2015). The first was to drive value for money for both students and taxpayers, while the second was to introduce a TEF. On Johnson's view, this change would incentivize universities to 'devote as much attention to the quality of teaching as fee-paying students and prospective employers have a right to expect'. The third pledge was to remove the cap on student numbers and widen participation, and so 'remove barriers to ambition'. Taken together, Johnson claimed, these measures would 'consolidate and build on [the] achievements' of the past five years (2015).

To address concerns about value for money Johnson urged greater transparency, which in turn would enable prospective students to make an informed decision. Thus, he told his listeners that 'universities must get used to providing clearer information about how many hours students will spend in lectures, seminars and tutorials, and who will deliver the teaching', and he expressed agreement with the 75 per cent of undergraduate students who, according to a recent survey, wanted to know how their tuition fees were being spent (2015). To further increase value for money while raising standards, the Government would give students 'more choice over the type of education they receive by allowing more innovative and flexible institutions to enter the market' (Department for Business, Innovation and Skills 2016). This appeal for ideological identification was founded on the neoliberal values of choice, innovation and flexibility, which were also present in the speeches of David Willetts (2012a, b) and in the Conservatives' 2015 manifesto. Again like Willetts (2012b), the Cameron government augmented this strategy by inviting its audience to identify with the interests of students, and so offered a second, instrumental ground for identification.

By redressing the balance between teaching and research, the TEF would enable the sector to 'meet students' high expectations of their university years and to deliver the skills our economy needs' (Johnson 2015; see also Willetts 2012b; Conservative Party 2015: 35). In particular, it would give students the necessary information to judge teaching quality, which would include a 'clear set of outcome-focused criteria and metrics' and be supported by a process of external assessment. Unlike the existing Research Excellence Framework, the TEF would be 'proportionate and light touch, not big, bossy and bureaucratic' and, through this contrast, Johnson invoked the principle of limited government in a bid to create ideological identification (2015). Once again, this strategy was paired with an appeal for instrumental identification in a bid to maximize support for the measures. As the Department for Business, Innovation and Skills put it: 'Institutions which meet the high standards set by the TEF will be able to raise their fees in line with inflation, to help incentivize high quality teaching standards and protect financial sustainability of the sector' (2016; for discussion see UCU 2016; Collini 2017: 160–169).

According to Johnson, 'anyone with potential to benefit from university should not be prevented from going because of their background or ability to pay' (2015). With this end in mind the Government had decided to remove the cap on student numbers, and Cameron had set a target of doubling the proportion of students from disadvantaged backgrounds going to university by 2020. This commitment to 'fair access' was founded on the 'new' progressive definition of fairness as individual opportunity, on which basis Johnson sought to create ideological identification (see Willetts 2012b). He also invited university leaders to identify instrumentally with the reforms, telling them that: 'I expect our new Teaching Excellence Framework to include incentives that reward institutions who do best at retention and progression of disadvantaged students through their college years' (2015). Here, Johnson employed a terministic screen based on the principle of continuity to link the TEF to widening participation, a strategy that mirrored the Coalition's pairing of higher tuition fees and improved access. In both cases, the Government perhaps intended to make the controversial aspects of its proposals more palatable to critics, though these efforts met with varying degrees of success.

The university mission groups broadly welcomed the Government's proposals, with the President of UUK and the Chief Executive of MillionPlus endorsing its commitments to protect the interests of students and improve access (see Department for Business, Innovation and Skills 2016). As such, they demonstrated instrumental and ideological identification with these aspects of the reforms. However, the University and College Union (UCU)[1] distanced itself from the Government on instrumental grounds, claiming that 'market-based reforms [such as increased tuition fees] are likely to deliver worse outcomes and value for students, employers and taxpayers' (2016; see also Collini 2017: 172–173). While expressing their ideological consubstantiality with the value of opportunity for all, critics also objected that the Bill did little to address the real barriers to higher education. In particular, it 'offers nothing new to part-time or older students; and, while it continues to trumpet the benefits to the economy of expanding higher education, it goes on loading the cost on to the individual' (Editorial 2016; see also UCU 2016). Underpinning these objections is a belief that higher education is an 'essential public good' (UCU 2016), which is fundamentally at odds with the Government's pursuit of marketization. It is too early to say how—indeed, if—this tension will be resolved, but it is likely to pervade the area of higher education policy for the foreseeable future.

The 2016 Referendum on Britain's Membership of the EU

Despite their status as Britain's most pro-European party, the Liberal Democrats were virtually invisible in the referendum campaign (Russell 2016: 83). In contrast, Cameron took centre stage and he presented a 'big, bold patriotic case for Britain to remain a member of the EU' (2016). The economy lay at the heart of this argument and, drawing on the technocratic/modernist account developed during the Coalition's term of office, Cameron asserted that Britain's membership meant 'continued full access to a growing single market, including in energy, services and digital, together with the benefit of the huge trade deals in prospect' (2016). Alongside these economic advantages, remaining in the EU facilitated co-operation with other member states to tackle such issues as human trafficking, terrorism and cybercrime. This is the argument that Clegg made at Chatham House in 2012 and, for Cameron, such collaboration was 'far more important than sovereignty in its purest theoretical form' (2016). He thus distanced himself ideologically from Leave campaigners, for whom parliamentary sovereignty was a core principle, while inviting instrumental identification with the claim that security co-operation was in the national interest. Finally, Cameron drew on the pro-European interpretation of the global power/exceptionalism narrative to argue that, rather than diminishing Britain, 'our membership of the EU is one of the tools—just one—which we use, as we do our membership of NATO, or the Commonwealth ... to amplify British power and to enhance our influence in the world' (2016). Paraphrasing Clegg's view that the UK should be strong in Europe 'for the sake of our security, our prosperity and our place in the world' (2012a), Cameron invited his listeners to identify instrumentally with his contention that 'Britain is stronger and safer in the EU, as well as better off' (2016), and to vote Remain.

The economy dominated the arguments of the official Remain campaign, Britain Stronger in Europe, in which senior Conservative figures played a leading role. Their core contention was that leaving the EU would be a 'leap in the dark', and they employed a negative version of the technocratic/modernist narrative to highlight the damage it would cause to the nation's interests (a strategy dismissed as 'project fear' by Vote Leave). Thus, their campaign literature included a letter from the businessman Lord Sugar, which stated that: 'Leaving the EU is a gamble we cannot afford to take. Less trade plus less investment, equals fewer jobs, lower wages, less growth and a weaker country' (Britain Stronger In 2016), while the Conservative Chancellor, George Osborne, produced a paper in which he described an exit as 'the most extraordinary self-inflicted wound' (quoted in Shipman 2016: 243; see also Clegg 2013). Underpinning this economic argument was the conception of human nature embodied in the narrative of incremental pragmatism, according to which the public were risk averse (Martin 2016: 21; see also Oliver 2016: 385), and therefore would choose the status quo. Consequently, Remain opted for a single-issue campaign based on the economy, to the detriment of matters such as immigration (Shipman 2016: 301, 364).

As James Martin points out, 'the strength of Leave's argument lay in the purported self-evidence of its premise—that the EU restricted the UK's capacity to succeed on its own' (2016: 21). This assumption was rooted in the narratives of global power/British exceptionalism and parliamentary sovereignty which, together with a conception of the 'national interest' as self-determination, informed the arguments of Eurosceptic Conservative backbenchers examined in Chap. 5. These elements also informed the vision of the Anglosphere espoused by Leave campaigners such as Nigel Farage, according to which Britain could 'prosper outside the EU by ridding itself of costly regulations and promoting free trade with third countries, especially in the Commonwealth' (Bevir et al. 2015: 11).[2] The slogan 'Vote Leave and take back control' fused the three elements, and campaigners thus urged voters to regain control of Britain's economy, sovereignty and borders from the unelected bureaucrats in Brussels (Hewitt 2016).

According to Tim Shipman, Vote Leave's Campaign Director, Dominic Cummings, saw 'the linkage between immigration and control as the key to a referendum victory' (2016: 40). This pairing had a strong presence in the run-up to the referendum, with the non-party campaign Better Off Out asserting that: 'Once we vote to leave the European Union, the British Parliament will regain democratic control over immigration and other matters' (2016). However, Vote Leave's 'masterstroke' was to link immigration to the economy and public services by means of a terministic screen based on continuity. Priti Patel MP, for instance, claimed that 'the shortage of primary school places is yet another example of how uncontrolled migration is putting unsustainable pressures on our public services' (quoted in Shipman 2016: 263), while Vote Leave maintained that, on leaving the EU, 'we can spend our money on our priorities—like the NHS, schools, and housing' (2016). The campaign also exploited the interpersonal division between the electorate and the political class, which had previously been highlighted by Eurosceptic Conservative MPs. Thus, they argued that the promise to reduce net immigration to the tens of thousands was 'plainly not achievable as long as the UK is a member of the EU and the failure to keep it is corrosive of public trust in politics' (Vote Leave quoted in Shipman 2016: 284).

The referendum produced a narrow victory for the Leave campaign, a result that continues to be analysed by scholars and commentators alike. Although the reasons behind it are myriad and complex, a contributing factor might be the rhetorical path dependency that shaped the language of the Remain side. Throughout the Coalition's term of office, Cameron repeatedly advanced the technocratic/modernist argument that EU membership was in Britain's national interest, and he invited instrumental identification on this basis. However, his defence of exceptionalism (2013, 2016) set Britain apart from the EU, and so limited the possibility of making a case for membership on ideological grounds. This is borne out by Roland Rudd, the Treasurer of Britain Stronger In, who reflected that:

> We needed a really good, positive agenda about how Europe was really good for Britain, why we shared similar values and why we had to be for our own, why it was good for Britain to be at the heart of Europe, and we never sold that as a package at any stage really during the campaign. (Quoted in Shipman 2016: 248; see also Clegg 2016: 196–197)

In contrast, the Vote Leave slogan 'take back control' encapsulated the values of democracy, sovereignty and self-determination, which had proved effective in achieving ideological identification for Eurosceptic Conservative MPs under the Coalition. This message was 'much more intuitive and straightforward' than that of Remain, and it was 'highly emotionally charged'. Furthermore, its inherent ambiguity (take back control of what?) permitted multiple interpretations, and so broadened its public appeal (Polonski 2016: 94; see also Oliver 2016: 403).

The success of Vote Leave's campaign is in part attributable to deep-seated attitudes towards Europe. Nathaniel Copsey and Tim Haughton explain that, rather than seeing 'Europe' as an essential part of their identity, 'Britons—or perhaps more accurately the English—tend to see *Europe* as a threat to national identity. They have difficulty reconciling themselves to the idea of being both British and European' (2014: 81). This distinction is, of course, reinforced by the narrative of British exceptionalism and the concomitant belief that 'we are special, different, unique' (Cameron 2016). Writing of Britain in 2004, Nick Clegg notes that 'there is no other member country of the European Union that suffers remotely the same intensity of emotion and fear, even now as attitudes towards the EU are taking a significant nosedive in almost all member states' (2004: 80). Given this visceral response to 'Europe', it is perhaps not surprising that Remain's logical, fact-based arguments about an abstract 'national interest' failed to triumph over emotional appeals aimed squarely at the electorate's heart.

THE CONSERVATIVE-DUP MINORITY GOVERNMENT

On 24 June 2016, Cameron resigned as Conservative Party Leader and Prime Minister and, following a short leadership campaign, he was replaced by Theresa May. Although May had publicly supported the Remain side, on 5 July 2016 she categorically stated that: 'Brexit means Brexit .... there must be no attempts to remain inside the EU, no attempts to rejoin it through the backdoor and no second referendum' (quoted in Blair 2016). This certitude did not translate into a clear plan for the UK's departure, in spite of which May triggered Article 50 of the Treaty on European Union on 29 March 2017, and so initiated a two-year negotiating period that would conclude with the UK's withdrawal from the EU. Within a month, on 18 April, May announced that she was calling a snap general election to strengthen her hand in the upcoming negotiations (2017a). The vote took place on 8 June and, in the wake of what was widely seen as a disastrous campaign, the Conservatives lost 13 seats, leaving them eight short of an overall majority.

After two weeks of talks, the Conservatives reached a confidence and supply agreement with Northern Ireland's DUP, which had won ten seats in Parliament. Under such an arrangement, as Robert Hazell and Akash Paun explain, 'governments can ensure they have the support of external parties on crucial votes in exchange for policy or other concessions' (2009: 7). Thus, the DUP agreed to support the Government on the Budget and the Queen's Speech, and on 'legislation pertaining to the United Kingdom's exit from the European Union; and legislation pertaining to national security' (Prime Minister's Office 2017). In this way, the two parties would 'deliver a stable government in the United Kingdom's national interest for the duration of this Parliament'. Additionally, the Conservatives and the DUP agreed to work towards the 'early restoration of inclusive and stable devolved government in Northern Ireland', as well as to spend two per cent of GDP on the armed forces, and to leave unchanged the Pensions Triple Lock and the Winter Fuel Payment for older people. The agreement would be reviewed at the end of each Parliamentary session (Prime Minister's Office 2017).

In a display of ideological identification with the DUP, May referred to the Conservatives as the 'Conservative and Unionist Party', their full name. She then claimed the agreement would enable the parties to 'work together in the interest of the whole United Kingdom, give us the certainty we require as we embark on our departure from the European Union, and help us build a stronger and fairer society at home' (2017b). Likewise, the DUP leader, Arlene Foster, asserted that the deal would 'operate to deliver a stable Government in the United Kingdom's national interest at this vital time', and identified as both parties' guiding principle a 'commitment to acting in the national interest in accordance with our shared objectives for strengthening and enhancing our precious Union' (2017). These statements suggest that the two leaders had reached a shared understanding of the challenges confronting the UK, and attained instrumental consubstantiality based on a mutually acceptable conception of the 'national interest'. Equally, it may be indicative of limited common ideological ground, a possibility that is explored below.

There are clear similarities between these early statements and those made by Cameron and Clegg in 2010. Of particular note are the reiteration of the 'working together in the national interest' mantra and the promise to provide stable government, through which the parties demonstrated their instrumental consubstantiality. However, aside from May and Foster's shared commitments to the Union and to the delivery of Brexit, there was little evidence of ideological identification between them at this stage. To an extent, this may have stemmed from their differences of principle on issues such as abortion rights and equal marriage, but it might also have been a reflection of the looser nature of a confidence and supply arrangement. Unlike in a full coalition, where ideological proximity is advantageous in developing and delivering a full policy programme, the Conservative-DUP arrangement covered only a few areas. Their ability to find points of common interest was sufficient for them to reach a limited agreement of this kind, and so public displays of ideological consubstantiality were arguably unnecessary (see Hazell and Paun 2009: 44).

The 2017 confidence and supply agreement was criticized across the political spectrum. Within the Conservative Party, MPs distanced themselves ideologically from the DUP, citing their views on abortion and LGBT+ rights. In the words of one parliamentarian, the fear was that the deal could 'wash away what's left of Cameron's legacy' and so herald the return of the 'nasty party'. Furthermore, some Conservatives raised concerns about the impact of the agreement on the Northern Ireland power-sharing talks. Of these, the most prominent was the former Prime Minister, John Major, who sought to create instrumental division by warning that the deal could compromise the UK government's impartiality and endanger the 'fragile' peace (both quoted in Eaton 2017). For other parties, the primary source of contention was May's pledge to give £1 billion of extra funding to Northern Ireland over two years. Thus, the then Liberal Democrat leader, Tim Farron, argued that: 'While our schools are crumbling and our NHS is in crisis, Theresa May chooses to throw cash at ten MPs in a grubby attempt to keep her Cabinet squatting in Number 10' (quoted in Asthana et al. 2017). Here, he accused May of prioritizing partisan concerns over the national interest, and so rejected her appeal for instrumental identification. Whether the Conservative-DUP arrangement will endure for a full parliamentary term is an open question at the time of writing, but the experiences of the 2010–15 Coalition offer a number of lessons for multi-party governments.

Lessons for a Future Multi-party Government

The preceding chapters highlight the importance of ambiguity and the ordering of reality in coalition politics. Indeed, the inherent contestability of political concepts enabled the (prospective) partners to reach agreement on contentious issues, as well as to reaffirm their party's distinctive identity. Various conceptions of the 'national interest' proved crucial in this and, through multiple (re)definitions of the concept of fairness, the Conservatives and the Liberal Democrats were able to negotiate a compromise on constitutional reform, win parliamentary support for their higher education policy and, for the larger party, to campaign against AV. The analysis also calls attention to the role played by ordering devices in creating unity and division. Here, we saw that the storylines of the deficit and the 2003 Iraq war were critical to uniting the partners against the Labour Party, while their choice of terministic screens underpinned the inter-party conflict over House of Lords reform. The skilled use of these techniques could be of considerable benefit to a future multi-party government at all stages of the coalition life cycle.

The formation of the Coalition was facilitated by the discovery of common ideological ground between Conservative modernizers and the *Orange Book* Liberal Democrats. While this enabled them to co-operate effectively in areas such as higher education and foreign policy, the parties' ideological proximity made it difficult for the Liberal Democrats to maintain their distinctive identity. Moreover, their acceptance of the Conservatives' austerity agenda did serious damage to their image as the party of social justice, as they would discover during the 2015 general election campaign. Differentiation is almost always a problem for the junior partner in particular (Hazell and Yong 2012: 202), but it is an important means of preserving credibility and maintaining trust. Consequently, the smaller party in a future coalition must be wary of sacrificing too many of its core values for the sake of government unity.

The attainment of ideological identification will be more difficult for some (potential) governing partners than others. As noted in the previous section this may prove problematic for the Conservatives and the DUP, given that many of the former party's MPs do not share the latter's socially conservative values. The technique of instrumental identification may prove invaluable in such situations, as it affords the parties an alternative means of presenting a united front to a wider audience. For Cameron and Clegg, it enabled them to frame the Coalition as the 'new politics' that placed the national interest before partisan concerns and, moreover, would give Britain the strong, stable government it needed to overcome the challenges ahead. The case of the Conservative-Liberal Democrat government also highlights the power of appeals to the 'national interest' in quelling dissent over matters such as the allocation of ministerial portfolios, as MPs risk appearing self-interested and petty if they openly criticize the leadership at such an early stage.

In addition to these strategies, senior Coalition figures employed identification through antithesis to bring the two parties together in opposition to Labour. This was the function of the storyline of the deficit, in which immediate reductions in public expenditure were framed as consistent with not only the Coalition's commitments to freedom and responsibility, but with the leadership's conception of the 'national interest'. Meanwhile, Britain's problems were blamed on the previous Labour government, whose allegedly reckless spending had destroyed the economy and necessitated the Coalition's austerity programme. However, there was a danger that the Liberal Democrats' willingness to reproduce this storyline would come back to haunt them in the event of the 2015 general election producing a hung parliament with Labour as the largest party. That Ed Miliband reportedly ruled out a deal with the Liberal Democrats if Clegg remained as leader suggests that sustained, aggressive attacks on the Opposition should be left mostly to the larger party, as the junior partner may later be confronted by the prospect of coalition talks with the former adversary.

On entering into a coalition, the smaller party needs to be realistic about what it can achieve in government (Hazell and Yong 2012: 203). While the prizes for Cameron included 'government, not opposition; stability, not chaos; [and] joint responsibility for tough decisions' (Laws 2010: 51), the Liberal Democrats gravely overestimated the benefits they would derive from the arrangement. At root, their miscalculation was attributable to an ideological and instrumental preoccupation with electoral reform, which blinded them to the possibility that they would lose the AV referendum (see Laws 2016: 92). This is evident in Chris Huhne's statement that:

> Our historic mission is to create a British Liberal party whose influence will be embedded in our politics through a reformed voting system ... Only a Conservative coalition now offers ... the prize of a guaranteed place in British politics for a strong liberal force. (Quoted in Laws 2010: 158)

In their efforts to realize this goal, the Liberal Democrats broke a number of pre-election pledges, 'most obviously over tuition fees, but also over the "U-turn" on dealing with the fiscal deficit' (Hazell and Yong 2012: 130). Their perceived partisan interest in making a success of coalition government thus resulted in an early loss of distinctiveness from which the Party never recovered.

Both partners need to be alert to the danger of being assigned a brief that is difficult for them to defend. This clearly was not the case in 2010, as the Liberal Democrat Business Secretary, Vince Cable, found himself in the uncomfortable position of having to steer through Parliament the higher education reforms he had previously opposed. As Cable was one of only five Liberal Democrat Cabinet ministers, he had a prominent role in the government and so was visibly associated with the policy in the eyes of the public. Given that memories of the Liberal Democrats' ill-fated pre-election pledge were still fresh, no amount of rhetorical manoeuvring would have enabled them to avoid the accusations of hypocrisy that followed the introduction of higher tuition fees. Even though the changes had little impact on student numbers—contrary to the predictions of critics—the widespread sense of betrayal would endure beyond the lifetime of the Coalition.

As Arthur Lupia and Kaare Strøm correctly point out, previous bargains between coalition partners may shape future outcomes (2008: 59). However, the present study shows that this observation is equally applicable to broken agreements. A case in point is Cameron's apparent violation of his commitment to play a limited role in what would be a bitter campaign against AV, which created friction with Clegg and emboldened

Conservative MPs to rebel on the House of Lords Reform Bill (see Clegg 2016: 134). The consequences of this were significant, as the Liberal Democrat leader retaliated by withdrawing his party's support for the proposed equalization of constituency boundaries. On Clegg's view, this move would 'restore balance to the Coalition Agreement' (2012b), but it also ensured that neither party secured the outcome that would benefit them electorally in the longer term. Therefore, a party in a subsequent coalition government should think carefully before breaking an agreement as it may prompt their partner to do the same, potentially to the detriment of both.

Relatedly, the analysis calls attention to the importance of the interpersonal mode of identification and division. Although Cameron and Clegg maintained a good working relationship on the whole, there were deep-seated tensions between the Prime Minister and sections of his parliamentary party. This friction was evident in relation to Europe, as some Conservative MPs were unable to forgive Cameron for breaking his promise to hold a referendum on the Lisbon Treaty, and there was also considerable backbench disquiet over his handling of the Syria vote in August 2013. Compounding Cameron's difficulties was the ever-present suspicion among his MPs that 'the larger party [had] compromised its ideals and conceded too much to the junior partner' (Hazell and Yong 2012: 207). While some doubts are inevitable, they can be mitigated through careful party management. One option would be to extend the formation process, so giving the negotiators more time to consult with their parliamentary parties. In contrast with the Conservative Party's 1922 Committee, which only met twice in May 2010, the Liberal Democrats held several meetings and their MPs were able to read the text of the Interim Coalition Agreement. The benefits of this consultation process were clear, as it 'helped the Liberal Democrat leadership through all the tribulations of the Coalition that the party voted strongly to endorse it in the first place' (Hazell and Yong 2012: 200). By giving their MPs a stake in a future partnership, party leaders can reduce internal tensions and so smooth the process of coalition governance.

Despite early predictions to the contrary, and conflicts over issues such as constitutional reform and Europe, the Coalition endured for a full five-year term. Although the establishment of formal and informal machinery for resolving disputes was undoubtedly important (see Hazell and Yong 2012: Chap. 4), it is perhaps not too much of a stretch to suggest that rhetorical strategies also had a role to play in keeping the partnership together. By invoking values, goals, the 'national interest' and a common enemy, senior Coalition figures were able to invite identification on a variety of grounds, and thus to appeal to multiple audiences. Beyond the formation stage, this approach may have created the possibility of the basis of identification changing over time. So, an individual who initially identified with the Coalition's ideological commitments may later come to identify primarily with its antipathy towards Labour. It is likely that the provision of several bases for identification contributed to the longevity of the Conservative-Liberal Democrat partnership, and indeed that the use of similar rhetorical strategies would be similarly beneficial to the parties in a future coalition government.

AREAS FOR FURTHER RESEARCH

The framework elaborated in this book opens up several avenues for future research. For instance, the negotiation dialogue that takes place within minority governments or surplus governments warrants academic attention, on the ground that much of the existing literature is concerned with minimal winning coalitions (but see Strøm 1984, 1990). An interesting case study would be the arrangement between the Conservatives and the DUP, the first such since 1977–78 when Labour entered into a confidence and supply agreement with the Liberal Party. This in turn opens up the possibility of a comparative historical analysis. It would also be instructive to compare the rhetorical strategies of the May government with those of the Cameron-Clegg partnership. The preceding discussion of the Conservative-DUP confidence and supply agreement shows that there were clear similarities in their early rhetoric of unity, which could indicate that the parties had learned lessons from the 2010 to 2015 Coalition. It would be worth assessing the extent to which these overlaps persist through the governance and termination phases of the May administration.

Additionally, scholars might investigate the strategies of identification and division employed by multi-party governments within the devolved legislatures of the UK. This is a potentially fruitful field of inquiry, as Scotland has had two coalitions since 1999 and Wales currently has its third multi-party government since 2000. The Northern Ireland Executive is rather different, as power has been shared between the five largest parties in mandatory coalitions since 1998 (see Geoghegan 2016). In contrast with voluntary arrangements there are no initial negotiations, and academics might examine how the unchosen nature of the partnership affects the rhetorical dynamics of coalition politics in Northern Ireland. The three polities could be analysed as single cases or comparatively, though it would be necessary to take into consideration the distinct social, political and rhetorical cultures of each.

Another area of interest is local government. There is a small literature on coalitions at this level but, as with the scholarship on national politics, it focuses on payoff distribution (e.g. Laver et al. 1987) or the determinants of government formation (e.g. Debus and Gross 2016). Once again, the rhetorical dimension of coalition bargaining is overlooked. The fact that coalitions are more common at this level means the negotiating dialogue that takes place within UK local government is ripe for investigation. Indeed, at the time of writing, possible case studies include Cumbria County Council, which is controlled by Labour and the Liberal Democrats, and the unitary authorities of the Isle of Anglesey and Stoke-on-Trent. These authorities respectively are run by Plaid Cymru, Independents and Welsh Labour, and by Independents, the Conservative Party and UKIP. This relative ideological diversity makes local government a worthwhile area for further study.

Finally, the framework could guide research into the rhetoric of coalition bargaining in democratic societies beyond the UK, and so pave the way for international comparative studies. At present, the literature on Western Europe is dominated by large-n comparisons involving the use of quantitative methods. Among the variables measured are the party system, institutions and 'critical events'—many of which are beyond the control of political agents (Hazell and Yong 2012: 5). A comparative analysis of the negotiating dialogue that takes place between governing partners in different European polities would shift the focus onto actors, and so begin to redress this imbalance. Alternatively, researchers might compare the UK's experience with that of New Zealand, which had its first coalition in 1996, and so explore how strategies of identification and division helped or hindered the transition from single- to multi-party government. Such research would complement existing scholarship on the bargaining process, while prising open the 'black box' of coalition politics a little further.

NOTES

1. UCU is 'the largest trade union and professional association for academics, lecturers, trainers, researchers and academic-related staff working in higher and further education throughout the UK' (UCU 2016).

2. This idea also found expression in the Leave campaign's belief that, on leaving the EU, Britain could immediately secure a trade deal with the US (Oliver 2016: 197).

REFERENCES

Asthana, A., McDonald, H., & Carrell, S. (2017, June 26). Theresa May Faces Backlash from Scotland and Wales Over £1bn Tory-DUP Deal. *Guardian.* Retrieved from https://www.theguardian.com/politics/2017/jun/26/tories-and-the-dup-reach-deal-to-prop-up-minority-government

Atkins, J. (2011). *Justifying New Labour Policy.* Basingstoke: Palgrave Macmillan.

Better Off Out. (2016). *Is Britain Getting Too Crowded?* Retrieved from https://digital.library.lse.ac.uk/objects/lse:bun833zaj

Bevir, M., Daddow, O., & Schnapper, P. (2015). Introduction: Interpreting British European Policy. *JCMS: Journal of Common Market Studies, 53*(1), 1–17.

Blair, O. (2016, July 5). Theresa May Meets with Richard Branson After Brexit for 'Secret Talks'. *Independent.* Retrieved from http://www.independent.co.uk/news/people/theresa-may-richard-branson-brexit-meeting-over-fears-eu-referendum-a7121016.html

Britain Stronger In. (2016). *From Lord Alan Sugar.* Retrieved from https://digital.library.lse.ac.uk/objects/lse:fit752gel

Cameron, D. (2013, January 23). *EU Speech at Bloomberg.* Retrieved from http://www.newstatesman.com/politics/2013/01/david-camerons-speech-eu-full-text

Cameron, D. (2016, May 9). *Speech on the EU Referendum.* Retrieved from http://www.conservativehome.com/parliament/2016/05/camerons-speech-on-brexit-full-text.html

Clegg, N. (2004). Europe: A Liberal Future. In P. Marshall & D. Laws (Eds.), *The Orange Book: Reclaiming Liberalism* (pp. 69–103). London: Profile Books Ltd.

Clegg, N. (2012a, November 1). *Nick Clegg Speech on His Vision for the UK in Europe.* Retrieved from http://www.libdems.org.uk/nick_clegg_speech_on_his_vision_for_the_uk_in_europe#

Clegg, N. (2012b, August 6). *Statement on House of Lords Reform.* Retrieved from http://www.bbc.co.uk/news/uk-politics-19146853

Clegg, N. (2013, October 8). *In Europe for the National Interest.* Retrieved from http://www.libdems.org.uk/nick_clegg_speech_on_a_richer_stronger_safer_greener_europe

Clegg, N. (2016). *Politics: Between the Extremes.* London: The Bodley Head.

Collini, S. (2017). *Speaking of Universities.* London: Verso.

Conservative Party. (2015). *The Conservative Party Manifesto 2015.* London: The Conservative Party.

Copsey, N., & Haughton, T. (2014). Farewell Britannia? 'Issue Capture' and the Politics of David Cameron's 2013 EU Referendum Pledge. *JCMS: Journal of Common Market Studies, 52*(Annual Review), 74–89.

Debus, M., & Gross, M. (2016). Coalition Formation at the Local Level: Institutional Constraints, Party Policy Conflict, and Office-Seeking Political Parties. *Party Politics, 22*(6), 835–846.

Department for Business, Innovation and Skills. (2016, May 16). *Press Release: New Universities to Deliver Choice and Opportunity for Students.* Retrieved from https://www.gov.uk/government/news/new-universities-to-deliver-choice-and-opportunity-for-students

Diamond, P. (2014). *Governing Britain: Power, Politics and the Prime Minister.* London: I.B. Tauris & Co., Ltd.

Eaton, G. (2017, June 16). Tory MPs Fear the Price of a Deal with the DUP Is Too High. *New Statesman.* Retrieved from http://www.newstatesman.com/politics/uk/2017/06/tory-mps-fear-price-deal-dup-too-high

Editorial. (2016, May 16). The Guardian View on the Higher Education White Paper: The Customer Is Always Ripe—For Fleecing. *Guardian.* Retrieved from https://www.theguardian.com/commentisfree/2016/may/16/the-guardian-view-on-the-higher-education-white-paper-the-customer-is-always-ripe-for-fleecing

Foster, A. (2017, June 26). *DUP Deal with Conservative Party: Arlene Foster's Speech in Full.* Retrieved from https://www.irishnews.com/news/political-news/2017/06/26/news/dup-deal-with-conservative-party-arlene-foster-s-speech-in-full-1067253/

Geoghegan, P. (2016, May 27). Northern Ireland's New Normal Normal. *Politico.* Retrieved from http://www.politico.eu/article/sinn-fein-good-friday-democratic-unionist-uk-politics-into-the-shadows-northern-irelands-new-politics/

Hazell, R., & Paun, A. (Eds.). (2009). *Making Minority Government Work: Hung Parliaments and the Challenges for Westminster and Whitehall.* Retrieved from https://www.instituteforgovernment.org.uk/sites/default/files/publications/Making%20minority%20government%20work.pdf

Hazell, R., & Yong, B. (2012). *The Politics of Coalition: How the Cameron-Clegg Government Works.* Oxford: Hart Publishing Ltd.

Hewitt, G. (2016, April 14). EU Referendum: Don't Discount Raw Emotion. *BBC News.* Retrieved from http://www.bbc.co.uk/news/uk-politics-eu-referendum-36029874

Johnson, J. (2015, July 1). *Teaching at the Heart of the System.* Retrieved from https://www.gov.uk/government/speeches/teaching-at-the-heart-of-the-system

Laver, M., Rallings, C., & Thrasher, M. (1987). Coalition Theory and Local Government Coalition Payoffs in Britain. *British Journal of Political Science, 17*(4), 501–509.

Laver, M., & Schofield, N. (1998). *Multiparty Government: The Politics of Coalition in Europe*. Ann Arbor: University of Michigan Press.

Laws, D. (2010). *22 Days in May: The Birth of the Lib Dem-Conservative Coalition*. London: Biteback Publishing Ltd.

Laws, D. (2016). *Coalition: The Inside Story of the Conservative-Liberal Democrat Coalition Government*. London: Biteback Publishing Ltd.

Lupia, A., & Strøm, K. (2008). Bargaining, Transaction Costs, and Coalition Governance. In K. Strøm, W. C. Müller, & T. Bergman (Eds.), *Cabinets and Coalition Bargaining: The Democratic Life Cycle in Western Europe* (pp. 51–83). Oxford: Oxford University Press.

Martin, J. (2016). Rhetoric of Excess. In D. Jackson, E. Thorsen, & D. Wring (Eds.), *EU Referendum Analysis 2016: Media, Voters and the Campaign* (p. 21). Poole: The Centre for the Study of Journalism, Culture and Community, Bournemouth University.

May, T. (2017a, April 18). *Theresa May's General Election Statement in Full*. Retrieved from http://www.bbc.co.uk/news/uk-politics-39630009

May, T. (2017b, June 26). *PM Statement on Confidence and Supply Agreement with the DUP*. Retrieved from https://www.gov.uk/government/news/pm-statement-on-confidence-and-supply-agreement-with-the-dup

Oliver, C. (2016). *Unleashing Demons: The Inside Story of Brexit*. London: Hodder & Stoughton Ltd.

Polonski, V. (2016). Impact of Social Media on the Outcome of the EU Referendum. In D. Jackson, E. Thorsen, & D. Wring (Eds.), *EU Referendum Analysis 2016: Media, Voters and the Campaign* (p. 94). Poole: The Centre for the Study of Journalism, Culture and Community, Bournemouth University.

Prime Minister's Office. (2017, June 26). *Confidence and Supply Agreement Between the Conservative and Unionist Party and the Democratic Unionist Party*. Retrieved from https://www.gov.uk/government/publications/conservative-and-dup-agreement-and-uk-government-financial-support-for-northern-ireland/agreement-between-the-conservative-and-unionist-party-and-the-democratic-unionist-party-on-support-for-the-government-in-parliament

Richards, S. (2013, August 30). For a Fragile Leader Like Cameron, the Past Can Be a Treacherous Guide. *Guardian*. Retrieved from https://www.theguardian.com/commentisfree/2013/aug/30/fragile-leader-david-cameron-past-treacherous

Russell, A. (2016). The Liberal Democrats: The EU Referendum's Invisible Party. In D. Jackson, E. Thorsen, & D. Wring (Eds.), *EU Referendum Analysis 2016: Media, Voters and the Campaign* (p. 83). Poole: The Centre for the Study of Journalism, Culture and Community, Bournemouth University.

Shipman, T. (2016). *All Out War: The Full Story of How Brexit Sank Britain's Political Class*. London: William Collins.

Strøm, K. (1984). Minority Governments in Parliamentary Democracies: The Rationality of Nonwinning Cabinet Solutions. *Comparative Political Studies, 17*(2), 199–227.

Strøm, K. (1990). *Minority Government and Majority Rule.* Cambridge: Cambridge University Press.

UCU. (2016, May 16). *UCU Briefing on the Higher Education White Paper.* Retrieved from https://www.ucu.org.uk/media/8156/Briefing-on-the-higher-education-white-paper/pdf/UCU_briefing_on_the_Higher_Education_White_Paper_May_2016.pdf

Vote Leave. (2016). *5 Positive Reasons to Vote Leave and Take Back Control: Europe Yes, EU No.* Retrieved from https://digital.library.lse.ac.uk/objects/lse:sav235yoh

Willetts, D. (2012a, September 13). *'A World Without Boundaries': Speech at UUK Conference.* Retrieved from https://www.gov.uk/government/speeches/uuk-conference-a-world-without-boundaries

Willetts, D. (2012b, April 18). *Speech to the HEFCE Annual Conference 2012.* Retrieved from https://www.gov.uk/government/speeches/hefce-annual-conference-2012

Index[1]

---

[1] Note: Page numbers followed by 'n' refer to notes.

© The Author(s) 2018
J. Atkins, *Conflict, Co-operation and the Rhetoric of Coalition
Government*, Rhetoric, Politics and Society,
https://doi.org/10.1057/978-1-137-31796-4

CPI Antony Rowe
Eastbourne, UK
January 24, 2020